Global Ser

Moving to a level playing field

The British Computer Society

BCS is the leading professional body for the IT industry. With members in over 100 countries, the BCS is the professional and learned Society in the field of computers and information systems.

The BCS is responsible for setting standards for the IT profession. It is also leading the change in public perception and appreciation of the economic and social importance of professionally managed IT projects and programmes. In this capacity, the Society advises, informs and persuades industry and government on successful IT implementation.

IT is affecting every part of our lives and that is why the BCS is determined to promote IT as the profession of the 21st century.

Joining BCS

BCS qualifications, products and services are designed with your career plans in mind. We not only provide essential recognition through professional qualifications but also offer many other useful benefits to our members at every level.

BCS Membership demonstrates your commitment to professional development. It helps to set you apart from other IT practitioners and provides industry recognition of your skills and experience. Employers and customers increasingly require proof of professional qualifications and competence. Professional membership confirms your competence and integrity and sets an independent standard that people can trust. Professional Membership (MBCS) is the pathway to Chartered IT Professional (CITP) Status.

www.bcs.org/membership

Further Information

Further information about BCS can be obtained from: The British Computer Society, First Floor, Block D, North Star House, North Star Avenue, Swindon, SN2 1FA, UK.

Telephone: 0845 300 4417 (UK only) or + 44 (0)1793 417 424 (overseas)
Email: customerservice@hq.bcs.org.uk
Web: www.bcs.org

Global Services
Moving to a level playing field

Mark Kobayashi-Hillary and
Dr Richard Sykes

To John,
Best Wishes,
Mark.

First South Asian Edition 2008

The British Computer Society
First Floor, Block D
North Star House,
North Star Avenue
Swindon SN2 1FA
UK
www.bcs.org

ISBN 10: 1 902505 83 2
ISBN 13: 978 1 902505 83 1

This edition is for sale in the Indian subcontinent only. Not for export elsewhere.

British Cataloguing-in-Publication Data
A CIP record for this book is available from the British Library.

Disclaimer

Typeset by Lapiz Digital Services, Chennai, India.
Printed and bound in India by Saurabh Printers, New Delhi, India.

Contents

List of Figures and Tables

Authors

Mark Kobayashi-Hillary is a British consultant and researcher based in London where he lives with his wife Nobumi and a Staffordshire bull terrier named Matilda. Mark is the author of *Outsourcing to India: The Offshore Advantage* first published by Springer in 2004 and updated to a new edition in 2005. He contributed a chapter on offshoring to Peter Brudenall's book *Technology and Offshore Outsourcing Strategies* (Palgrave, 2005) and has edited the forthcoming *Building a Future with BRICs: The Next Decade for Offshoring* (Springer, 2007) and written *Who Moved my Job?* (TBA, 2007).

Mark is the offshoring director of the UK National Outsourcing Association (NOA) and is a founding member of the British Computer Society working party on offshoring. He is a visiting lecturer at London South Bank University where he is focused on contributing outsourcing knowledge to the MBA programme.

Mark is a non-executive director of foreign exchange firm FXA World and research firm Brainmatics. Mark has an MBA from the University of Liverpool.

Mark also writes a regular outsourcing blog for the leading technology magazine *Computing*, is editor of the NOA podcast, and occasionally writes other media features when he can find the time. He can't really play guitar, but enjoys trying to.

www.markhillary.com

Dr Richard Sykes is a business counsellor, trusted advisor and strategic coach with a particular focus on the globalization of the ICT services and business process markets. A Brit, he lives in London with his Kiwi partner, Penny Mason, in a Georgian terrace house, home to their collection of contemporary art.

He chairs the Outsourcing & Offshore Group of Intellect, the UK trade association for the IT, Telecoms and Electronics industries, and also the De La Warr Pavilion Trust, responsible for the stewardship of the Grade 1 listed icon of the Modernist movement at Bexhill-on-Sea on the UK south coast.

A scientist by education (his undergraduate years at Clare College, Cambridge and his PhD from Yale University), Richard has held senior executive roles in ICI plc (he was Group VP IT in the 1990s) and the

IT industry (non-executive Chairman for both the outsourcing consultancy Morgan Chambers plc, 1999–2004, and Site Confidence Ltd, 2001–2004). He has lived and operated internationally, including in Japan. He currently chairs Solcom Ltd, has an advisory non-executive role at the Indian venture Quickstart Global Ltd and is an Associate at CSC's Leading Edge Forum.

www.dr.richard-sykes.com

Foreword

A few years ago, a British management magazine published a cartoon about outsourcing. It showed a large office in which there was a single desk with one young woman sitting at it, and one telephone. Standing over her in a 'boss-like' pose was a man saying: 'And I want you to talk in an Indian accent so people think we are big enough to have a call centre in Bangalore.'

Not everyone in boardrooms or Trade Unions in Britain or other developed countries has taken such a wry and relaxed approach to outsourcing. Often it has been seen as a significant threat to employment and to wage rates in developed countries. And urban myths have grown up about taxi routers 5,000 miles from the city of operation, or financial sector back offices vulnerable to fraud, or perhaps moving important functions overseas in an attempt to escape the appropriate regulatory jurisdiction.

The reality of outsourcing and offshoring is quite different. Companies' motives are very varied, and the types of service they relocate are remarkably diverse. Outsourcing is now about much more than call centres and back offices. The great merit of Kobayashi-Hillary and Sykes' work is that they present a thoughtful and detailed taxonomy of the global trade in services, which carefully distinguishes the reality from the myth. Unusually, it is a book that will be helpful both to companies themselves, as they think through the structure of their operations and try to make decisions that will maintain their competitiveness, and also to those involved in the debate on globalization itself – whichever point of view they currently adopt. It deserves a wide audience.

Sir Howard Davies
Director of the London School of Economics

Acknowledgements

Writing a book is a thankless task. Hours of solitary research and writing that stretch into days, weeks and months of effort even before worrying about whether anyone will actually like the result. It becomes even more complex when it is the effort of more than one author, so we are pleased to find that the outcome of this project has answered the questions we set out to address. It is largely thanks to our tireless editor Matthew Flynn that everything worked out in the end, so thank you Matthew.

We would like to thank Thomas Friedman for summarizing the issues surrounding the 'flat world' in his book of the same name. Some commentators have criticised Friedman for oversimplifying the issues of globalization, and global trade in particular, but regardless of any shortcomings he not only managed to summarize the key issues in a single volume, he generated enough interest to sell several million copies. Those who choose to cast stones might want to sit down and try crafting their own volume in response.

Mark and Richard would like to thank (in no particular order): Nobumi, Matilda, Ourah, Jadoo, Ben and Luke, John and Carol Uncle, Penny, the Arctic Monkeys, all the commentators who helped by talking to us or contributing their thoughts, the British Computer Society, Intellect, The National Outsourcing Association, Professor Leslie Willcocks and Professor Patrick Humphreys at the London School of Economics, all the LSE Institute of Social Psychology PhD students, Dr Frédéric Adam at University College Cork, George Bell and Alan Hovell at London South Bank University, Professor Phanish Puranam at London Business School, Anil Kumar and B.M. Suri at CTR Manufacturing in Pune, Marc Vollenweider and his great team at Evalueserve, Elizabeth Sparrow, Hilary Robertson at Xansa, David Moschella, Kirt Mead, Lem Lasher, Doug Neal and other key colleagues (co-thinkers!) at CSC's Leading Edge Forum, Andrew Fairburn at Hill & Knowlton, Kully Dhadda at Flame PR, Dr Mohan Kaul at the Commonwealth Business Council, Dalim Basu, Vijay Kumar at FXA World, Carl Stadler and Ravi Pandey at NIIT Technologies, Andrea Murphy at Richmond Events, the late Sunil Mehta at NASSCOM, Professor Mari Sako at Oxford University, Mike Scott, Keith Sharp, Charlotte Poskitt, Arun Aggarwal, A.S. Lakshmi – and of course Marta Dziedzicki for all the help getting served at The Talbot – at TCS in London … the list could go on because so many have helped, but at some point the BCS would like the manuscript! Many apologies if you have helped us in any way, but have not enjoyed a mention.

Mark would like to add an extra special note of thanks to Mahesh Ramachandran, a Sloan fellow of London Business School and director of FXA World. Mark has travelled to India several times with Mahesh gathering research on this industry and enjoyed many long conversations over a 'Cobra' on where this is all headed. It was over these conversations with Mahesh that the concept for this book was really formed.

Abbreviations

3G/4G	third/fourth generation
A&R	Artists and Repertoire
ASP	application service provider
B2B	business to business
B2C	business to consumer
BCP	business continuity planning
BOT	build–operate–transfer
BPM	business process management
BPO	business process outsourcing
BPR	business process re-engineering
BRIC	Brazil, Russia, India and China
BSI	British Standards Institution
C2C	consumer to consumer
CBC	Commonwealth Business Council
CeFA	Certificate for Financial Advisors
CeMAP	Certificate in Mortgage Advice and Practice
CFA	client file assessment form
CIO	Chief Information Officer (Chief Investment Officer in financial services
CMM	capability maturity model (Software Engineering Institute–Carnegic Mellon)
CMMI	capability maturity models integrated
COBIT	Control Objectives for Information and related Technology
COPC	Customer Operations Performance Center Inc.
CRM	customer relationship management
CSR	corporate social responsibility
EBIT	earnings before interest and tax
EPOS	electronic point of sale
ERP	enterprise resource planning

eSCM-SP	e-sourcing capability model for suppliers
ESR	electronic staff records
EU	European Union
F&A	financial and accounting
FM	facilities management
FSA	Financial Services Authority
FTE	full-time equivalent
GATT	General Agreement on Tariffs and Trade
GDM	global delivery model
GDP	gross domestic product
GE	General Electric
GMAT	Graduate Management Admission Test
GNDM	global network delivery model
HR	Human Resources
HTML	HyperText Markup Language
ICT	information and communications technology
IFA	independent financial advisor
IFS	Institute of Financial Services, UK
IM	instant messaging
IMF	International Monetary Fund
IP	Internet Protocol
IPO	initial public offering
IS	information systems and services
ISACA	Information Systems Audit and Control Association
ISO	International Organization for Standardization
ITES	Information Technology Enabled Services
ITGI	IT Governance Institute
ITIL	Information Technology Infrastructure Library
ITO	IT outsourcing
IVR	intelligent voice response
JV	joint venture
KPI	Key Performance Indicator
KPO	knowledge process outsourcing
LPO	legal process outsourcing

Mbps	megabits per second
MGI	McKinsey Global Institute
MRI	Magnetic Resonance Imaging
NASDAQ	National Association of Securities Dealers Automated Quotations
NASSCOM	National Association of Software and Service Companies, India
NHS	National Health Service
ODC	offshore development centre
OECD	Organisation for Economic Co-operation and Development
ONS	Office of National Statistics, UK
PC	personal computer
PDA	personal digital assistant
QCA	Qualifications and Curriculum Authority, UK
R&D	research and development
ROI	Return on Investment
RSS	really simple syndication
S/ITS	Software and IT Services
SaaS	software as a service
SEI	Software Engineering Institute
SFIA	Skills Framework for the Information Age
SLA	Service Level Agreement
SMEs	small and medium-sized enterprises
SOA	service-oriented architecture
T&M	time and materials pricing
TCS	Tata Consultancy Systems
TEBS	technology-enabled business services
USB	universal serial bus
VOIP	voice over internet protocol
VPN	virtual private networks
XML	eXtensible Markup Language

Glossary

Application professionalism   The human contribution and expertise required for the delivery of a particular service.

Blog   A weblog, or online diary. Blogs are online journals that can be updated immediately and can be used for personal opinions and views, or for serious online debate.

Brand guardian   A holding company that preserves and cultures a brand ethos, setting strategy and managing various operating companies that exploit the group brand.

Captive   A captive is the offshore service delivery unit for a company, where the offshore unit remains a part of the company group and the employees in both offshore and onshore locations work for the same company, or same corporate group.

Captive facility   The office facilities used by a captive service provider.

Clickstream   The record of websites visited by any particular user; now a sought-after commodity as knowledge of a user's clickstream can improve advertising to that user.

Cost-plus   The most basic method for pricing a service by calculating the cost of delivery and then adding a margin to ensure a profit.

Dashboard   A system used for reviewing project status; most managers will use a dashboard to analyse a lot of information quickly, so only the urgent issues can be given attention, in much the same way as a car dashboard conveys a great deal of information in a summarized form.

Dot com   Shorthand description for a company that uses the internet as the main delivery channel or marketing and promotion channel.

Due diligence   The process of discovery or detailed analysis when engaging a partner company in a service relationship. Due diligence is the process of cross-checking the claims they made during the sales process, to ensure that all the facts are on the table and visible.

End-user driven   Ability of the actual user of a technology platform to define how it works and what services can be offered, rather than to just accept what is on offer.

Experiential depth   Depth of experience within a particular product or service, as opposed to a broad range of services.

Experiential intimacy   Deep experience of a product or service within a particular industry, rather than just the IT tools that under-pin that service.

Fixed-cost model   Where a service provider will quote a fixed price for a service, regardless of the time and effort involved, which may change as the work progresses – in much the same way as a decorator may charge a fixed price to paint a house, regardless of any snags or problems that may be encountered during the work.

Gainsharing   The concept of working together with another organization and creating measurable cash benefits from the partnership that can be used as payment to the service provider, rather than charging in the more usual way for time and materials.

Joint venture   A business venture where two organization join forces as partners to create a shared third-party organization with goals that meet the needs of both founding partners.

Knowledge economy   As many service-based jobs have been created requiring no more than the knowledge inside a person's head, the term knowledge economy has grown in usage to describe the jobs these people perform and their value to the wider economy.

Legacy systems   Old, generally proprietary systems that cannot be upgraded or improved without replacement.

Micropreneur   American writer Daniel Pink has used this term to describe very small companies; generally single-person entrepreneurial outfits that can give the impression of being a much larger company through the use of a professional website, phone answering service and good stationery.

Millenium bug   The problem of computer software written in the 20th century using only two digits to store year values – such as '75'. This became a major problem, as the fear in the late 1990s was that many systems would not be able to distinguish between 2000 and 1900.

Moore's law   The theory proposed by Gordon Moore of Intel that the data density achievable on an integrated chip doubles approximately every 18 months.

Multisourcing   The use of several service partners within a single contract, to extract value or to ensure each can offer their key strengths.

Offshoring   The process of working with an offshore partner for service delivery, usually where the partner is a third party, but this term also applies to offshore services delivered from within the same company (a captive unit).

Outsourcing   The process of purchasing a service from a third-party supplier; usually distinguished from procurement by the consideration that most outsourced services remain a part of the supply chain.

Podcast   An audio or video broadcast designed for use on an MP3 player. Named after the Apple iPod, the most important distribution channel remains the Apple iTunes system, where podcasts from individuals can be found alongside all the major global broadcasters.

RSS   Really Simple Syndication, a system that allows the easy republishing of material from news websites or blogs, so you can subscribe to content that you are interested in and updates will take place automatically.

Run-rate reduction   Reducing the amount of actual outgoing costs.

Technological professionalism   The measurement of technical proficiency, as opposed to business proficiency.

Telcos   Telecommunications companies.

Time and materials   T&M is the most basic method of charging for a service contract; basically it is nothing more than a unit cost for time (amount per day usually) plus expenses.

Utility computing   The concept of making computing power available and charging for it in the same way as other utilities, such as electricity or gas. Compared to present models of building immense infrastructure, the idea of paying only for what you need is quite innovative.

Value chain   The chain of services that connect together everything your company does from one department or process to the next, and how they add value to whatever it is that you do.

Value-add   The measurement of where value is added to a process or service.

Value-minus pricing   Pricing a service by quantifying the value it will create and using this figure to place a price on the service; the agreed price for the service will be this total value created figure minus a figure agreed by the two parties. For instance, if a new scheduling system might be projected to save a company £5 million per year, they might offer an IT group £3 million to produce the system, but with payment based on the projected savings being achieved – rather than time and materials payment of £1 million.

Water-cooler comment   The real intelligence in any company is always the discussion around the water cooler.

Wiki   A wiki is a type of website that allows very easy contribution, editing and changes. It encourages collaboration by making it easy for multiple parties to contribute to a single project or repository of information.

XML Extensible Markup Language, a formal markup language that facilitates the sharing of information across different types of system using the internet as a distribution platform.

Useful Websites

24/7 Customer	www.247customer.com
British Airways	www.ba.com
BrainMatics	www.brainmatics.net
BT Global Services	www.btglobalservices.com
Cognizant Technology Solutions	www.cognizant.com
Computing Business	www.computingbusiness.co.uk
Datamonitor	www.datamonitor.com
eBay	www.ebay.co.uk
Economics UK	www.economicsuk.com
EquaTerra	www.equaterra.com
Evalueserve	www.evalueserve.com
Firstsource	www.firstsource.in
Flickr	www.flickr.com
FXA World	www.fxaworld.com
Greynium	www.greynium.com
Intellect (UK trade association for hi-tech industries)	www.intellectuk.org
ITC Infotech	www.itcinfotech.com
IT Directors Network	www.itdirectorsnetwork.co.uk
Lulu.com	www.lulu.com
Magellan Consultancy Services	www.magellancs.com
Myspace	www.myspace.com
NASSCOM (National Association of Software and Service Companies)	www.nasscom.org
neoIT	www.neoit.com
NIIT Technologies	www.niit-tech.com
IAOP (International Association of Outsourcing Professionals)	www.outsourcingprofessional.org
RentACoder	www.rentacoder.com
Royal Mail	www.royalmail.com
Salesforce.com	www.salesforce.com
Second Life	www.secondlife.com
small business service	www.sbs.gov.uk
silicon.com	www.silicon.com
Times Online	www.sunday-times.co.uk
Tata Consultancy Services	www.tcs.com
Xansa	www.xansa.com
YouTube	www.youtube.com

Preface

We would like to thank you for choosing to purchase or borrow our book and we hope you find it a useful addition to the knowledge of what exactly is happening in services today – particularly the creation of a global market in services through the use of technology. We have tried to avoid producing a lengthy didactic tome describing in minute detail what is happening and why – it's just impossible. This market is changing so fast that a book is not even the natural format for comment: the internet and quality news journals are far superior if you just want to keep track of industry trends and what individual companies are up to.

So why bother reading the book at all if everything can be found online? Services are the major engine of the contemporary economy – services are now the predominant face of the IT industry and global trade in them is growing fast. Both of us feel that there are some significant lessons to be learned from other industries and the history of other industrial developments, such as the globalization of manufacturing. There is an interesting framework of trends that is developing – and is sometimes ignored in the furore over offshoring – and is worth exploring in broad concept. We have attempted to be as succinct as possible, with sufficient detail to illustrate and emphasize. This book is intended to spur further debate on the reality of global services and to help reduce some of the noise – we hope it can sit as a manifesto for reality, cutting through the hype and opinion.

Mark and Richard met thanks to the circuit of 'outsourcing' conferences Mark was attending to promote his *Outsourcing to India* book and Richard was attending in his role for Intellect, the UK trade body for hi-tech companies. Both found a lot of common ground in their views that offshoring was about more than just jobs vanishing offshore, about more than just a race to the bottom, about more than just slashing costs, and about more than just India and software development. The offshoring backlash really reached a peak in the UK in 2003 with union members dressing as elephants to highlight the perceived 'flood' of jobs racing to India, followed by a similar reaction in 2004, as offshoring became a 'dog-whistle' campaign issue in the US Presidential election. Both Richard and Mark felt that it was time someone expressed the complete picture of services globalization without boring the non-economist audience, and as nobody else appears to have made that statement, we hope that this book covers most of our thoughts on the subject and resonates with you.

The book flows together in a series of eight chapters covering the issues we feel are of most importance and a ninth that summarizes the learning from the book. It's not a book about outsourcing or offshoring or even information technology alone, though these are all key enablers to the way global services are changing today. All these topics are covered in the context of examining just what is happening to the global services marketplace today and why this affects all of us. You can read the book straight through for a complete picture, or single out key chapters that might be of most interest to you.

Mark Kobayashi-Hillary and Dr Richard Sykes
London, March 2007

1 The Millennium

The level playing field agenda: The fixed deadline of the millennium gave a boost to all offshore technology groups offering help to those fighting to prove that their technology could withstand the 'millennium bug'. Now that the offshore model has been accepted for technology-related services it can be observed that the UK has greatly benefited from an increased willingness to buy services remotely, rather than the opposite situation that most had feared.

With the benefit of a half-decade's worth of hindsight, the millennial divide was very real as far as the – still very young – world of information technology was concerned. Not as real as the dot-com visionaries tried to persuade us in 1999, but real in other significant ways whose impact in 2007 is becoming increasingly apparent.

It was not that some exciting new technology suddenly appeared on 1 January 2000. Quite the reverse, to the degree that technology had a hand at all in the huge shifts that this book sets out to explore, the underlying innovations were already well in place, and well exploited, by New Year's Eve 1999.

The quite fundamental shifts that we can now see accelerated in 2000 and beyond, lay in two significant changes in the wider information technology marketplace, underwritten by a very important third, the development of the internet as a global utility.

What was the first significant shift? People – users – moved to the front line in selecting, influencing, shaping and exploiting through their priorities what was on offer in the world of applied information technology (IT). Two groups in particular were involved: the consumer (especially the younger consumer) and the non-IT professional (in contrast to the IT professional).

For the first time the consumer (and the explosion in text messaging amongst the young is a classic example) began pulling the IT industry in new directions that it had neither foreseen nor had intended to pursue – and feeding the rapid growth of a new generation of IT companies targeted at responding to the individual consumer's requirements. After decades during which the industry (the supply side) had taken the lead in setting the agenda, the user (the demand side), under the guise of the consumerization of IT, started taking control.

As the contemporary capabilities of the technology became more integral to the operation of an increasing diverse range of business and professional operations, from accountancy to medicine to architecture and to the law, non-IT professionals themselves increasingly became the lead creators and innovators of how technology would be put to work in their corner of the economy.

What was the second significant shift? A new generation of entrepreneurs emerged in countries such as (and in particular) India to call the new world of the developing economies into play to redress the competitive balance of the old. By 2005 a clutch of new global players, powered by impressive margins and strong balance sheets, were rewriting the rules on the back of business models based on the concept of offshoring – exploiting the international arbitrage of the IT professional. Manufacturing had earlier globalized by exploiting the international arbitrage of the factory worker – now the higher-level skills of the young engineering graduate and IT professional were put to work in a similar fashion. An IT industry globalization that had hitherto been essentially transatlantic in its nature suddenly widened to be genuinely global in its scope.

The purpose of this book is to argue that these two fundamental millennial shifts, enabled and underwritten by a third (the rapid development of the internet as a public utility), are rewriting the competitive landscape for the information technology industry more fundamentally than is yet understood or being allowed for, and to outline the new rules of the game that will scope the competitive global battlefields of the near future.

INFORMATION TECHNOLOGY: FROM INFANCY TO TEENAGE KICKS

The infant IT industry of the 1950s to 1980s was (perhaps inevitably) an aggressive purveyor of new technologies, often unproven, untested and uncertain in their application. Promise routinely exceeded delivery, actual business impact generally narrowed that scope, and progress from merely automating the old to enabling the new came in slow steps. The industry sold kit (hardware) and software (competing operating systems and bespoke applications). The customer was the corporation, and its IT department, and the prime focus of the IT industry was its business customers. Telephone companies, a distinct breed, sold voice and some data network services to anyone, whether corporation or house owner.

The 1990s, with the arrival of the standardized software package to challenge the economics of the bespoke, with the emergence of the distributed server and mobile laptop to allow the user to escape the restraints of the centralized mainframe, and the initial convergence of computing and network technologies, saw the first evidence of the consumer taking charge – i.e. the pornography-funded emergence of the web from its academic and defence roots as a public facility – and the first evidence that business change was the real objective (rather than the technology itself) – i.e. the arrival of Amazon.com as the new bookshop to the world, genuinely rewriting the retail model.

So the application began to define technological intent, rather than vice versa, and the user began to take charge, selecting and rejecting from the capabilities offered, and defining the preferred way forward. New-generation IT companies such as eBay, Google and Yahoo! launched business models focused on the individual consumer, and the arrival of the mobile phone and the laptop confirmed 'the consumerization of kit'.

In equal measure, the infant IT industry of the 1950s to 1980s was the creature of the technologically mature economies of North America and Western Europe – soon joined by the post-war Japan. The technologically precocious industrializing nations of South Korea and Taiwan were, by the 1980s, also starting to edge into the camp. The 1990s saw the established transatlantic version of the globalization of the electronics and hardware sectors of the industry rapidly morph into a more genuinely, Asia-encompassing reality. The sourcing and outsourcing of the manufacturing of hardware in its full diversity became an established norm by the end of the decade – and the norm was to so do on a global scale. The scene was set for the new decade.

The foundations were laid for the two millennial shifts outlined above. The third enabling factor, the pornography-funded emergence of the web from its academic and defence roots to work as a de-facto public facility, was key to the consumerization of the industry by the likes of Amazon. It also served as the vector on which to align much key industry technological and operational innovation – both in globally recognized standards (the Internet Protocols) and in the open-systems capabilities required to ensure that the exponentially expanding whole of converged network and computing power grew unhindered. And in so doing it provided a global capability to underpin the impact of the two millennial shifts as they gained momentum into the new decade.

Seen in the context of the year 2000, the web and its capabilities appeared vital to the dot com e-revolution fostered in the final years of the old decade, promising in the opening years of the new to sweep away all before it. In short order, the subsequent collapse of the dot com bubble in March 2000 destroyed much of the new e-vision, re-injecting a new sense of realism (or perhaps a more classic commercialism) into the industry. This false dawn at the millennium's edge distracted attention from the more fundamental revolution that was taking shape – and within a very few more years was significantly reshaping the global playing field.

ENTER THE NEW MILLENNIUM AND THE INDIAN TIGER

In the circumscribed 1990s world of corporate information technology, the approach to the millennium was particularly dominated by the apparent global challenge of the millennium bug. A tight-fisted approach to the use of scarce coding space in the early days of the IT industry had, it was feared, left a legacy at the heart of corporate IT systems across the world that threatened paralysis on the stroke of midnight 31 December 1999 – an inability for the software to 'know' whether it was now 1 January 2000 or 1 January 1900.

The need to review the coding of millions of software structures, to 'seek out and fix', called for a massive, almost military-style campaign. The foot soldiers of this campaign were the experienced creative minds of the IT world – the developers. The demand for such resource in the western economies outstripped supply, causing a huge increase in contractors' rates – and providing the first major opportunity for the small but growing band of Indian IT companies to drive hard into their prime export markets – English-speaking North America and the UK. Offshoring to India was born as a significant reality.

The companies, lead by the venerable TCS (Tata Consultancy Systems – an offshoot of the diversified Indian industrial conglomerate Tata) had spent the 1990s developing a first-world industrial export sector in the midst of India's third-world economy – building on the ample availability of young, well-educated and English-speaking engineers pouring out of the major Indian universities and institutes, whose earning expectations massively undercut those of their American and European peer group. Entrepreneurial leadership, seeing the emerging opportunity, focused on assembling well-regimented armies of IT professionals, with an emphasis on project management and quality delivery skills that outranked the western competition with a strategic determination to kill from the start the idea that low cost meant low quality. The millennium bug fed the opportunity, and the first Indian company ever to list on the US NASDAQ exchange, Infosys, signalled the arrival of the new competitors on the world stage.

History has yet to determine with any confidence the degree to which the millennium bug was or was not for real – the world certainly did not come to a juddering halt at that midnight hour – but a few years on, four Indian companies passed through the 1 billion dollar annual sales mark (TCS, Infosys, Wipro and Satyam) as leaders of a half dozen or so Indian ventures that are now recognized as heavyweights in the global IT industry. Their endeavours have reignited the globalization of the industry and redrawn its boundaries. Major American and European suppliers and customers have moved to expand into India, and the Indian example has speeded a wider globalization, with countries such as the Philippines and Russia entering the market.

The roots of these new Indian companies may have been in the offshoring of development, but all have worked hard since the millennium turn to develop their major cost advantage into a broadening geographical footprint with a far more complete range of services than they initially offered in the 1990s.

To further define the terms outsourcing and offshoring for the purposes of clarity, throughout this book 'offshoring' refers to the use of some offshore resource that is remote from the location purchasing the service; regardless of whether the resource remains within the same company or is purchased from another ('outsourced') we would still term the service as having being offshored.

Making use of their competitive cost advantages, the top three of TCS, Infosys and Wipro have consistently delivered earnings before interest and tax (EBIT) margins well above 20 per cent, and delivered revenue growth of 30 per cent, 40 per cent and even 50 per cent per annum. They have positioned themselves particularly in the US market (contributing 60–65 per cent of their revenues in 2005), with more recent growth in Europe (25–35 per cent of their revenues in 2005). As Anthony Miller, partner of Arete Research, noted recently:[1]

> **In so doing, they have, over the space of an accelerated decade, in fact conservatively copied, with much commercial brilliance, the journey though an evolution of business models that their older, maturing American and European competitors shaped and developed through the 1980s and 1990s.**

OUTSOURCING: THE EMERGENCE OF REMOTE SERVICES

As already noted, the post-war IT industry grew initially as an innovator and purveyor of its core technologies, particularly mainframe computers and their associated peripherals (card readers, tape drives, printers and so on) along with associated operating systems and some bespoke application software. 'Corporate IT' evolved to purchase, use and manage this equipment and software, to furnish the corporation, and to create and deliver technology-based services internally. The founding model of the IT department was established – the in-house team of business and systems analysts, programmers and computer operators who created the (generally bespoke) business systems and delivered the associated services across the company.

In parallel, the much older and quite separate telecommunications industry grew as a technology-based – usually a regulated monopoly – service provider. The telcos (telecommunications companies) offered a source of point-to-point telecommunications services, for voice (analogue signals) and then a growing business also in digital data transmission. Large corporations purchased bandwidth and constructed their own internal networks in order to reduce costs. The ever-expanding IT department then moved to take the burgeoning telecoms services under its wing, the better to integrate with the fast-growing diversity of information systems and services (IS) it was now responsible for.

In the 1990s the digitization of telecoms networks fed the initial stages of technological convergence, and with it development, for major corporations, of the service offer of virtual private networks, or VPN services – what today can be labelled as the very first 'e-service'. Convergence brought the once very distinct disciplines of the IT professional and the telecommunications engineer together within the fast expanding information and communications technology (ICT) industry.

The 1980s had already seen the foundation and rapid growth of a new dimension to this industry. The concept of outsourcing developed as an extension of facilities management (FM) and of bureau services. The latter was a natural form of shared service for those companies whose size (or business focus) did not justify the cost burden of their own expensive IT resources. The former grew around the offer by outside organizations to 'take responsibility for and manage' the IT assets (kit, software and people) of a company, justifying the move through the benefits of the critical mass and professional management that a specialist player such as EDS would bring to the game.

This newer breed of IT company took the FM model into the management, maintenance and development of the corporate computing resource. Established purveyors of technology, most especially IBM, recognized the importance of this new market, and diversified into it. By the mid 1990s, the outsourcing sector was strongly established across the American and European ICT markets – and with the privatization of the telecommunications industry across Europe (and the break up of AT&T in the USA) the outsourcing model developed into an increasingly integrated ICT model.

During the 1990s, this market evolved into the broadly defined area of IT outsourcing (ITO), starting with infrastructural operations and growing to include the applications run on the infrastructure. The next natural development was the move 'up market' into the outsourcing of not just the application but also the processes the application enabled – usually known as business process outsourcing (BPO). A snapshot of the progress of this development is given in Figure 1.1, drawn from a CSC/FT corporate survey made in Europe in 2004.[2]

The Indian companies moved with determination to climb the same path, so that by 2006 they have become competitive players across all sectors of the ICT market, from systems development (code-cutting), integration and maintenance through a wide range of ITO services, to more recently developing strategies that have taken them rapidly into the BPO market.

Within the ICT industry, the FM model still remains central to ITO and BPO thinking, with the associated language of outsourcing and, when the outsourcing involves the use of overseas resources, offshoring. The working assumption is that there is a corporate IT resource that is doing the work, which is then outsourced to a third party in whole or in part.

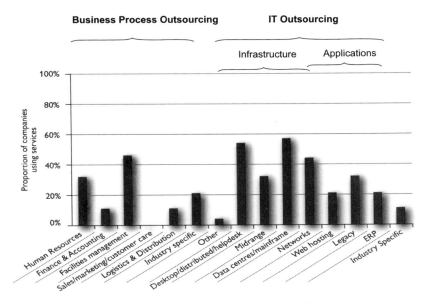

FIGURE 1.1   *The migration to technology-enabled services*
Source: *CSC Leading Edge Forum, www.lef.csc.com*

In contrast, the more recent consumerization of IT services, from Google onwards, has been articulated in terms of online services, sourced off the web by the consumer – through the laptop, increasingly through the mobile phone, and through the personal digital assistant (PDA) and its relatives. No one talks of the consumer outsourcing his or her search requirements to Google.

Our choice of language to describe a particular reality both reflects our understanding of the reality, but can also influence how we think about it. In practical terms, the act of outsourcing involves the client purchasing back a service or services. Within the broader categorizations of contemporary commerce, these services are defined as business-to-business (B2B) services. The consumerization of the IT 'offer' has involved from the start the rapid growth in business to consumer (B2C) services. Equally, these particular B2B services can be further usefully categorized as technology-enabled services, reflecting their dependence on the exploitation of the underlying ICT technologies.

Where the outsourcing involves offshoring, the purchasing back of the service or services involved, or the B2B commerce, becomes categorized as a part of the international trade in services. As we will argue further below, this proper categorization of offshoring as, in essence, a particular category of the international trade in services, is an important step, treating offshoring as a quite natural development in the ongoing globalization of trade and commerce rather than some challenging novelty to be feared.

THE USER IS ALWAYS RIGHT

As already noted, the commerce of B2C services is mainly delivered over the web. In contrast, corporate IT has usually delivered services to its internal customers over the telecoms network – and classic ITO and BPO B2B-sourced services have also been network-delivered and accessed, rather than over the web. Halfway through the first decade of the new century, this is now all changing. One consequence of the consumerization of the ICT 'offer' has been the rapid take up by the corporate employee of a wide range of hardware, from home computers to laptops to mobile phones to PDAs, and their associated B2C services. This increasing consumption of the B2C web-enabled services on offer in the wider world has increasingly risked clashing with the tightly controlled 'inside world' of corporate IT's B2B network-based service paradigm.

Perhaps the best example of the emergent new world is a decision by the oil company BP to encourage its employees (for a once-a-year lump sum payment of £1,000) to eschew the services of BP's IT department and become self-sufficient in their purchase and maintenance of IT kit and associated web-enabled B2C services.[3]

But wait a moment. A large company like BP is offering its employees money to just go away and support their own kit. Isn't that madness? Most IT departments strictly lock down the platform and reduce what users can do with their equipment. There is your problem – nobody wants to be told what to do by someone who probably doesn't understand your job anyway. This is particularly applicable to the young, who have never lived without access to consumer electronics. It's becoming increasingly common for companies to follow the BP lead though, especially in the financial services companies in the City. Once all your internal applications are web-enabled then any employee can use any piece of kit to access your company tools just as they would access Amazon or Google.

A good example of IT department bureaucracy can be illustrated by the policy of a firm that one of the authors used to work for. This company insisted that employees going out to meet clients used a laptop PC to run PowerPoint presentations, yet they refused to purchase the kit for the staff – insisting that a shared pool was enough. Most of the staff involved in regular client meetings just bought their own PC, from their own hard-earned and taxed cash. Yet the IT department refused to allow the staff to connect these 'non-compliant' PCs to the office network, so copying presentations was always a nightmare (this was before the easy availability of universal serial bus (USB) memory sticks).

At the root of the BP decision on staff IT requirements is a recognition that the contemporary employee uses their kit as much for their private lives as their business lives and has a diversity of personal requirements that standard company-issued kit rarely matches. Many employees, corporate IT has rapidly learnt, are willing to invest in higher-quality kit than the company historically has been willing to supply. More importantly, the contemporary browser allows the employee ease of access to BP's internal systems across the web, through agreed web portals – protected by effective security systems – when company business is to be done.

Accessing the systems required to work for BP becomes just one more online, web-enabled service, alongside Google, MySpace and eBay, that the employee exploits. The industry's consumer services 'offer' aligns alongside the industry's corporate services 'offer'. The proactive corporate user, long the bane of the corporate IT department, is at long last recognized and empowered.

Switching to the language of services, as we have done above, in our view helps untangle the conceptual jungle of contemporary ICT developments that otherwise risks nothing but confusion. Services are what people exploit and consume, whether as private citizens or corporate employees. In this book we are treating the development of the commerce of technology-enabled services – whether B2B or B2C. By switching to the language of technology-enabled services, we correctly position the role of technology – the underlying capabilities that enable the service to be created and delivered. The hierarchy is clear: the service is the purpose, the master; the technology is the servant. In the words of the 20th century Hungarian modernist artist, Laszlo Moholy-Nagy: 'Technical progress should never be the goal, only the means'.[4]

APPLICATION PROFESSIONALISM

In the opening paragraphs of this chapter, we have discussed the impact of the non-IT professional alongside that of the consumer as users, moving to the front line in selecting, influencing, shaping and exploiting through their priorities what is on offer in the world of applied IT. We note that, as the contemporary capabilities of the technology became more integral to the operation of an increasing diversity of business and professional operations from accountancy to medicine to architecture and to the law, non-IT professionals themselves increasingly became the lead creators and innovators of how technology would be put to work in their corner of the economy.

This insight into the wide range of the human contribution to value creation from contemporary IT is mapped in Figure 1.2, developed by one of the authors in his work with CSC's Leading Edge Forum. The human contribution comes in three main forms: innate competencies (people tend to have them or not – e.g. an attention to detail, or a strategic mind-set); skills that can be trained; and (perhaps most importantly) accumulated experience. In the early days of the IT industry, the human contribution grew with a very strong technical professionalism at its heart. Our argument in this chapter is that the last decade has seen the rapid extension of the human spectrum to the right, into application professionalism. This spectrum is a very real one: people will position themselves on it in their work, and one individual alone cannot span the whole spectrum. (In practice, we will argue below, companies also face a real challenge to position themselves across the full spectrum: a company's core competencies at their heart are accumulations of the human contribution – and focus on the core competencies is about focus on a particular part of the spectrum.)

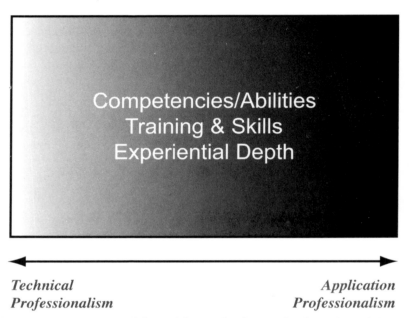

Technical   *Application*
Professionalism   *Professionalism*

FIGURE 1.2 *Human capabilities deliver value from technological capabilities*
Source: *CSC Leading Edge Forum, www.lef.csc.com*

A clear insight into the importance of the contribution of the non-IT professional (application professionalism) came in a report published in 2004. The rapid growth of offshoring in the early years of the new millennium led to wide concern in the UK (and in the USA) over the jobs of IT professionals being lost to workers overseas. The debate was (and remains) strong enough in the USA to have a significantly political dimension, including a fierce debate during the 2004 US Presidential campaign. In the UK the debate has been more muted since a peak of union protests in 2003. This fear has acted, nonetheless, as a significant brake on the exploitation of offshoring by the public sector.

In November 2004 Professor Mari Sako, of SAID Business School at Oxford University, and her colleagues published a report that presented a very different picture and gave a clear insight into the importance of the contribution of the non-IT professional (application professionalism).[5] Based on a detailed analysis of UK employment and trade statistics, it suggested that far more employment was being created through a fast-growing export performance than was being lost through offshoring. At the heart of the study was a presentation of the trade statistics for a significant sector of the UK economy, business services (see Figure 1.3).

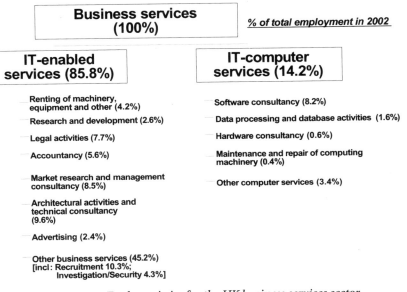

FIGURE 1.3 *Trade statistics for the UK business services sector*
Source: *UK Government Business Statistics, courtesy of Professor Mari Sako, SAID Business School, University of Oxford and AIM Research*

The category of business services in Figure 1.3 are B2B services characterized by a significant professional content, and nowadays generally enabled by the capabilities of contemporary ICT. This is a part of the white-collar sector of the B2B services market, distinguished from blue-collar B2B services such as catering, cleaning, building maintenance and security. One sub-sector, IT-computer services, is recognizably the home of the IT professional (technical professionalism).

The other sub-sector listed in Figure 1.3, IT-enabled services, is the home of the non-IT professional (application professionalism) – though building on a close collaboration with the IT professional. A fuller characterization could therefore be as professionally rich, technology-enabled B2B services – a characterization that better emphasizes that these services are as much as about applied IT as the services categorized under the IT-computer services rubric – which in turn are also characterized as professionally rich, technology-enabled services – with the emphasis of the professionalism perhaps more in the exploitation of the technology per se rather than its particular end application.

Such is the importance of the City to the UK economy that the statistics for financial services, which can in parallel also be characterized as professionally rich, technology-enabled services, are categorized and reported separately. The City, in its broadest sense (from banking to insurance, and incorporating its close links to other major UK geographical clusters of financial and insurance services such as Edinburgh and Leeds) delivers both B2B and B2C technology-enabled services.

The business services sector of the UK economy covered by the Sako study:

- employs 4 million people – one in seven jobs in the UK;
- has generated 50 per cent of UK job growth over two decades;
- provides a strong trade surplus (~£18 billion) – even as offshoring fuelled a fast growth in imports to ~£14 billion in 2004, exports grew even more rapidly to ~£32 billion;
- has a trade surplus across all sub-sectors, both IT-computer services and IT-enabled business services;
- has rising sector productivity, broadly matching that of the US (the other major net exporter of business services amongst the other Organisation for Economic Co-operation and Development (OECD) economies).

The importance of this study, and a similar study performed by the OECD in 2006, is that it represents the world of outsourcing and offshoring in a new light.

First, it reminds us, as noted above, that when a company outsources IT operations, it buys back IT-enabled services. Outsourcing as ITO, it buys back technologically enabled services where the professional focus is on the delivery of the IT service: outsourcing as BPO, the bought-back service requires a blend of professionalism in IT operations plus professionalism in their application in, say, payroll or invoicing.

Second, it demonstrates that there is a significantly broader market space in these IT-enabled services than the FM model of ITO and BPO may suggest – engineering services and architectural services are two examples, both rooted deeply in specific professionalisms, and both, in the 21st century, equally deeply rooted in applied ICT in their modus operandi. The strong UK trade performance reflects in good part the global competitiveness of its professionalism in these and other disciplines.

Third, it reminds us that, in a broad marketplace of technology-enabled services, the option exists to purchase the services, to source them, alongside the option of outsourcing: the existence of a marketplace in professionally rich, technology-enabled services that can be sourced as such.

The hallmark of these business services is that they bring together a blend of the specialized exploitation of technology in a particular discipline (application professionalism) with the delivery of the capabilities of the underlying IT (technological professionalism). In the main, the companies that deliver these business services are not necessarily IT companies: they are companies like Arup Partners (architectural engineering) or Schlumberger (oil and gas exploration and production technology), companies integral to, and identified with, their particular industries rather than the ICT industry.

Over the last decade, the exploitation of the capabilities of IT has become increasingly diverse and increasingly embedded across the whole of the modern economy. Applied IT has penetrated deeply into the many 'professionalisms' that support the modern economy – from accountancy to architecture, from construction to consultancy, from engineering to education, from logistics to law, from marketing to medicine, and from retailing to research. In each profession 'learning by doing' has developed a wealth of new capabilities, each carrying the clear mark of the profession – while subverting more broadly available generic IT capabilities (such as spreadsheets or email) to their particular needs.

In so doing, on the 'front line' of these operations, the way that IT is exploited has become increasingly distinct, increasingly shaped by the special nature of the profession or the business itself. In the 1980s, most businesses used IT to automate back-office functions that were much the same from business to business. By the start of the new decade the process of differentiation, industry-by-industry, had accelerated.

The importance of application professionalism is that it identifies that a major source of value creation (or 'value add') in these IT-enabled services lies outside the expertise of IT – and instead lies in how the IT is exploited for value in the end market. It lies in the professional user expertise, exemplifying the first of the two millennial shifts identified in the opening of this chapter.

Against this background, the work of Mari Sako and her colleagues importantly points to this broad market for B2B technology-enabled business services – more conveniently labelled as TEBS. TEBS cover a broad market spectrum, ranging from the strongly technological (server farm services, VOIP telecoms services) to the highly application specialist (legal patenting services, oil and gas exploration services). The market incorporates the spread of ITO and BPO – but as sub-sectors of a much wider market.

If we now take industry differentiation as increasingly rooted in application professionalism, and look to the way that technical professionalism is exploited – to deliver generic technologies effectively and efficiently, or to deliver special technologies that differentiate in particular ways – then the professionalism spectrum introduced above can be developed into a wide analysis of how different kinds of companies focus the use of their human resources (Figure 1.4).

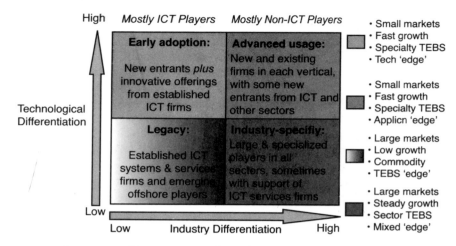

FIGURE 1.4 *How companies focus their use of human resources*
Source: *CSC Leading Edge Forum, www.lef.csc.com*

In the lower left quadrant of Figure 1.4 are the emerging commodity players – classic ICT companies whose real focus will be on 'making the technology deliver' in the form of commoditized infrastructural and transactional services (from the desktop to payroll, as two examples). In the lower right are the volume markets where a deeper understanding of how a given industry sector 'ticks', an intimacy with that industry, is key to success – application professionalism rules! The ICT companies (including the young Indian offshore tigers) envision their future here in the higher-value services that exist 'up the value chain': but in reality this is more the home of the Schlumbergers, the Uniparts and the Hewitts, companies with deep experience in their core competencies, expressed in specific application professionalisms – experiential depth that the ICT players lack (whether Indian, American or European), and can only gain speedily by acquisition or by being acquired.

The upper left is the home of the technically innovative (e.g. Skype), whose ultimate business success lies in 'crossing the chasm' and dropping to the big volume generic applications in the lower left quadrant. The most interesting quadrant is the upper right, where technical specialism is intimately blended with business specialism. It is worth exploring a couple of examples of companies that illustrate the difference between the upper right and lower left quadrants. Attenda Ltd runs server farms to deliver commoditized transactional services over the web for companies such as the airline bmi and the car rental company easycar. Attenda is positioned in the lower left quadrant – its ability to simultaneously run its server farms to very high reliability, very high loadings and very high flexibility delivers market-beating economics.

They are all about very high asset productivity. In contrast, Ffastfill Ltd specializes in serving the derivatives marketplace in the financial industries – highly specialized software technologies tightly aligned to the very special needs of the derivatives trader, and with the ability to rapidly change and adjust to new trading models. The difference is clear: the service provided by Ffastfill requires a deep intimacy with the derivatives trading process. The competencies, skills and experience of the staff employed by Attenda are very different from those of the people employed by Ffastfill. Each company has (and nurtures with great care) the human profile it requires to deliver a competitive edge through its chosen business model. Each delivers services (TEBS) that have competitively very distinct blends of human, technical and application professionalism.

Earlier in this chapter, we discussed the importance of moving to the language of services. The TEBS concept provides a useful bridge between the world of corporate ITO and BPO (technology-enabled) services and the world of consumerized online (technology- and web-enabled) services:

- it disengages from the FM model, replacing the concept of outsourcing with the concept of service sourcing;
- it underlines the importance of application professionalism as a major source of value creation in addition to/alongside the value creation provided by the capabilities of the ICT technologies exploited;
- it recognizes that TEBS are globally tradable goods, a natural component of the continual development of international trade.

The factors that will increasingly shape the developing international commerce in TEBS will be developed below. But first we need to consider the infrastructure, the utility, across which a growing portion of the commerce of TEBS is being conducted.

WEB 2.0 AND THE MYSPACE GENERATION

In the opening of this chapter, the emergence of the web from its academic and defence roots as a de facto public facility has been described – as has its vital role in providing a technological vector on which to align much key ICT industry innovation – both in globally recognized standards (the Internet Protocols) and in the open-systems capabilities required of an exponentially expanding whole of converged network and computing power. In so doing it has provided a global communications capability, and an emergent platform for services delivery, whose sophistication and capacity has been rapidly developed and evolved in the last half decade.

The contemporary web is in essence a public infrastructure of wired connections to widely distributed and interconnected computing power that scales to meet the needs of hundreds of millions of users. It is based on the widespread use of architectures designed as components and layers that can be easily accessed and recombined without prior coordination. 'Web 2.0' has been adopted as the shorthand for the newer standards and technologies now being exploited. Its development has been rendered even more potent by the rapid expansion of broadband and wireless access to the web across most of the OECD economies.

The lead players in this new world have been companies such as eBay, Google and Yahoo!, whose business models have grown initially around the demands of the individual consumer and, in responding to and learning from their needs, fired the development of an increasing sophistication of their 'offer'. Most particularly, unlike the classic hardware and software pricing models adopted by the IT industry of the previous decades, these consumer-oriented businesses have developed innovative advertising-funded business models more tightly aligned to their consumer services nature.

In parallel, development of the web's ability to offer access to and delivery of content in the widest sense – from textual 'stuff' to music, from the graphic to the photographic to the animated graphic to the full-scale video film and movie – has been enabled by the carrying capacity of both the web itself, and the means of access (from broadband to wireless broadband to third/fourth generation (3G/4G) mobile telephony).

Consumer services have classically been people-intensive, and thus expensive to deliver in the modern, developed economy. The story is told of a Victorian-era head of the Post Office who saw no future in the telephone given his easy access to messenger boys who, for a pittance, would run handwritten letters all over the City at the snap of his finger – the Victorian instant messaging (IM) service? A key feature of new-generation web-based services has been the ability to automate them and deliver them over the web in ways designed to make it easy for the user to do most of the hard work.

The cost-volume economics of capital-intensive and software-based services are very strongly volume-driven. Unit costs drop sharply with increasing volumes: the marginal costs of software itself are close to zero once it is in place and in operation. By contrast, people-rich services have cost-volume economics that drive up unit costs with increasing volume, because of the need to organize and manage the human dimension in which the (intangible) assets reside.

Automating the human contribution thus shifts the service model from a one-to-one, high people-to-capital ratio whose unit costs tends to rise with volume, to a one-to-many, high capital-to-people ratio, where unit costs rapidly drop to almost zero at the margin (Figure 1.5).[6]

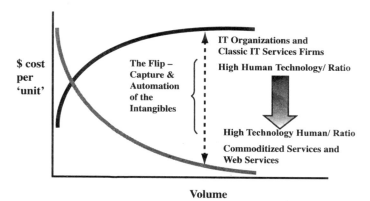

FIGURE 1.5   *Automation of the human contribution*
Source: *CSC Leading Edge Forum, www.lef.csc.com*

One significant development of the new decade has been the ability to capture and automate human (intangible) experiential assets, delivering them as services over the web. The commercial drivers are clear from Figure 1.5: the economics of the service 'flip' from the top curve to the bottom curve, radically rewriting the cost structure of the business model.

One of the fundamental questions organizations need to address at the outset of any outsourcing decision making is 'Why are we outsourcing?' and the answer one receives is different depending on who you ask within an organization.

Is it tactical? – 'We need to cut costs.'

Is it strategic? – 'We are growing and hence need to find the right partner or new location for us to site operations.'

If it is a tactical decision and an organization needs to dramatically reduce costs – and speed is of the essence – then an offshore third-party arrangement may deliver better short-term returns than a trying to build operations in an offshore, lower-cost environment. However, if the answer is strategic and an organization is looking to change its business model, then more time needs to be taken in understanding what is core to the business and what can be outsourced/offshored dependent upon the skills in particular locations.

The next piece of analysis will be to understand which processes are to be outsourced/offshored, and how. Again, a common pitfall that

(Continued)

17

(Continued)

organizations fall into is either trying to outsource the end-to-end process without any view on ownership, management and controls, or over-engineering the process to such an extent that the supplier is actually hamstrung in being able to deliver the service.

Knowing the actual capabilities of the supplier is vital in defining what they will be performing on your behalf and what will remain in-house. Our experience shows that many suppliers often claim to already be performing all of the processes you wish to outsource, but the reality is somewhat different. However, irrespective of whether the suppliers claim they already perform the processes for other parties, processes that add competitive advantage to your organization or have a high element of your organization's intellectual property should not be outsourced to a third party.

Kesh Sharma, Director, Magellan Consultancy Services (Magellan won the National Outsourcing Association 2004/2005 'Best Outsourcing Advisor' award), www.magellancs.com

The new business models thus enabled range from relatively straightforward 'self-services' such as online airline ticket and rental car booking, to significantly more sophisticated services such as eBay and salesforce.com. The latter brings to the screen the digested experience of decades of professional selling, expressed in a complex of rules embedded in the operating software, combined with a diversity of analytical tools that can be put to work by the user – all delivered over the web as 'software as a service' (SaaS).

The 1990s saw the development of the service bureau model (introduced, as noted above, alongside the FM model) into the concept of the application service provider (ASP) – a contemporary version of the service bureau in which a particular software application (such as an accounting suite) would be run for a number of clients with online availability. The Web 2.0 developments give new impetus to the ASP model, and most software providers are now actively moving to create SaaS offerings, requiring new business models that charge for usage 'by unit transaction' rather than an up-front licence fee and annual maintenance charge.

In parallel, these developments support the commercial evolution of commoditized transactional services: standardized services in areas such as accounting that can be tightly specified, and thus highly commoditized, for delivery at very low cost over the web. These web-delivered services (web services) are also a class of TEBS. Very clearly the TEBS family can now be widened to include the great diversity of B2C (business to consumer) TEBS and the fast-growing families of C2C (consumer to consumer) TEBS that the internet enables.

A further feature of the Web 2.0 revolution is that the service offerings are increasingly two-way in the fullest sense. Availability of the services on the web enables full customer interaction with them – as with airline booking systems where search, enquiry, and options development and evaluation are now the norm before the actual booking is made. The capabilities of the web allow remote management and servicing of kit, including upgrading software, adding new software, trouble-shooting, maintenance and backup. The TEBS universe merges seamlessly with the virtualization of process and de-localization of location.

Thus the twin capabilities of Web 2.0 and broadband fuel the second of the two discontinuities that this chapter has set out to discuss:

- the strengthening of the internet as an essentially (global) public infrastructure through which web-enabled services can be delivered and accessed with increasing ease;
- the power of contemporary software to capture human-based (intangible) intellectual property and commoditize it into a whole range of services whose economics of production and delivery are highly competitive.

THE LEVEL PLAYING FIELD: A GLOBALIZATION OF SERVICES

In this chapter, we have explained how the rapid growth in business to consumer (B2C) services over the recent decade has been enabled by – and speeded the development of – the web, the internet, into an increasingly powerful public utility. We have shown how the established phenomenon of outsourcing, based on the facilities management (FM) model, is now better understood as a sub-sector of the fast-developing market in business-to-business (B2B) technology-enabled business services (TEBS), and that the performance of these services rests not only on the contributions of technological professionalism (in making the technology perform) but also the contributions of application professionalism (in delivering market-valued performance).

The more recent strengthening of access to the internet through wireless and broadband, and the development of Web 2.0-enabled infrastructural capabilities, now provides an essentially public and global infrastructure of 'industrial' capacity and strength that increasingly allows TEBS to be offered and sourced irregardless of location or distance, while Web 2.0-enabled web service capabilities open the door to the commoditization of an ever-growing diversity of services that start with a high human (expensive) content and are reshaped as automated low human (highly cost competitive) services.

Let us therefore set out some key features of a new model, a new paradigm that describes how the individual and the corporate will increasingly source and access the contemporary capabilities of the ICT industry.

1. A marketplace for services, technology-enabled services, that are increasingly internet-accessible or delivered over the web, and increasingly globally traded – a global marketplace.

2. The contemporary internet, combined with increasingly powerful means of access (e.g. broadband, wireless) creates the potential for a level playing field for this global marketplace in terms of access.

3. As the ICT industry matures from 'purveyor of kit, bits and bytes' to a 'purveyor of services', and as the journey through ITO to BPO educates and develops both the industry and its corporate customer, the distinction between the value-adding contribution of technological professionalism (making the technology perform) and the value-adding of application professionalism (delivering market-valued performance) becomes sharper – one important competitive differentiator.

4. In turn, this value creation from the contribution of application professionalism means that the ICT industry finds itself joined by a widening phalanx of new competitors whose background is more embedded in the business of sectors other than ICT. The boundaries of the (technology-rich) TEBS services marketplace are set far wider than the ICT industry can scope or address.

5. The distinction between B2B and B2C services will blur, as many B2C technology-enabled services are and will be exploitable in the corporate environment – a service is a service is a service.

In the chapters that follow, the issues raised by the developments need to be addressed, scoped and freed into these new contexts. What factors will influence the growth and development of the world trade in technology-enabled services? What will be the impact on the maturing global vendor community? Beyond Web 2.0, what are the full ranges of technological enablers that potentially can reshape the global level playing field further? And what will be their impact? What will a fully globalized service economy look like? And what skills will it demand and reward? What are the new messages for the modern IT professional? How will the global delivery model work, and what business models may emerge?

As business process outsourcing becomes increasingly commonplace, the discussion is shifting from debating its merits, to trying to better understand how BPO may redefine the future shape of business.

One example we can look to as a guide is manufacturing, especially in the electronic manufacturing services industry. What happened there was that companies first outsourced the fabrication of specific components – a chip here, a board there, a cable set somewhere else. But, over time, and especially as new competitors entered the industry seeking to rapidly capitalize on a breakthrough product idea, this selective approach gave way to a more integrated relationship with just one or maybe a couple of top-tier suppliers.

These top-tier suppliers, companies like Solectron, Flextronics, and Jabil, now often manage the entire manufacturing supply chain for some of the very largest companies in that industry. And, their services have expanded over time to start at the moment of product inception and continue all the way through to the support of the product in the field and even its disposition at the end of the product's useful life. Essentially, the electronic manufacturing services companies have become the real manufacturers, while the companies we generally think of as the manufacturers have become market-savvy product innovators and solution integrators for their customers.

BPO service providers may eventually do the same thing for the services side of the business as these top-tier electronics suppliers have done for manufacturing. After all, internal services operations are essentially factories. They produce the product used by the business's internal and external customers. It's reasonable to project out to the day when that 'factory' isn't even part of the company anymore, but is instead run by BPO's future equivalent of today's top-tier manufacturing services providers.

Michael F. Corbett, Executive director of the International Association of Outsourcing Professionals (IAOP) (www.outsourcingprofessional.org), and the author of *The Outsourcing Revolution*[7]

2 Business Processes Develop into Knowledge Processes

The level playing field agenda: The remote delivery of services is a proven business model. Companies across the world are already engaged in business process outsourcing, yet the goalposts are moving daily. As service providers start offering patent writing, research and other high-value services, where will the new boundaries of the retained organization be located?

In August 2005, Kiran Karnik, president of the Indian National Association of Software and Service Companies (NASSCOM), predicted that the country's IT exports would grow by 32 per cent to touch US\$22.3 billion by the end of the year. After he quoted the positive predictions from various market analysts and displayed ever-upward charts to the assembled journalists he made an interesting statement: he said that knowledge process outsourcing (KPO)[1] was set to outgrow the BPO sector in coming years.

Although Mr Karnik did not quantify the potential of the KPO industry he claimed that a lot of foreign companies were looking at India for setting up research and development services. China and East European nations were the major states that were well poised to give a tough fight to India in the sector, he observed.

In general, as has been observed since the millennium in India, the global business process outsourcing sector continues to go from strength to strength, with high levels of activity – both onshore and offshore. Complementing this growth is the spurt in new suppliers offering highly complex services, such as research or analytics. This trend is often termed 'moving up the value chain' – a dreadful cliché uttered far too often by commentators who forget that less complex services can also be of great value.

However, it remains a fact that suppliers are moving up the value chain and offering more complex services. The increased nature of global competition and subsequent impact on profitability has forced many service companies to expand their range of services, with the move to offering more complex tasks being a natural next step where they have already established credibility in other areas.

KPO is merely a continuation of BPO, though with rather more business complexity. The defining difference is that KPO is usually focused on knowledge-intensive business processes that require significant domain expertise (application professionalism in the language of Chapter 1). The offshore team servicing a KPO contract cannot be easily hired overnight as they will be highly educated and trained, and trusted to take decisions on behalf of the client.

As we highlighted in the opening chapter of this book, IT outsourcing is strongly focused around technical professionalism, and the migration to business process outsourcing introduces this extra dimension of application professionalism. Ever more complex services, as implied by KPO, demonstrate this very well. The profile of people being hired to serve within KPO service companies are more diverse than just being drawn from technical IT services – these are people with MBAs, and medical, engineering, design or other specialist business skills.

KPO delivers higher value to organizations that offshore their domain-based processes, thereby enhancing the traditional cost–quality paradigm of BPO. The central theme of KPO is to create value for the client by providing business expertise rather than process expertise. So KPO involves a shift from standardized processes to advanced analytical thinking, technical skills and decisive judgement based on experience.

THE MAIN DRIVERS

There are a number of reasons for the rapid growth of the market for international and offshore KPO services:

- **BPO suppliers seeking better profits** from higher-value services. It is clear that the profit margin on high-cost services is much better than very basic, repetitive services. Suppliers offering quite basic services, such as tape transcription, can improve profits by offering intellectual services such as research that have a stronger value to the client.
- **Buyers saving more** may seem counter-intuitive given the previous bullet point, but the cost of securing the services of an MBA in the USA is very different to the same service in a developing region. The difference for these skilled resources or services is more than the difference between lower-value resources, for example a local call centre agent compared to an offshore call centre agent.
- **Existing suppliers spreading the range of their service** provision to capture an increase in similar, but more complex, business. Suppliers in the offshore services business are constantly spreading their wings into new areas in an effort to be able to offer the exact service a client will ask for the next time the telephone rings.
- **Existing clients** of BPO services often ask the service provider to take on additional services. As the supply chain has been increasingly outsourced suppliers have gained KPO skills, often without an explicit strategy to do so. This is very common where the relationship between client and supplier is healthy; both will

work together to increase the load on the supplier, in their mutual interest.

- **Global competition is getting cheaper.** This means that basic BPO services can often be performed elsewhere for less, so suppliers need to raise the level of service that they can offer. Even a country such as India, which enjoys a large share of the offshore BPO market, cannot avoid the reality that other locations are cheaper – and provide good service. For basic services, cost is the deciding factor; for KPO, value is more important than cost.
- **Skills shortages** in many developed regions in specific industries are making it attractive to consider either controlled immigration or selective offshoring in order to remain competitive in a global market.

THE UPWARD TRENDS

Global demand for outsourcing continues to grow with organizations looking to outsource more of their business functions, often moving beyond traditional outsourcing segments. The global demand for IT services and BPO is naturally hard to pin down as different analysts use different measurements and some exclude IT. However, there is a consensus that this market should be worth around US$1 trillion by 2008.

This estimate is not the total amount of services that are offshored, it represents outsourcing where the supplier can be local or remote. However, the growth of KPO and the maturity of offshore suppliers mean that the potential for offshoring BPO is rapidly increasing. It is true that there is a natural limit to what can be offshored as not all processes are suitable for a variety of reasons, such as labour intensity, interdependency, continuity, risk, availability of skills, requirement for local knowledge, or regulatory constraints. Some companies have a perception that offshoring carries a high risk and some still doubt that the capabilities to perform their particular task can exist in another location. When a task requires complex decision making and complex communications then the ability to send it to an outsourced supplier, especially one that is offshore, reduces dramatically – yet the growth in KPO shows that the boundaries of potential are shifting.

In our view, around 60 per cent of tasks that are presently outsourced could be sent to remote offshore locations – theoretically. As KPO continues to mature it is likely that this figure will increase to around 85 per cent. This is the potential for KPO seen by many suppliers, eager to enter the market during this period of rapid growth. Actual market penetration is likely to be much lower, as it is unlikely that the potential for offshoring will ever be achieved by those who want to see a 'perfect' market environment, where the best-value provider always wins the contract.

> KPO firms offer a host of knowledge-based services ranging from analytics and equity research to patent-writing and radiology. Most of these services require resources with more specialized business and technical knowledge than a basic BPO service.
>
> Unlike BPO, where cost arbitrage is the main driver, KPO offers a more enriched value proposition. Firms can outsource modules of their own supply chain to 'knowledge-partners' elsewhere in the world and get the same, if not better, quality insight, guidance and consulting for their business. Consequently, intellectual capital becomes a key driver of KPO growth.
>
> In the long-term, many companies selling services on cost arbitrage benefits alone are likely to struggle from the sheer scale of global competition, but those KPO suppliers with specific knowledge and expertise will succeed. The future of KPO lies in making global talent available for business problems anywhere.
>
> B.M. Awadhesh, Chief Executive Officer, Brainmatics (A division of CTR Mfg. Ind. Ltd.) www.brainmatics.net

To use India as an example, NASSCOM estimates suggest that offshore penetration is likely to increase from an estimated 6.3 per cent of the global IT services and BPO market in 2004–2005 to 8.8 per cent by 2007.[2] The value of the global services delivered from offshore locations is forecast to rise from US$39.6 billion in 2004 to nearly US$74 billion by 2007. Because of this immense potential and genuine market growth, the KPO market continues to grow at a rapid double-digit pace across the world.

The Indian BPO industry achieved revenues of US$5.2 billion, recording a growth of 44.5 per cent in the full year 2004–2005. NASSCOM has forecast that the Indian IT-ITES (Information Technology Enabled Services) industry will grow at approximately 44.4 per cent and reach US$5.7 billion by the end of the 2004–2005 financial year – a compounded annual growth rate of 56.4 per cent over 2000–2005. These trends are startling and, with the addition of KPO growth and the compound factor, it is certain that India will continue to lead the offshore BPO market for some time.

India is rather a special case as it has a 'mature' BPO industry ready to feed the ambitions of fledging KPO suppliers. Local entrepreneurs such as Raman Roy, formerly of Citigroup and Wipro,[3] have entered into the national psyche as heroes to be admired. Who can argue that Mr Roy does not cut a dashing figure with his psychedelic braces, large cigar and wide grin, but it would be considered slightly deviant for British undergraduates to be pinning photographs of Sir Richard Branson inside their business school locker.

25

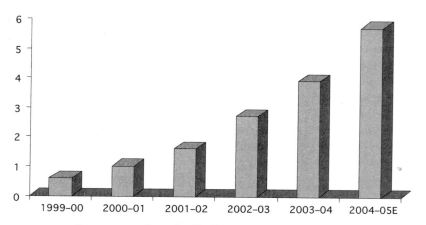

FIGURE 2.1   *Growth of Indian ITES-BPO, 2000–2005*
Source: *NASSCOM*

The key driver for this BPO growth is the supplier company's ability to rapidly build up the scale of operations to match the increasing breadth of and demand for services in order to provide an integrated single contract. The major visible trends are a maturing supplier landscape, high levels of technological absorption, continued market consolidation, increased breadth of services offered to include KPO, widening of the customer base, and relatively stable pricing levels. The industry is witnessing the first major shakeout as those who have attempted to board the BPO gravy train in search of riches see their companies fail, merge or be acquired by a rival.

SHIFTING SANDS FOR BPO

The reasoning behind offshore BPO has formerly been one of cost, cost and then cost. It remains so in many quarters and many less experienced service companies continue to preach the low-cost mantra failing to understand that, across the world, their clients have moved on. BPO itself is shifting away from being purchased only because of a need to reduce operational costs. KPO can never really be purchased because of price alone because of its very nature. Comparative cost analysis may play a role in KPO purchasing decisions, where different organizations are offering the same service at different prices, but it is unlikely to be the primary driver behind to move to offshore an intellectual service.

Some of the key changes in the BPO industry at present that are influencing the greater development and adoption of KPO services are discussed next.

Cost structure

The comparative cost advantage was one of the major reasons that brought outsourcing to many offshore locations such as India or the Philippines. Any European or American company outsourcing to these offshore locations would usually like to achieve cost savings in the region of 50 per cent. However, the salaries of these offshore professionals are rising and overseas clients are unsure whether the cost savings are attractive enough anymore; the savings must be substantial to justify the risk of major change. With the rising salaries and infrastructure costs in many offshore locations and the increase in competition between these regions it is becoming harder for suppliers to price services at the low prices seen just a few years ago.

City infrastructure

Metropolitan areas have dominated the offshore outsourcing industry. The relentless growth of business in these limited regions is stretching the fragile infrastructure of several countries, including the leader of the pack, India. Indian international airports are atrocious by international standards and gleaming offices packed to the hilt with BPO employees sit cheek by jowl with desperate shantytown dwellers. In many regions a lack of adequate trained manpower is increasing the rate of attrition and stimulating the corresponding cost of constantly hiring, just to stand still.

Many companies see the future as smaller, more remote towns, yet these 'second-tier' towns often have a less developed infrastructure than the major cities.

Data security

A key issue in the area of data security is the lack of any global guidance or comprehensive international legislation. In the absence of it, customers are cautious to outsource work that involves any personal customer data. However, this information is usually essential for any back-office work – especially in the financial services industry.

Data protection is easier to guarantee if operations remain within the European Union countries because the EU data protection directive has harmonized laws throughout Europe. Personal data can flow from the 25 EU member states and three EEA member countries (Norway, Liechtenstein and Iceland) and to a select few other nations without any further safeguards. The EU has recognized Switzerland, Canada, Argentina, Guernsey, Isle of Man and the US Department of Commerce's Safe Harbour Privacy Principles as providing adequate data protection.

Ultimately though, most crime involving information is performed by employees, regardless of where they are located. Improved procedures can help to prevent most data theft, but a determined criminal will circumnavigate the rules. Implementing the kind of anti-social-engineering procedures outlined by Kevin Mitnick in his book *The Art of Deception*[4] can protect corporate data to a far greater extent than any basic security practices, but it will be some time before all offshore service providers are as conscientious as this.

Increasing market

Companies have noticed that continued good performance in current projects can lead to the customer getting more convinced about the outsourcing model and therefore confident enough to outsource higher-level or more complex work. This is particularly significant in the context of increased competition because the additional experience at many levels of the supply chain is allowing some service providers to differentiate themselves in the market, though they may have started by offering very basic tasks. Market growth is stimulated by addressing new services and eventually the services rise far enough up the supply chain to require enough responsibility on the service provider to be considered KPO.

Threat of improved technology

Basic back-office BPO is a commodity service and can be commoditized and broken into a series of steps in the same way that basic manufacturing can. When organizations such as British Airways have already transferred all the services their call centre agents perform to their ba.com website one has to wonder if the traditional call centre is no longer required. Of course, companies such as British Airways will continue to answer the phone, but a large number of customers are likely to switch to self-service because it is faster and easier than calling and asking someone to perform a basic service you can do yourself with the click of a mouse.

Intelligent voice response (IVR) is heralded as a technology that will also make the call centre agent's job a thing of the past. At present these systems remain an annoying nuisance ('press 1 to hear Mozart for 15 minutes, press 2 if you are losing the will to live ...'), yet voice recognition technology is improving to the point where basic services can be requested without the need for a human operator through voice commands.

Technological changes of this nature may bring the entire model of outsourcing low-value tasks to a lower-cost location into question. If commoditized work is automated then the services performed by humans will only be those tasks where intelligence or decision making is required, hence the desire to grow expertise in KPO from many companies who presently specialize in basic services.

THE POTENTIAL KPO MARKET

While many regions continue to exploit the ongoing outsourcing of low-end commodity services, there is also a clear view emerging that the cost argument, so long the driver for offshore outsourcing, cannot be used as a primary driver any longer. In addition, new market entrants will almost certainly be cheaper than those presently offering offshore services so any region currently achieving success in this industry must seek to tap into the growing market for KPO services, exploiting their existing experience and client base to move beyond very basic services.

One glance at the Evalueserve data in Figure 2.2 makes the case even stronger for a focus on KPO – it is growing much faster than BPO services. The predication is for global BPO to increase year-on-year by about 26 per cent to 2010. The same statistic for KPO is 45 per cent.[5]

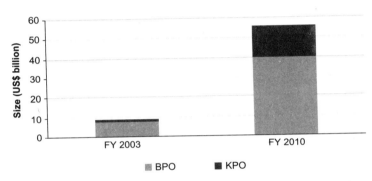

FIGURE 2.2   *Expected growth in global offshore BPO and KPO Markets, 2003–2010*
Source: *Evalueserve Analysis*

Clearly for the outsourcing of low-end, non-strategic processes, the future is nothing but commoditization and automation. Creating non-cost-oriented differentiation in the market is where most suppliers of note are focused at present. There is a focus on high quality for many companies, rather than a repeated analysis of cost alone. This trend can be observed as many companies that started outsourcing non-core functions to offshore partners have now started outsourcing complete end-to-end processes.

In their research paper 'India in the new knowledge economy',[6] the Confederation of Indian Industry estimate that the global KPO industry will grow at 46 per cent to reach US$14–17 billion by 2010, with India's share hoped to be around 70 per cent. This could be possible as India now has years of experience in delivering offshore IT and BPO services – moving to provide more complex services is much easier if you have experience in a similar market. However, a lot of Indian companies have failed to move on from the low-cost BPO strategy and continue to market their services as cheap, not something the KPO buyer wants to see. With countries like Ukraine, Hungary, Poland, the Czech Republic and the Philippines offering

BPO services at a lower rate – before even thinking of any one of dozens of African nations – Indian companies have to shift their focus to KPO or risk being washed away from the global services industry by a storm of lower-priced equally capable opposition.

NASSCOM have created their own estimate of demand in India for KPO services and broken it down across very specific types of intellectual service, as demonstrated in Table 2.1.

TABLE 2.1 *Market potential forecast for emerging KPO services, 2003–2010*

Service line (US$ billion)	2003	2010	CAGR*
Basic data search, integration and management	0.3	5.0	50.0%
Market research and competitive intelligence	0.02	0.4	54.0%
Equity research, actuarial analytics and data modelling	–	0.4	NA**
Engineering design	0.4	2.0	29.0%
Animation and simulation	0.1	1.4	46.0%
Medical content and services	–	0.3	NA
Remote education and publishing	–	2.0	NA
Research and development (non-IT)	0.1	1.0	39.0%
Biotech and pharmaceuticals	0.28	3.0	40.0%
Total	**1.2**	**15.5**	**43.5%**

Source: NASSCOM
* Compound Annual Growth Rate
** Not Available

From these estimates, it seems that the typical users of KPO services globally are market research agencies and consulting firms, investment banks and financial services institutions, legal firms, telecoms, engineering design, automotive firms, publishing houses, data aggregators and corporate planning departments of large organizations. Many smaller companies may consider KPO services for very specific project-based tasks.

It is clear that any global region with expertise in such sectors as banking, health care, pharmaceuticals or biotechnology should be considering how to offer that expertise remotely. The market for high-value services is growing much faster than the more general BPO market and will do so for many years to come.

As we prepared the final version of this text, Evalueserve managed to provide an interesting addition to their detailed 2004 report.[7] Especially for inclusion in this book, their researchers went back to the initial analysis and revisited their predictions for the growth of the global KPO industry, both in terms of dollar value and also the numbers of people involved in providing high-end KPO services.

Table 2.2 lists the KPO activities, with the original 2004 predictions alongside the revised prediction from August 2006.

Though most of the predictions remain valid, there are a few downward revisions that are also reflected in the numbers for India alone (see Table 2.3). What is most interesting about the global figures in Table 2.2 is that the research into lead optimization is revised upwards, although the figure for India remains static, which indicates that there clearly is market growth outside India.

Table 2.3 shows the same information, but focused on India alone. As India is offering such a large proportion of the global market in KPO services, it is interesting to analyse the prediction changes here as well.

The main casualty in India has been data searching, warehousing and analytics, with the revised prediction being less than half that of the 2004 analysis. Remote logistics, marketing and medical processes have also been revised downwards. Although these sectors are still growing, it is clear that the Evalueserve researchers feel that they are not growing at the rate expected back in 2004. In general, there is a slightly tempered prediction from the Evalueserve team for a few areas of KPO, but the majority of growth predictions remain valid – and the growth predicted for this sector is significant.

KNOWLEDGE PROCESS OUTSOURCING CASE STUDIES

This chapter has reported on the reasons for the growth of KPO and how the international market for high-value services is developing, but to fully understand the relevance of KPO and why it is important, it is useful to illustrate the argument with some case studies of various services. Two projects from two different companies will be used to demonstrate the type of services that can be performed from a remote location.

Evalueserve

Evalueserve (website www.evalueserve.com) base their delivery from Gurgaon, close to Delhi, although most of their senior directors are spread across the USA and Europe. Evalueserve has published some of the most interesting research on outsourcing in the past year including detailed analysis of the effect of offshoring on the US and UK economies, the impact of the Indian diaspora on development at home, and specific work on the rise of KPO. They offer several KPO services in addition to their

TABLE 2.2   *Comparison of predicted worldwide KPO activities, 2004 and 2006*

Description	FY-2010 revenue: estimated at April 2004 (in US$ million) Worldwide	Number of professionals: estimated at April 2004 Worldwide	FY-2010 revenue: estimated at August 2006 (in US$ million) Worldwide	Number of professionals: estimated at August 2006 Worldwide
Investment research	400	8,000	400	8,000
Data searching, warehousing, analytics	4,000	80,000	**1,750**	**35,000**
Business research	1,000	20,000	1,000	20,000
Human resources – research and analytics	200	4,000	200	4,000
Market research and computing intelligence	400	10,000	400	10,000
Engineering design and architecture – research and communications	2,000	42,000	2,000	42,000
Designing, animations and video gaming	1,400	33,000	1,400	33,000
Legal and intellectual property	350	7,000	350	7,000
Medical content and process offshoring	250	6,000	**150**	**3,500**
Remote education, publishing, technical writing	2,000	40,000	2,000	40,000
CROs*, lead optimization and analytics	3,000	60,000	**5,250**	**105,000**
Translation and localization	1,100	27,500	1,100	27,500
Support for marketing and sales	200	4,000	200	4,000
Remote logistic services and procurement	500	12,500	**300**	**7,500**
Network optimization and analytics	200	3,500	200	3,500
Total	17,000	357,500	16,700	350,000

* Contract Research Organizations

TABLE 2.3 *Comparison of predicted KPO activities for India, 2004 and 2006*

Description	FY-2010 revenue: estimated at April 2004 (in US$ million)	Number of professionals: estimated at April 2004	FY-2010 revenue: estimated at August 2006 (in US$ million)	Number of professionals: estimated at August 2006
	India	India	India	India
Investment research	350	7,000	350	7,000
Data searching, warehousing, analytics	3,000	60,000	**1,250**	**25,000**
Business research	400	8,000	400	8,000
Human resources – research and analytics	100	2,000	100	2,000
Market research and computing intelligence	300	7,500	300	7,500
Engineering design and architecture – research and communications	1,500	30,000	1,500	30,000
Designing, animations and video gaming	1,000	22,500	1,000	22,500
Legal and intellectual property	300	6,000	300	6,000
Medical content and process offshoring	200	4,000	**100**	**2,000**
Remote education, publishing, technical writing	1,000	20,000	1,000	20,000
CROs*, lead optimization and analytics	2,250	45,000	2,250	45,000
Translation and localization	900	22,500	900	22,500
Support for marketing and sales	150	3,000	**100**	**2,000**
Remote logistic services and procurement	400	10,000	**200**	**4,000**
Network optimization and analytics	150	2,500	150	2,500
Total	12,000	250,000	9,900	206,000

* Contract Research Organizations

research services. Interestingly, their senior management team had never all been together in the same room at the same time until a strategy conference in Cambridge, UK in January 2005 – a real virtual success story.

Alok Aggarwal and Marc Vollenweider set up Evalueserve in December 2000 with the intention of capturing the high-value and high-complexity end of the BPO value chain. The company has grown steadily since then and accelerated in the past couple of years.

Evalueserve has now delivered work in 192 different countries and in 65 different languages. Their research team in India is very well educated and a third of them are graduates of the Indian Institutes of Technology and the Indian Institutes of Management (the elite 'Ivy League' schools of India), each with potential GMAT (Graduate Management Admission Test) scores of between 680 and 720.

Case study 1: Market prioritization

This project involved calculating the market prioritization for a leading chain of fast-food restaurants to enable the client to identify attractive markets for future expansion.[8] Evalueserve approached the task of identifying markets that the client should consider for expansion by analysing both the demand and supply side. Demand-side analysis required the formulation of a model that could predict 'consumption propensity' for the core product categories. The demand-side diagnostics were calibrated with supply-side dynamics (competition, marketing and retail investment costs) to formulate a model that could assign a weighted attractiveness score to various markets.

The client provided access to sales data across markets and consumer level data (which included demographics, behaviour and attitude). The sales data was mapped with consumer-level data to identify consumption drivers and to create a profile of consumer segments (both core consumers and those who exhibit poor receptivity). The consumption propensity in each market is factored along with the prevailing competitive environment to construct an 'attractiveness index' for each market. The attractiveness index is used as a decision rule to shortlist markets for future expansion.

The client has used and continues to use this analysis to devise their retail expansion strategy, a clear example of a knowledge service driving the strategy of a restaurant business.

Case study 2: Customer retention analysis

This project involved the analysis of customer churn (ongoing loss and replacement of customers) and retention using historic data to predict content response rates, for designing future content strategies for a large internet media client.

The analysis of consumer churn was based on past account and usage data to provide a more detailed analysis of correlations between content usage and churn in both the US and Europe. The data for analysis consisted of over 120 million account records, making a data size of over 180 Gb to be analysed systematically.

The Evalueserve team created a large data warehouse by merging weekly data for internal product usage of over 100,000 accounts. Measurements were developed to assist in predicting the correlation between content use and churn rates. For example, one group of consumers might be those who spend 20–40 per cent of all online time using email – this online behaviour can be correlated to the churn rate, forming the ability to predict which consumer may leave the service soon. A 'dashboard'-type overview was created using PowerPoint to present the information in an intelligent manner with qualitative inputs based on the quantitative analysis.

The client has used the results from this analysis to devise the content development and marketing spend strategy for their global customers.

NIIT SmartServe

NIIT SmartServe is a global business process management organization based in India.[9] NIIT SmartServe's integrated suite of services blends state-of-the-art technology and business process expertise to deliver significant identifiable cost savings to its customers.

NIIT's facilities at Gurgaon (near New Delhi) bring together the benefits of an advanced telecommunication infrastructure and an enriching partnership with top-tier IT service providers. The human resource at NIIT SmartServe is a differentiator – a pool of hand-picked talented and professional personnel, eager to be on a steep learning curve. With a rich employee development and training culture inherited from NIIT Ltd (NIIT is well-known across India as a training company), the ability to 'skill' and 'scale' manpower strength is a big asset for NIIT SmartServe in the outsourcing arena.

NIIT operates in 44 countries, providing learning, software and knowledge solutions to customers in Asia, Europe, India, Japan and the USA. NIIT is the first and so far only Asian education and training organization to feature among the IDC Top 20 Global IT training market leaders for three consecutive years.

Case study 3: Financial services compliance

Sesame is the leading provider of support services to 7,000 financial advisers across the UK. Some of the services provided include compliance and regulatory support, access to the latest product research, training and development technical seminars and access to cutting-edge technology that allows advisers to write business more efficiently. The Sesame organization achieved a turnover of £335 million in 2003–2004. Sesame is a part of the Misys Group (turnover £900 million in 2003–2004). Misys primarily provides software solutions to the banking and securities, health care and financial sectors.

Most financial and insurance products marketed in the UK are now regulated by the FSA (Financial Services Authority). Sesame provides a range of support services to its customers to enable them to operate safely within the regulatory framework. One such service is checking point-of-sale documentation and the suitability of advice. Sesame's customers provide a broad range of financial advice to their clients. Records of this advice have to be retained. These records are checked in order to protect the interests of the end clients from unsuitable or inappropriate advice, and reduce Sesame's exposure to the cost of rectifying 'bad' business.

Before NIIT SmartServe could undertake the service for Sesame from a remote location they first had to ensure that personnel carrying out the compliance work were trained and certified on UK financial regulations, products and services. Exams had to be conducted by the IFS (Institute of Financial Services, UK) and approved by the Qualifications and Curriculum Authority (QCA, UK). All staff, even in India, needed to be qualified to the same professional level as the financial advisors in the UK itself.

The primary objective of the compliance service is to assess the point-of-sale documentation and the 'suitability of the advice'. The offshore team check on the advice being given (Figure 2.3) and determine whether the product or service meets the client's needs and requirements and that all factors and alternatives have been considered. For example, they have to consider the following:

- the client's ability to pay;
- that the benefits are appropriate to the client's circumstances;
- that the investment funds are commensurate with the client's stated risk profile;
- if any other product would have been a better choice;
- any specific requirements or instructions stated by the client.

The case is then checked against a CFA (client file assessment form). There are five types of CFA:

- basic CFA (points would differ for savings and investments, protection, pension);
- equity release (now called lifetime mortgages);
- execution only;
- mortgage;
- general insurance.

The basic CFA has 10 sections covering the important elements of the advice process, each of which will have a number of related points. A case would typically be checked on over 100 technical points. Turnaround times are very good, especially compared to the client requirements, as demonstrated in Figure 2.4.

process overview

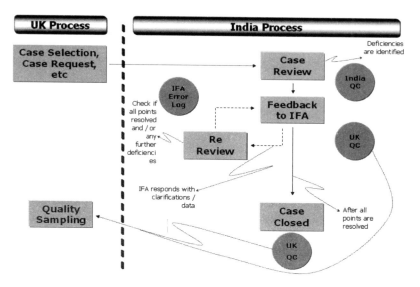

FIGURE 2.3 *The Sesame process overview*
Source: *NIIT SmartServe*

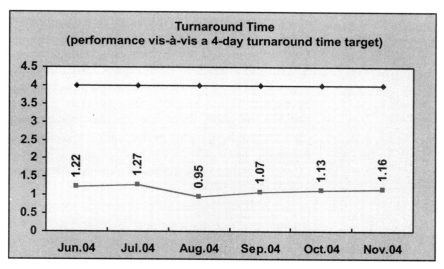

FIGURE 2.4 *Turnaround time – performance compared to four-day target*

In the two years that the process has been based in India a number of process improvements have been initiated to increase the level of service offered to Sesame:

- Abby baby – a package developed in-house to minimize errors in free-text entry during the review process.
- Tracker software – built in-house by NIIT, this helps in monitoring cases and individual performance.
- Key account management – an enhanced service provided by NIIT SmartServe towards the management of key independent financial advisors (IFAs).
- Redefining quality – ensuring a better service to Sesame and IFAs. Quality redefined to include the case management perspective.
- The entire process has been mapped, allowing a visual overview of the entire process with flow charts and documentation.
- SMEs – introduced the concept of subject matter experts (confusingly, NIIT use the acronym SME for subject matter expert where it would usually mean small and medium-size enterprise for most readers) on the floor; there are six SMEs now operational. Their job entails conducting research in their specific domain, getting updates and guidance from Sesame UK, sharing the knowledge with the floor and assisting case reviewers.
- Commenced quality checking three months ahead of time.
- The various learning styles and training styles have been analysed and improved leading to improved staff retention and performance quality.
- Improved the pass percentage in Certificate for Financial Advisors (CeFA) and Certificate in Mortgage Advice and Practice (CeMAP) exams (as compared to performance in these exams in UK), generally because the resources taking the exam must pass in order for them to become chargeable resources – there is greater pressure to pass.
- All measurements and performance indicators (metrics) under control.
- Commenced call management and query handling three months ahead of schedule.
- Achieved 98.42% availability of both hardware and network.
- Business continuity planning (BCP) and disaster recovery tested.
- Reduced the number of staff in the business monitoring unit (BMU) in the UK to six, excluding one who is involved with transitioning new processes and one who is in charge of offshore support.

The development of the service quality and consistency of the checking service are compared with the earlier standards in Figure 2.5, which shows a clear rise.

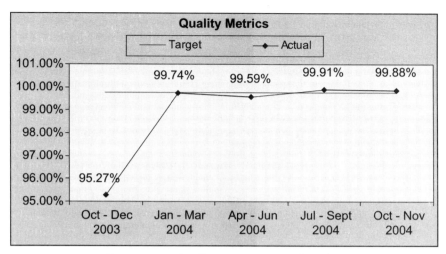

FIGURE 2.5 *Quality measurements (metrics)*

When auditors travelled from the UK to India to review the entire process they made several positive comments on the project. The auditors noted that the quality of resource in the Indian BMU unit and the associated Indian and UK Quality Assurance teams seemed appropriate to conduct business monitoring activity on UK financial services business in the future – a strong vote of confidence in the ability of the offshore team to offer this type of complex remote process. The auditors also noted that the outsourced unit had strong procedures, and the staff complied with them well.

The project continues to grow and additional processes have been added to the initial contract, including new tasks such as mortgage and general insurance case checking; advertisement approvals (to ensure that all advertisements released and stationery used by IFAs meet the FSA and other relevant regulatory requirements); and reviewing Precipice Bonds procedures.

The Sesame project is strong proof that an offshore service provider can work within a detailed and controlled regulatory environment. The service-level measurements demonstrate that Sesame delivers a better service to the community of independent financial advisors using their compliance service and clients of Sesame clearly approve of the service provided by NIIT SmartServe as the scope of the project is increasing. As described earlier, a satisfied client will often ask the service provider to take on more and more complex tasks, and this is an excellent example of the concept.

Case Study 4: A closed-book insurance back office

When a leading financial institution with an existing insurance business acquired a new insurance company, it decided to concentrate its efforts on growing the business using the recently acquired company and make the operations of the original company 'closed-book', meaning that no new business would be written into either company. However, the existing insurance company had commitments of 1.75 million existing life and pension policies from a large customer base, to whom continued levels of high service needed to be maintained. In addition, the earlier operations needed a technological overhaul that was not financially viable without revenue generated from new customers.

The organization therefore created three strategic objectives for outsourcing the servicing of its 'closed-book' life and pensions policies: it would improve service levels, cut costs, and provide a stable work environment for employees. To achieve these objectives the organization chose to outsource all aspects of the life and pensions policy servicing for the 'closed-book' business to a leading global ebusiness solutions company. A separate insurance subsidiary was created to manage this large and complex operation.

More than two years into the contract and with the technology migration well underway, an offshore business case emerged. The vision was to create an offshore 'life and pensions centre of excellence'. After a review, NIIT SmartServe was chosen to manage the offshore operations. The contract encompassed servicing part of the closed-book account for the company's insurance policies involving all aspects of life and pension policy processing: general servicing, amendments, and payments in and payments out.

After carefully studying the requirements, a comprehensive solution was designed for offshore processing, encompassing all dimensions of performance: technology, people, operations and quality. All process documentation is available online on the client intranet system and policy information is held and updated on the client proprietary database system. Any policy and client details can be searched using a separate search engine.

Procedures and processes are modified as required on the basis of updates received from the client to ensure that all work types adhere to the latest regulatory changes, including changes related to anti-money laundering and data protection. To ensure a continued level of high productivity and efficiency, individual performance reviews of all employees are conducted every month by their team managers.

There are numerous quality checks for any newly migrated processes and NIIT SmartServe also uses the six sigma path as a framework to improve process understanding and quality. The percentage of work checking reduces to a predetermined level based on the increased proficiency displayed by an individual agent, monitored at regular intervals.

During the initial stages of the establishment of the offshore centre, the processing included simple work types related to policy administration. As confidence in the levels of proficiency and quality increased, more complex work types were migrated to the new system, including those involving transfers, and payments out and payments in. Significant achievements include the following:

- Indexing of work migrated successfully and significant quality improvements seen in offshore processing.
- Moving further from the stabilization of work types to migration of more complex work types and processes and a significant increase in team size.
- Error analysis using six sigma has lead to improved process understanding and better quality.
- Training material prepared offshore added to client process documentation via the company intranet.
- Disaster recovery drills successfully conducted to check business continuity infrastructure – an audit by the onshore audit team of all aspects of offshore processing, including regulatory compliance, operations, technology, facilities and the human resources system, reported no significant risk issues.

WHAT LIES AHEAD FOR KPO?

The future is apparently bright for KPO. Growth is strong and customers of services are increasingly aware of what can be performed from an offshore location. As the case studies have shown, research or analysis-based projects can be successfully delivered as can ongoing services where offshore teams are trained to local standards.

However, there are some formidable challenges in the path of KPO development, some of which are outlined below.

- Processes executed within the KPO domain require higher quality standards because the stakes for the clients are high. Furthermore, the clients are likely to be apprehensive about the quality of services delivered (especially in view of the fact that these services are being provided by low-cost destinations) and these may be difficult to alleviate.
- In some cases, investment in KPO infrastructure is expected to be higher than with traditional BPO. For example, a company involved in simulation and finite-element analysis will require high-end workstations, whereas one involved in simple data collection, sorting and analysis may require moderate capital. Similarly, contract research organizations are likely to require higher amounts of capital.

- The lack of a good talent pool for the execution of projects may often prove to be a hindrance in many countries.
- KPO projects require a higher level of control, confidentiality and enhanced risk management. Laxity in any of these parameters will not only jeopardize the KPO services being provided, but may also affect the entire business conducted by the client.
- In comparison to traditional BPO services, scaling up of KPO operations will be difficult, primarily owing to difficulty in finding highly trained professionals.

In their 'From BPO to KPO' research mentioned earlier, Evalueserve has predicted a total global market in the region of US$14–17 billion by the end of the present decade, spread across the sectors outlined in Table 2.4.

TABLE 2.4   *Comparative opportunities in the KPO Market, 2003–2010*

KPO sectors	FY-2003	FY-2010	CAGR*
Equity, financial, insurance research	0	0.4	N/A
Data search, integration and management	0.3	5.0	50%
Research and information services in HR	0	0.2	-
Market research and competitive intelligence	0.01	0.4	70%
Engineering and design	0.4	2.0	29%
Animation and simulation services	0.1	1.4	46%
Paralegal content and services	0	0.3	N/A**
Medical content and services	0	0.3	N/A
Remote education and publishing	0	2.0	N/A
Biotech and pharmaceuticals (CRO,*** lead optimization, and manufacturing processes)	0.28	3.0	40%
Research and development	0.2	2.0	39%
Total (USD billion)	**1.29**	**17.0**	**46%**

Source: *Evalueserve Analysis*
* Compound Annual Growth Rate
** Not Available
*** Contract Research Organization

The founders of the contact centre industry in India – GE Capital, American Express and British Airways – created reliable back-end operational infrastructure. Then came the independent service companies like Spectramind and Daksh – now purchased by Wipro and IBM respectively. Soon, international service organizations such as Accenture and IBM joined the party. The sophistication level of independent service providers is very high and can only extend further into high-value KPO services if they want to increase their market share. With more and more KPO business coming into India, BPOs will try to upgrade themselves into KPO units as revenue per unit is more in the latter than former. And the first to benefit will be those already working in a BPO, with some degree of specialization.

CONCLUSION

Given the potential for KPO in the outsourcing sector and the huge, growing world market, the long-term strategy for any service provider in this market must be to move toward high-end services. While it is important for regions with existing and mature BPO industries, such as India, to consider a focus on KPO this need not be at the expense of losing the high volume, low-end business. From the point of view of employment, the low-end services not only provide large-scale employment, but do so for a class of young people who would otherwise not find jobs in the white-collar sector. In many cases, these unemployed and frustrated youths might be ideal recruits for crime or terrorism. Therefore, even the low-end IT or BPO jobs are an important contribution to social stability and economic well-being.

The days of cost arbitrage as a unique selling proposition are dead. It's cheap and offshore has had its day. Instead, any region or company seeking to be a serious player in the KPO market must consider quality, productivity and efficiency. KPO is not a commodity business – it's a premium service where every action counts and suppliers will live or die by their ability to take decisions and deliver a service as if they were the client themselves.

> The KPO (knowledge process outsourcing) industry, defined as offshoring of high-value-added complex processes is poised for massive and sustained growth at around 50 per cent per year to reach about US$14–17 billion by 2010, starting from US$1.5–2.0 billion as of today. India is likely to take a 70 per cent market share in this emerging global KPO industry.
>
> Currently, two major trends characterize the industry: the emergence of a strong third-party vendor base next to a further increase in captive activity predominantly in highly sensitive areas, an increasing complexity of already available process such as R&D, data management and analytics, business and investment research, clinical trials support, insurance underwriting etc. and the creation of several new sectors such as LPO (legal process outsourcing) and intellectual property asset management, and multi-lingual services for European and Asian clients. However, several areas are already maturing quickly, e.g. business and investment research, where a set of about 5–10 players dominate the industry, because client requirements have reached levels which do not allow fresh start-ups to win KPO deals any more. Additionally, there will be a wave of consolidation in the industry and IPOs [initial public offerings] led

(Continued)

(Continued)

by large BPO vendors, which will reduce the number of independent KPO players by about 50 per cent during the next five years. Moreover, finding and training professionals, the most important ingredient in KPO, will become a major challenge. Only companies that manage to create a grow-your-own people-centric model will continue growing. Clients will ask for significantly increased standards in terms of data security and compliance, which can already be witnessed in KPO for Investment Banks. Additionally, KPO players will be required to globalize their operations and offer solutions to large companies, as well as SMEs.

Marc Vollenweider, Chief Executive, Evalueserve, www.evalueserve.com

3 The Maturing Vendor Community

The level playing field agenda: The suppliers are getting smart. They are no longer into just undercutting the price or claiming a project will be delivered quicker than a rival, they are developing partnership models. This has the potential to become a genuine win–win situation, where the suppliers win more contracts and earn more from that work, but also the clients gain more committed suppliers, who have a better understanding of their clients' needs. Sharing in the benefits created from global services is the new order of the day.

For those who bemoan the current state of corporate greed and globalization it is worth a reminder that the situation is not new. This passage from the *Communist Manifesto*, written by Karl Marx and Friedrich Engels back in 1848, should resonate:

> **The exploitation of the world market has given a cosmopolitan character to production and consumption in every country ... All old-established national industries have been destroyed or are daily being destroyed. They are dislodged by new industries, whose introduction becomes a life and death question for all civilised nations ... In place of the old local and national seclusion and self-sufficiency, we have intercourse in every direction, universal interdependence of nations. And as in material, so also in intellectual production. The intellectual creations of individual nations become common property. National one-sidedness and narrow-mindedness become more and more impossible.[1]**

Marx and Engels could have been writing today. Their observation on the interdependence of nations and the creation of transnational companies could be a part of this book – which it now is. The obvious error is to assume that all those nations would get along and be happy to share intellectual property, but given that the quote is from more than 150 years ago, it's accurate enough.

The late Professor Sumantra Ghoshal of London Business School held the belief that big organizations such General Electric or Hewlett Packard, McKinsey, Disney or 3M have emerged as perhaps the most important social and economic institutions in our modern society. They are more than capitalistic devices for enriching shareholders. They are what binds a modern democratic society together and provide the whole of society with the means for progress and development.

Although Professor Ghoshal believed this of the companies themselves, he felt that many individual managers within those organizations were totally ignorant of their impact on society. This could create a source of friction at the point where the companies interact with the society around them, and lead to inefficiencies in their cash-generating activities.

The classic model for an organization that believes it can benefit from structuring operations around an outsourced or multilayered model would be to outsource a single, low-risk, pilot project. If the operation is fairly small and you don't want to go to the trouble of creating an offshore subsidiary then it makes sense to work with a vendor, so they manage the offshore headache. This is a well-beaten path and would normally apply until the vendor is managing a few hundred people on your behalf, at which point the finance director is likely to say something like 'we are paying for 250 offshore resources and the vendor is taking a margin on each, so why don't we just open our own office and go "captive"?'

So the next step would be the creation, by direct foreign investment, of a captive or wholly owned facility and these offshore service centres can grow very large indeed. GE Capital had many thousands of employees in their captive facility near New Delhi performing research and back-office functions before they sold off 60 per cent of their own operation for more than half a billion dollars.[2] GE Capital created value by pioneering business process outsourcing (BPO) offshoring in India and subsequently, through making use of a much lower cost base, saving process costs; they created further value by eventually selling a 60 per cent stake in the offshore company and now are free to compete in the global market as a service provider, generating additional profit for the parent company. With the GE reputation and the experience of their management team, the company – now known as GenPact – is likely to be a formidable force in the global services market.

Clearly the vendors are maturing and as global service offerings mature, the specifics of what can and cannot be outsourced shifts considerably. We are reaching a time where the boundaries of 'a company' may need to be redefined.

THE FUTURE SHAPE AND SIZE OF THE COMPANY

When asked to define a company, most people would describe something similar to the joint stock company. A joint stock company is basically a form of partnership. This form of company has a common capital called the stock. Each partner within the company is called a shareholder, since they receive shares for their contributions to the stock. Shares express an ownership and give decision-making power in the company. Shareholders are free to transfer their shares to someone else without needing the consent of other shareholders. These terms are quite familiar to any viewer of business television channels, and even mainstream news sources report major share price changes and stock index performance – the Dow Jones Industrial Average, the FTSE100, the Hang Seng, and so on.

The joint stock company was – and remains – a financing model that allowed companies to raise large amounts of capital while lowering risk by diversifying contributed capital among multiple ventures.

Looking further into accepted corporate design it can be seen that companies are generally structured into one of several basic organization designs, simple, bureaucratic or matrix:

- **Simple:** the simple company will usually have a single owner or founder and a number of department heads reporting directly to the owner. For example, if this was a shop then the owner would head the organization and take all decisions, with all salespeople reporting to him. The simple structure is fast, flexible, inexpensive and easy to maintain. Accountability is always clear because the buck always stops with the boss.

- **Bureaucratic:** standardization of processes across a number of departments underlies the bureaucratic structure, so every section of the company needs to conform to centralized planning and control. Routine tasks, rules, and a grouping of tasks and specialities into functional departments with centralized authority are typical attributes of the bureaucratic organization. Many large organizations can be described in this way. Large departments such as IT, Sales, Accounts or Human Resources are all well structured with standard and routine processes and employees have little interaction with other departments.

- **Matrix:** the matrix organization takes the bureaucratic model and then cross-cuts the functional responsibilities with the processes required to deliver products or services. So it becomes possible for individuals to have multiple reporting lines, as they may operate within the sales division, but with a focus on a particular product. This model is increasingly common as it allows departmental specialists to work together in functional teams, all working with a common purpose regardless of their personal speciality.

Many new corporate structures are emerging as technology and strategies such as global sourcing allow the basic structures to be analysed and changed where the old methods are found to be inadequate. The most important emerging models include the following:

- **The team structure:** as mentioned within the matrix model, the idea of using product or service teams allows companies to break down the walls between departments, stimulating ideas and creativity by ensuring that staff with different skills can work together. Self-managed teams calling on the resources available within a bureaucratic structure are becoming relatively common.

- **Virtual organizations:** this is where the use of outsourcing can often come into play. The virtual organization can be best described by considering how a Hollywood movie is produced. A company is formed and every 'team' member is contracted to the company for a limited period of time while the movie is being produced, only to be released once filming is complete. At that point other professionals, perhaps with marketing expertise, are needed to sell the movie, but the actors, camera operators, and lighting and sound teams will have moved on to the next movie. The company changes its size as required and is extremely flexible, never wasting resources. The company structure is therefore entirely virtual and is reorganized as and when it is required.
- **Boundaryless organization:** Jack Welch, the former Chairman and Chief Executive of General Electric, coined the term 'boundaryless organization'. He was describing a vision where the departmental functional silos (such as sales, production) and team functions were entirely blended. Status and rank are minimal within such an organization, as there is no chain of command. Employees need to be appraised by the range of fellow staff and management (including those more senior and those more junior) using what is nowadays labelled as the 360-degree approach and uniformity of privilege is encouraged – so no corner office for line managers then.

For a number of years, companies have been experimenting with these new structures for a number of reasons:

- **Strategy:** the structure of the company has to contribute to the end objectives of the executive management. A strategy to reduce cost may be entirely different to a strategy designed to create an innovative environment. The strategy should balance risk and the opportunity for profit, or other desirable outcomes, against the planned company activities.
- **Organization size:** small companies will have a very different structure to larger ones. This seems to be an obvious statement but it is important to remember when considering corporate growth. A 10-person company cannot grow easily to a 500-person company in a year without a radical change in structure, most likely a shift from a very simple structure to something more bureaucratic, with standardization, departments and specialization. However, a company that already has a more complex structure and employs 500 people could double in size in a year without any complexity beyond the obvious Human Resources (HR) challenge of managing more people.
- **Technology:** within business and corporate structure, technology normally refers to the process of taking something into the company and generating an output. It does not refer to how many PCs are

wired up to the internet. Technology processes can be routine tasks such as making a sales call using a script, or very complex ones such as genetic research. The complexity of the tasks within a company, between taking information or raw materials in and producing products, services or new information, can entirely shape the structure of the company.

- **Environment:** the environment within which a company operates can affect how it should be structured. There are three dimensions to the environment in which a company operates: capacity, volatility and complexity. Capacity refers to how much the company can support growth; in some environments the company may have too many or too few resources. The stability of the business environment is referred to as environmental volatility. Major changes, such as wars or new inventions can change the stability of an entire industry. Complexity refers to the scale of heterogeneity and concentration of competitors. Some industries are simple, with clear competition and some are global and very complex.

It is worth examining the concept of the virtual organization in more detail because this is not only becoming one of the most popular business strategies, it is also the most conducive to global sourcing and remote offshore services. The level playing field is achieved through those service companies offering their wares to the greatest possible range of buyers.

In the early days of offshore outsourcing, businesses and their vendors experimented with various models, ranging from the very hands-off 'throw-it-over-the-fence' model, the 'low-hanging fruit' model, to the more mature 'extended enterprise' – which has proven to be a more stable and successful business model.

The challenge businesses now face, in a world where emerging technologies are rapidly breaking down traditional barriers to outsourcing, is the physical remoteness, which can restrict the activities that can be outsourced. The reliability of communication links and speed of response is essential for international services and ensuring the client gets what they expect.

I believe the heart of the matter is the challenge of integrating diverse human cultures and ways of working with the essential culture of the organization itself. Using the wizardry of technology that's what the extended enterprise delivers today. We should ask what will be the new avatar of this model tomorrow?

Hardeep Garewal, European CEO, ITC Infotech, www.itcinfotech.com

The virtual company has long existed in academic literature, with Charles Handy being one of the most well-known commentators to extensively describe different formats of company that we might now consider as normal, or just another example of global integration.[3] Examples within the UK might be Virgin or easyGroup. Both these companies have well established brands that generate trust and loyalty in consumers. The Virgin brand creates a sense of fun, excitement, and irreverence. Everyone who sees a Virgin logo thinks of Sir Richard Branson flying a balloon around the world or riding an elephant – the brand is strongly connected to the idea of having honest fun. The 'easy' brand has a rather different emotional response. It stands for great value, products at the right price, no-nonsense deals. The easyJet airline has pioneered low-cost air travel in Europe and the brand has now extended its reach across internet cafés, Mediterranean cruises, cinema, buses, pizza delivery, mobile telephones and even watches.

A company where a strong brand adds immense value can easily be structured in a virtual way, as it is the brand that is adding the most value to the services of the company. The structure of a virtual company will resemble that shown in Figure 3.1.

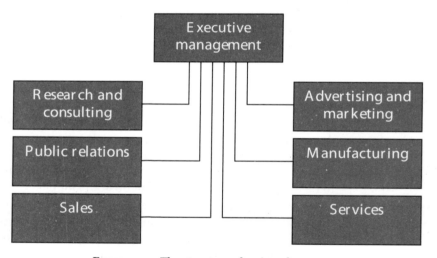

FIGURE 3.1 *The structure of a virtual company*

It is possible for the executive management to be the only paid employees of the company. All the other services, which might normally be considered to be company departments, can be outsourced to specialist partners in those fields, for example an advertising agency dealing with adverts and an offshore factory dealing with manufacturing.

Companies such as Virgin and easyGroup are in fact brand guardians. They consist of a relatively small holding company that owns the brand and employs the most senior management. Then a portfolio of companies within the group will be structured to offer specific services, all licensing the brand from their parent. In most cases, those companies themselves will utilize a virtual structure, for instance the Virgin Atlantic airline has service partners in India and South Africa for technology and back-office processes.

When companies move to a world beyond basic service provision, they will almost all be utilizing the virtual structure. The key advantage for an organization in seeking to structure their operations in this way is the focus it allows on their core competencies – those competencies that differentiate the company from its competition. As can be seen from the organizational chart in Figure 3.1, operations within a knowledge-based company can be agreed with a partner and outsourced to an expert provider.

While strategy and protection of the brand is managed by the executive team, who remain employed by the company, the operational management is outsourced to the various partners. Those partners then take care of hiring, firing and daily management of the rest of the employees.

Focusing on core competencies allows the executive management to remove distractions and to focus on what it is that adds value to their company. In the case of Virgin Atlantic, most passengers don't care who does their accounts or cleans the interior of the aircraft, but they are concerned about security, entertainment, in-flight service and food – so these might be areas the company can consider keeping a tight hold on while releasing some other tasks to partners.

The following comments from management thinkers all echo a similar view on how the organization is changing:

> Before very long, having a proper job inside an organization will be a minority occupation. What was a way of life for most of us will have disappeared. Organizations will still be critically important in the world, but as organizers, not employers.[4]

> By far the greatest number of jobs will take the form of non-standard employment.[5]

> [In] less than a century, 'mass' work in the market sector is likely to be phased out in virtually all of the industrialised nations.[6]

> What is disappearing today is not just a certain number of jobs, but the very thing itself – the job ... [Jobs are a] rigid solution to an elastic problem ... When the work that needs doing changes constantly, we cannot afford the inflexibility that the job brings with it.[7]

> All around the world, flexible work and insecure terms of employment are growing faster than any other form of work.[8]

> The society in which everyone could hope to have a place and a future marked out ... is dead. We are a society of phantom work.[9]

> The concept of a job as a more or less fixed package of tasks and responsibilities has gone ... more people work 'for' themselves rather than 'for' someone else.[10]

> America's new economic emblem is the footloose independent worker – the tech-savvy, self-reliant, path-charting micropreneur.[11]

Large virtual companies have already embraced the concept of outsourcing and a virtual structure, so to go one step further and consider the options for offshore or global delivery is not a giant leap, but what about smaller organizations?

THE SME MARKET

The main issue for a small company is that they may not have developed the scale or resources to build a complex internal structure that can support offshore outsourcing. There always needs to be some form of buffer zone between the executive management and the portfolio of partner organizations, even if this is just a small management control office where performance is monitored. The resource to monitor a partner relationship may be just too much for a small company, yet small and medium companies make up almost all of registered businesses.

There were an estimated 4.3 million private-sector business enterprises in the UK at the start of 2004.[12] This compares with an estimated 4.0 million comparable business enterprises in the UK at the start of 2003. Almost all of these enterprises (99.3 per cent) were small (0 to 49 employees). Only 26,000 (0.6 per cent) were medium-sized (50 to 249 employees) and 6,000 (0.1 per cent) were large (250 or more employees).

At the start of 2004, UK enterprises employed an estimated 22 million people, and had an estimated combined annual turnover of £2,400 billion. Small and medium-sized enterprises (SMEs) together accounted for more than half of the employment (58.5 per cent) and turnover (51.3 per cent) in the

UK. Small enterprises alone (0 to 49 employees) accounted for 46.8 per cent of employment and 37.0 per cent of turnover.

With such incredible statistics, it seems unthinkable that smaller businesses would not also be thinking of how they too can restructure to take advantage of global sales and sourcing opportunities.

Three major factors have now shifted in favour of the smaller company:

1. The service suppliers have already taken most of the easy outsourcing and process re-engineering business from large organizations. The last five years has been a lot of fun for these companies, as any competent services company could enjoy astounding growth helping all those large companies to review their own core competencies, resulting in several juicy projects and enough to go around for all the service providers. This situation has now changed and a wave of consolidation, mergers and acquisition is sweeping the vendor community as they seek to capture any remaining large deals. For this reason, many of the very experienced and well-respected offshore service companies are now willing to discuss smaller contracts that they would not have considered viable a few years earlier. You might only need a five-person back-office facility, but there is no need to consider a second-rate service provider, as the major companies will now welcome you with open arms – perhaps not all the top-tier firms, but respectable ones nonetheless.

2. The advisors and consulting community have realized what is happening and started creating fixed-price or success-based advice packages that are more suitable for smaller companies. Some consultants are even trying to act as aggregation points for specific services. The idea is to find many clients who want to outsource a very similar, small ongoing task. Let's say a small legal practice is interested in outsourcing the equivalent of one person who would be performing case research. If the consulting group can find more legal firms interested in the same kind of services, even just one or two researchers for every firm, then the contract can be bundled together allowing a better offshore deal to be negotiated.

3. To enable competitive economics for an SME to set up their own and directly managed (initially small-scale) offshore operations, the promise of the virtual is being now exploited by ventures such as QuickStart Global Ltd. These offer an established local corporate structure, local recruitment processes and fully serviced office space; an SME can thus rapidly establish its own directly managed offshore resource and expand as its business requirements demand. Once the directly managed operation has grown to a critical mass, separation and migration into a directly owned legal subsidiary is simply achieved.

The commoditization of many technology-enabled services, and their global availability over the networks and the internet, will also democratize the marketplace for the SME by making increasingly sophisticated capabilities available on-demand, to be paid for only when used.

This commoditization of services has already been introduced in Chapter 1, and in Chapter 5 the essential features of the very fundamental commercial revolutions in progress will be detailed further. The basic concept of on-demand or utility computing is to ensure that the company has enough computing power and application service capacity available, at all times. The concept works in the same way that you don't need to tell the electricity company how many electric fans you are going to plug into their system, you just do it and pay for the electricity used. Many commentators advocate that complex outsourcing agreements for IT don't help either the client or supplier. A more fluid relationship and technical infrastructure that allows the use of a system to be measured and billed, just like a water bill, would be a more effective way forward.

There are a number of new technologies that enable utility computing to become a reality, as expanded on in Chapter 5. These include the following:

- grid computing;
- blade technology;
- virtualization;
- web services and service-oriented architecture (SOA);
- service provisioning.

With these technological advances offering a more utility-like service for the IT division, it can only be a matter of time before some back-office service contracts become more utilitarian – and thus open the marketplace for even the smallest SME to 'source as required'.

In summary then, every indicator points to the virtual structure being the dominant business model for the company of the 21st century. The emerging use of cheap communications technology and transnationally traded technology services mean that this will be the structure of choice for the foreseeable future. Yet the virtual model risks being still based on relationships between client and vendor that must be managed in a traditional way. In the sections that follow, the development of newer client–vendor commercial models, more fit for purpose in the new market environments, is described.

PARTNERS, NOT VENDORS

Vendors are moving beyond the time and materials concept of outsourcing to a critical new role in the supply chain where they provide services and share the risk of the client company sourcing those services. (The example of British Airways having no food available for passengers during the Gate Gourmet dispute of summer 2005 is a classic example of not realizing how important one link in the supply chain really can be.) Companies are certain to become more 'layered', with some work processes performed internally and other work processes performed externally within the wider vendor marketplace, yet the required work process outcome is a result of the whole – with an emphasis on the importance of each layer working together and sharing risk along a single value chain.

The question of pricing for products and services is a subject that has been of interest to humans since the first cave dweller traded an attractive rock for a roast leg of rabbit. Pricing is the most basic of requirements, as every service has a price.

Yet as Hilary Robertson of Xansa describes in her contribution to this chapter, there is a huge difference between service provision when it remains internal to a company and an outsourced service. We all naturally know this, but the contracts, service level agreements (SLAs) and key performance indicators that typify an outsourced programme of work make the difference explicit.

When an organization is outsourcing a major business function such as their IT or finance and accounting service they will usually set out a requirements definition of the service. A period of due diligence takes place to validate this information as much as is practical, prior to – or in parallel with – developing the best and final offer the service provider can put forward. This creates a basic service level against which future performance gains can be measured.

When organizations are offshoring, however, most start by extracting smaller service elements from within a larger service or function. This can leave responsibility for the end-to-end service blurred, or shared between the client and the offshore provider. Organizations may in this case procure by identifying purely the input costs and base a supplier evaluation upon like-for-like labour cost savings. This can have consequences by not considering the sometimes considerable opportunity for value-add into the evaluation. In other cases, due diligence is undertaken, and again in others a pilot contract is created and a small pilot service is migrated to the offshore location and run for a limited period. During this period appropriate service levels are agreed between the client and service provider and form the final contract.

The process can be complex, but the consensus within the industry is that clients are moving away from a simplistic demand for nothing more than lower operational cost. Run-rate reduction is an attractive reason to consider outsourcing, but the opportunity to use the expertise of a supplier and create additional value is now becoming the compelling reason for considering third-party solutions.

THE PRICING FRAMEWORK

To find the right solution to a client's outsourcing needs a supplier should consider a range of inputs, including business environment, volatility and competition, business goals and strategy, current capability (experience of outsourcing, offshoring, third-party governance etc.) and risk assessment. The supplier should then work with the client to create a solution that offsets benefits against risk and encompasses the following:

- the service scope
- the timing of the service
- the shape of the delivery solution (over time), considering:
  - fully onshore delivery (with/without TUPE regulations for the UK, or equivalent labour legislation);
  - fully offshore delivery;
  - integrated on–offshore delivery;
  - with or without the underlying technology;
  - risk;
- projected service levels and key performance indicators;
- the proposed operating structure;
- the commercial arrangements (over time);
- commercial governance.

A spectrum of different pricing options can be considered when outsourcing, driven by the nature of what is being outsourced and the type of relationship, and represented by the continuum in Figure 3.2.

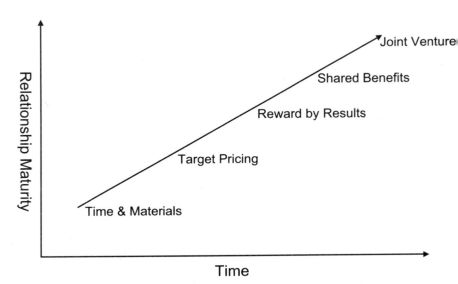

FIGURE 3.2 *Path of a maturing supplier relationship*

Commodity services may be bought in a transactional relationship using input measures such as daily full-time equivalent (FTE) rates. As the importance of each partner grows in respect to the other, however, there needs to be closer alignment of business goals in order that the commercial relationship survives change.

The continuum describes how the most basic relationship is one based on time and materials. A company asking a software firm to completely redevelop their website may receive a quote based on how long the job will take and the total chargeable cost is a simple equation based on the time, number of staff involved and the daily rate being charged.

As a supplier is used more often and becomes trusted, other pricing models can be explored, where the pricing of a service starts to be in the favour of both parties so they become more like partners. This can eventually be formalized by creating a joint venture (JV) company if the relationship is strong enough and the service is consistently required. It should be noted that anyone entering into a corporate joint venture because of overlapping objectives should consider a potential future divergence of interest – needs and attitudes change over time. There are many issues with JVs because the initial planning only looks at the present shared interest.

In order to outsource an existing service, the organization needs first to understand the value it contributes to the business – both direct and indirect. This requires definition and measurement. The question is, what to measure? The easiest answer is to calculate the cost inputs of the service: labour costs, fully loaded with benefits and charges for facilities, IT, HR, F&A [Finance and Accounting], management overheads etc. This becomes the comparator against the third-party costs. What's harder to measure, evaluate and compare are the service outcomes, risks and softer benefits.

A typical example of the latter might be: how to measure the value that the in-house service knowledge gives you to shape future business strategy or input to a regulatory review? How do you account for this value if outsourced and how do you evaluate options to address the risk?

Service outcomes are rarely measured in-house – measurement implies added cost – and their mostly intangible nature usually militates a subjective approach to quantification. In addition, this only gives you an 'as-is' comparator, whereas most buyers seek a transformed or at least improved future service.

(Continued)

(Continued)

In an outsourcing selection process, comparison of one set of costs and benefits against another is rarely about comparing apples with apples, but about evaluating different sets of service outcomes, risks and costs.

These can be envisaged on a spectrum that maps commodity services at one end through to complex services at the other. If the service is a commodity – simple and standardised – then the selection emphasis lies on cost and the most appropriate relationship is that of transactional buyer–supplier. At the other end of the scale, the more complex the service, the greater part value and risk play in the evaluation. It tends towards a closer, integrated partnership relationship, alignment of goals, and sharing of risk and reward to bind service value with cost and commitment. Ascribing and comparing values for complex service approaches is difficult. But if cost evaluation overly dominates the selection process, it can lead to mismatched expectations on both sides.

As outsourcing and offshoring of services accelerates in pace, scope and impact, the operating model of the future for many firms will integrate service components from multiple providers across different locations around the world. To benefit from the significant opportunities globalization offers in this respect, organizations will need to develop strong in-house capabilities in measurement, procurement and governance of complex services and structures.

Hilary Robertson, Offshore Development Director, Xansa plc, www.xansa.com

BUSINESS PROCESS BILLING MODELS

As indicated by the continuum presented earlier, outsourcing suppliers are now finding that pricing models can become more complex as their service matures. When a client is confident enough to work in partnership with a supplier and share the risk of a new service supporting a new business line or product, then great benefits can be shared by both sides. Most outsourcing remains driven by cost and the supplier market is still mainly using a cost-plus (margin) model, but there are interesting exceptions – a wind of change is sweeping through the industry.

Cost based

Consider the traditional idea of cost-plus pricing, the basic model used for pricing products or services and where a lot of sourcing remains at present. This model takes into account the cost of servicing the client and adds a margin on top, allowing the service provider to generate a profit. Quite often the profit might be a percentage of the cost, so the supplier may always try to charge a rate to customers that is cost plus 10 per cent – giving a 10 per cent profit on all income.

This model has naturally suited the offshore outsourcing market because it has been largely dominated by price and margins. Where competition for a particular service is very price-sensitive then it is likely that suppliers will cut their costs to the bone and then make a slim margin through a cost-plus strategy. This naturally works best for high-volume services – making a slim 1 per cent margin on revenues of several million pounds can support a service company. Making 1 per cent on small and sporadic contracts will rapidly lead to bankruptcy.

The PC hardware business is an excellent example of this pricing strategy. Companies such as Dell and Lenovo have very efficient manufacturing processes, allowing a new PC to be designed, manufactured and shipped to an end user for just a few hundred pounds. If you recall buying a PC just 10 years ago, the price then was many multiples of the present prices for hardware, not even accounting for the effect of inflation and the fact that comparing a PC from now to then is like comparing a Star Trek communicator with a walkie-talkie. Intense competition, fantastic manufacturing efficiency, and razor-thin cost-plus margins have allowed the PC manufacturing business to develop in this way.

Cost-plus pricing is often used for business process outsourcing. The supplier will determine the cost of paying people a salary, providing an office and all the related facilities for doing the job and will then charge a daily rate for a full-time equivalent. The rate is a fully blended price that includes the cost of everything from the salary paid to the office cleaner and the chairman's Mercedes. It will also include the profit margin.

Cost-plus pricing presents a number of key issues for the supplier:

- Brand value is hard to realize when profit is based only on the cost of delivering the service. If Louis Vuitton or Alexander McQueen only charged for their products based on the cost of manufacture, plus a small margin, then every other person would be carrying the distinctive brown bags or wearing loud clothes. (In some parts of Tokyo, every other person is wearing strange clothes and carrying Louis Vuitton products, but you understand the point.)

- Market positioning can be hard to control if your price is determined only by the cost of producing the service or product. Your position in the market is important as this is how a client perceives your service. Positioning is affected by the price you sell the service for, the quality of the service, how customized you make the service for each client, how clients find out about your service, and how you present the service to the market. Trying to pitch a great service of high value to potential clients at a rock-bottom price might seem like a great strategy, but it can affect the client's perception of the service quality.

- Hidden costs are everywhere in the outsourcing industry and within services it is particularly hard to price every cost into a fixed daily rate. Staff may not be utilized by a client project 100 per cent of the time and so a 'bench' must be financed where staff are paid, but are inactive. Having no bench at all is also dangerous as it becomes very hard to respond quickly to a client if no employees are free.

A similar model within the services industry is time and materials pricing, or just T&M. Time and materials pricing is common practice in the consulting industry, where the daily rate for a consultant is charged and an additional charge is made to the client for any expenses related to the use of that consultant, such as travel or sustenance.

Less common within the world of business process outsourcing is the fixed-cost model. This is where the supplier quotes a price to deliver a particular service and does not include details of time or resource used, because the supplier is giving a guarantee that the service will be delivered as expected for a fixed price, no matter how much effort is actually involved. Again, this is quite common with consulting services where a longer-term assignment may be agreed on a fixed price rather than daily rate terms. It's also common within the software industry, where a piece of bespoke software is agreed on and the software company guarantees to deliver the product as specified for a fixed price.

These forms of pricing generally work well for business process outsourcing because the market is fiercely competitive and it's simple for both client and supplier to understand what they are paying for. It would be normal to establish a pricing model along these lines when first entering into a relationship with a supplier. However, many client–supplier relationships are now maturing. Suppliers have become a critical part of the supply chain for some companies and so it makes sense to think beyond daily service rates and penalty clauses to an environment where both the supplier and client can benefit from the relationship.

Risk and reward gainsharing

If a supplier can share in some of the risk of doing business in the market their client is in then they deserve some of the potential gains to be generated by working together, not just a daily rate for their time. This is a concept that is becoming popular amongst many clients. According to Shiv Nadar, Chairman and Chief Executive of HCL Technologies, 'Clients are demanding this. They naturally want to share business risk together with their supplier and that also allows a shared upside. But it's important to say no if you don't feel you can offer the right service on time or to the right specification.' He goes on to say 'We are choosing to enter into these joint ventures. We are also asking clients about risk-sharing, just look at our partnership with NEC in Japan. If a product is not on time or does not do well then we will both suffer. We are good at saying no to an alliance, when we feel the risk is just too high to carry.'[13]

So gainsharing, as the concept is known, allows a supplier to offer their expertise to a client, but with the proviso that they can then share in the future improved performance of the client. Classic gainsharing works in a number of ways, though it's always essential to benchmark the existing status of the service for future measurement and comparison to the benchmark. This involves a consideration of the following aspects:

- **Salary costs as a proportion of sales revenue:** this is where a company selling £1 million of services with a salary bill of £400,000 may reduce the salary bill to £350,000 over a year allowing the £50,000 saving to be distributed to employees or the gainsharing partner.
- **Sales revenue minus cost of materials:** this is where a company selling £1 million of services with the cost of materials for the provision of those services at £400,000, reducing the materials bill to £350,000 over a year allowing the £50,000 saving to be distributed to employees or the gainsharing partner.
- **Key performance indicators (KPIs):** the KPIs are identified and measured at the start and end of the period, with a cash value calculated for each one allowing the bonus value to be calculated.

The offshore BPO industry is seeing exciting times with new pricing models emerging, thanks to the maturity of the industry, the ability of buyers to structure deals around specific service level agreements and the maturing performance capability of service providers.

While the existing pricing models have been serving the required purpose, pricing of services continues to evolve due to the following drivers:

1. **Change in buyer expectations:** more mature buyers who have experienced high-quality service output realize that there are more gains from offshore BPO vendors than just cost reduction and have raised the bar in expectations from vendors. This has driven vendors to invest in creating best practices such as six sigma, business continuity plans etc.

2. **Hidden costs:** some buyers underestimate the full impact of offshore cost management; the result is that they end up investing more than initially estimated, altering the cost attractiveness of offshore considerably.

(Continued)

61

(Continued)

3. **Value enhancement by vendors:** the competition amongst off-shore BPO providers has created the need for offshore players to differentiate themselves through innovation in order to stay in the game. Until recently vendors who were adding value through innovation have abstained from charging for the value created. However, offshore BPO service providers have begun to realize that 'value' prized is not 'value realized'.

Gainsharing, fixed cost reduction and charging for increased value creation will therefore become increasingly common as relationships mature.

Shanmugam Nagarajan, Co-founder and Chief Operating Officer, 24/7 Customer, www.247customer.com

Clearly for the outsourcing of services to a partner firm the use of KPIs is the method of most relevance. If a service provider has agreed to work on the finance and accounts of a client then the KPIs must be well designed so that both client and supplier are happy that the right processes are being measured.

Devesh Nayel, Finance and Accounting Practice Head of Infosys BPO, explains that good KPI metrics are the most important factor in the success of an offshore transition: 'Cost per payables transaction, cost per pay slip processed, cost per man hour or cost per accounting head are good metrics for an accounting project.' He added: 'One could also have subjective measures like the number of complaints in a month, or number of customer calls dropped in a month, or cycle time to resolve customer support queries. It really depends on the nature of the particular project.'[14]

Nayel is right to comment that KPIs can be very objective or highly subjective. While a basic framework of KPIs will be defined by the outsourcing supplier or captive offshore centre manager, it is essential to think further into the future. Think beyond the transition of services. It is fine to be worried about how you will move the tasks to an offshore location or distant supplier – it is a big transition project – but the KPIs will live on beyond the transition process; try thinking from a customer perspective as Nayel suggests.

It is worth reviewing the importance of the key performance indicators in measuring the value – or lack of – in structuring a company along the principles of outsourcing. KPIs are the benchmarks that will be used to measure whether the minimum service levels are met, or not. Prior to outsourcing an IT helpdesk function, the helpdesk manager may have received a number of vague complaints about service: calls take too long to be answered, email is not answered, emergency hardware problems take too long to resolve. None of these complaints are actually measured with any kind of indication of performance.

In contrast, relevant targets for these complaints might be:

- the support phone is always answered in fewer than three rings;
- all support email must be responded to within four hours;
- emergency hardware faults must be resolved within one hour.

These performance targets can be utilized as KPIs by recording how often the target was achieved within a certain time frame. With a Service Level Agreement (SLA) and suite of KPIs in place, the helpdesk manager could easily see exactly how often the phone was not answered quickly enough or emergencies not resolved.

It is clear that careful drafting of KPIs is essential, especially where the contract includes a gainsharing clause. The KPIs are also of use to both client and outsourcing supplier. The supplier is fully aware of what the client requires and where the minimum service benchmark exists. The client uses the KPIs to define what they want from the relationship in quantifiable terms. KPIs can easily translate into management reports or a 'dashboard' of the most important indicators.

Gainsharing is basically a partnering model and is therefore rather different to some of the more unscrupulous tactics being employed within the sourcing industry at present, particularly at the lower end of the market. Competition for these service contracts is intense and in some regions this has caused some service providers to take on contracts at such unfavourable terms that the entire risk of a business working or not is taken upon their own shoulders, rather than being shared between a client and their supplier.

A good example of this is the outbound call centre market, typically used for making cold-calls to consumers offering a new mobile phone or insurance quote. It's a wretched business model in the first place, very much like spam email (does anyone enjoy receiving unsolicited phone calls in the middle of dinner?). We have observed several smaller contact centres taking on these sales contracts on a commission-only basis, where there is no payment at all for the service provided, just a fee paid if a customer actually signs up for a phone after an unsolicited sales call. This is not a partnership model at all: it's the client passing all the risk off to a contact centre company. For the contact centre to be taking a contract on such unfavourable terms they must be desperate for the work and so the spiral towards bankruptcy accelerates.

Value creation

The major difference between the more recent pricing models for service outsourcing is the pricing of value. In his contribution to this chapter, Shanmugam Nagarajan from 24/7 Customer acknowledges that BPO service providers have not generally been able to price services based on value added or generated. Value has tended to be a rather vague concept, yet some vendors are now actively talking about the measurement of value when a service is priced. The main three ways in which this is happening are value-minus pricing, output-based pricing and joint ventures.

VALUE-MINUS PRICING

Value-minus pricing is almost the exact opposite of cost plus and refers to the concept of 'exchange value' defined by Karl Marx. A service has an intrinsic value to the purchaser, but it can create additional value. To give an example, a radio company may sell advertising space based on the random allocation of adverts. So an advertiser booking a commercial to be aired for a week has very little control of the timing of the commercial, except for perhaps the frequency it will be repeated during that week – let's say 42 times. If the radio company could commission a piece of software that could analyse the content of its shows and schedule commercials to be played at the most suitable time, based on some demographic connection between the product being advertised and each particular show, then this additional control would make the advertising space more valuable.

If this happened the radio company would have more control over its advertising, the rates could increase, the listeners would get more relevant commercials based on the show they are listening to and the advertisers could reach out to more potential customers. Everyone appears to win.

This piece of scheduling software might take a month to complete and test for two people. Now let's assume a 20-day working month and that the software company charges £1,000 a day. The total bill for the software development should be £40,000. In a regular scenario, the radio station would just pay the money and get the software for this price. If they considered a value-minus option then both the software company and radio station could potentially benefit.

To explain how this works, we first need to understand the baseline situation and the potential situation once the new system is in place. To make some assumptions, we could say the station is generating advertising revenue of £1 million at present and predicts that with the more sophisticated system in place, this could almost double to £1.9 million per year.

The predicted value of the system is therefore £900,000 to the radio station, though this can only be realized with £40,000 worth of effort. If the software company offers to share the risk of the business change with the radio station, so both companies agree on the predicted business increase then they might waive the £40,000 fee and complete the work for no charge. In return, they would be entitled to a share of the improved business.

If the radio station agreed to give the software company 10 per cent of increased advertising revenues then the software company would receive £90,000, providing the estimates are correct. So, in this case, the software company receives more money and the radio station gets their new system updated for no expense – and they only need to pay if the increased business materializes.

Value-minus pricing requires an acceptance of risk and trust. If the payment to the supplier is guaranteed then it may be just as attractive to the client to pay a fixed fee and to have no further relationship. The idea of this strategy is to examine the total value to the client of a new way of doing business and to then share some of that benefit.

In the example given the advertising revenue does need to increase considerably for the value-minus model to be worthwhile to the software company. The model works well for both parties, provided the targets are realistic and the accounts are open.

OUTPUT-BASED PRICING

This model reduces the business processes being performed into discrete services that can be charged by the unit. For example, when banks outsource the settlement of equity transactions they will usually pay the partner a fixed price for each trade settled as a unit of work. There is no additional charge for the resources or number of people required by the service provider to provide the service: each unit delivered is a fixed price.

This model is generally used for quite mature processes that require continuous delivery. Where the volume increases it is usual for a discount to be applied to the unit price.

Services such as accounting or payroll services can often be charged in this way. The service provider can guarantee a price per transaction because their expertise should allow them to transition and stabilize the business processes, creating an environment where unit costs are lower than when the services were performed in-house. By using people, process and technology and underpinning the design of the service with an integrated on–offshore delivery it should be possible to create added value for a client.

JOINT VENTURES

Our favourite reference tool *Wikipedia* defines a joint venture as follows:

> A joint venture (often abbreviated JV) is a strategic alliance between two or more parties to undertake economic activity together. The parties agree to create a new entity together by both contributing equity, and they then share in the profits, losses, and control of the enterprise. The venture can be for one specific project only, or a continuing business relationship such as the Sony Ericsson joint venture.
> Organizations can also form joint ventures, for example, a child welfare organization in the Midwest initiated a joint venture whose mission is to develop and service client tracking software for human service organizations. The five partners all sit on the joint venture corporation's board, and together have been able to provide the community with a much-needed resource. [15]

A successful joint venture is essentially the Holy Grail for outsourcing suppliers. It is the point where the interests of both supplier and client are aligned and the partnership ensures that it is in both of their interests to perform well.

As an example of a joint venture that also crosses the public/private divide consider how Xansa has worked with the British government's National Health Service (NHS). In March 2005, the NHS announced a joint venture with Xansa and the Department of Health to commence with 47 different NHS organizations. Xansa would operate several back-office functions for the NHS, such as accounting, finance and payroll.

The British public generally love their public health-care system and fight vehemently to keep it free at the point of delivery. One of the favourite complaints is the amount of 'pen-pushing' bureaucracy at the expense of using taxes to pay nurses and doctors. Commenting on the joint venture, UK Health Minister John Hutton said: 'Moving ahead in this way will help the NHS streamline back office functions, reduce bureaucracy and generate substantial savings for reinvestment in front-line services. The joint venture will generate significant cost savings – enough to pay the annual salaries of over 3,000 GPs or 12,000 nurses.' (Politicians often know the soundbites that will make the front page.) Mr Hutton added: 'By entering into this partnership, we are utilizing private sector experience to both improve and expand the range of corporate functions provided for the NHS. It's good news for the NHS and for taxpayers.'[16]

Since the NHS joint venture was launched in 2005 it has been extended to 71 different NHS trusts across the UK. The joint venture is also increasing in complexity of services as the partners grow closer and create centres of service excellence. As well as offering services on existing payroll platforms, the joint venture has started offering a full range of services utilizing the new national ESR (electronic staff records) payroll system, which is geared specifically to the needs of the NHS.

Joint ventures don't happen overnight, however. As outlined at the start of this chapter, reaching a position where the supplier and client are working together to provide a service is usually the result of a relationship built up over time and on more basic terms, lower down the continuum. A basic outsourcing relationship based on charging for time and materials may have been in place for some time, followed by a modest shift to gainsharing and then a desire to make the relationship work harder and in the favour of both parties.

TRANSITION FROM COST-BASED TO VALUE-BASED PRICING

Clearly there are some examples where a shift to a closer and better relationship may not be appropriate. For non-strategic or short-term projects it makes no sense to engage in a long-term partnership that may even lead to a joint venture. For the majority of business process outsourcing, however, there is an ongoing relationship between client and supplier. They depend on each other. There should only be benefits for both by examining how they can shift further along the continuum from time and materials pricing to a joint venture.

Establishing trust between client and vendor is one of the most difficult things to achieve in an offshore partnership. Many offshore providers are often blamed for this lack of trust: the tactics of some providers during the outsourcing boom created some mistrust, and many providers still only keep their clients updated strictly on a 'need to know' basis.

One way to build trust in an offshoring partnership is to ensure transparency in every aspect of the business relationship. This means, for example, having transparent risk assessment and sharing procedures, open estimating and pricing models, and transparent governance.

Over the past years NIIT Technologies has fully embraced the concept of partnering with our clients and we have adopted a flexible and open approach to commercial arrangements. In the case of the former, this sometimes results in operating several different billing arrangements within a single account to reflect the different types of engagement, ensuring value can be tracked and measured.

A transparent, trusting relationship has long-term benefits for offshore vendors and clients alike. The relationship will move from one based simply on tactical supply to a strategic partnership that encourages the creation of added value and proactive problem solving.

Once the requirements for cost savings and how they will be used have been established, offshoring partners need to agree the most appropriate framework for making the relationship work for both sides. The providers who can demonstrate clear benefits, beyond cost alone, will be the long-term winners in this dynamic market.

Ravi S. Pandey, Senior Vice President and Head of NIIT Technologies UK, www.niit-tech.com

There are some fundamental questions a company needs to consider before moving away from paying for services by cost to thinking of them in terms of value:

- What is value-based pricing?
- How can value be measured?
- When should this strategy be implemented?

These are discussed next.

What is value-based pricing?

It is essential to consider this question in the context of your own services, or the services you are buying. This chapter has outlined some of the steps towards a joint venture, including gainsharing. But, how does this apply to your own environment? Are the management team prepared to think about how pricing models can be changed or how to structure their own company? Many companies prefer to find a model that works and then to stick to that plan forever, with new ideas being treated as a distraction. The idea of pricing by value rather than cost can appear to be radical when first introduced, but remember that this is a strategy creating value for both supplier and client. You must create a situation where the new pricing model allows both parties to benefit.

How can value be measured?

Again, if the present value is not being measured and there is no baseline to go from then it will be impossible to measure value within an outsourcing deal. Value is hard to define due to differing perceptions. In the earlier example of the radio station, it could be argued that if the radio station is so sure they can create a huge amount of additional revenue then their best option would be to pay a fixed price for the project, rather than giving the software company a share of the increased advertising revenue. In Britain many people pay for private health insurance, yet the free NHS already exists. This is because the individual wants to ensure that if they ever get diagnosed with a life-threatening disease then they can go straight to the top of the queue at the hospital of their choice, not rely on the lottery of living near to a hospital with doctors specialized in their particular ailment. Is the extra monthly payment good value? It depends on your perception of risk and the same is equally true within an outsourced service; just ensure a baseline is measured before any transfer takes place.

When should this strategy be implemented?

It is highly unlikely that an organization with no experience of partnering or outsourcing will seek to enter into a joint venture with a strategic partner. The most likely routes to more innovative billing for services are from basic cost plus moving to a gainsharing model or when a company tenders for a new contract and offers a value-minus model as an alternative to charging for time. Once any partnership has enjoyed some form of benefit sharing for a period of time it is likely that a joint venture can be explored, though clearly this is a major step that should be strongly in the interest of both parties.

MULTISOURCING

Outsourcing is a strategic operating decision and yet many executive decisions are ad hoc in nature without due consideration being given to the full range of options available. The ad hoc decision-making process can often be exacerbated where outsourcing is a strategy mandated from on high.

The benefits of multisourcing can be summarized as follows:

- **Value creation through specialization:** the 'best of breed' effect is encouraged through a process of choosing suppliers based on their specialized expertise and execution capabilities, rather than an ability to service every possible function, regardless of quality.
- **Risk reduction:** you can hedge your bets by utilizing a basket of expert suppliers, rather than a single behemoth. It's a lot easier to replace a supplier failing in a single service than to negotiate with a large supplier failing in key areas, but satisfactory in others.
- **Obtain competitive pricing:** your scope to select specialist suppliers is wider and allows increased competition for services provision, before selection and once service commences.
- **Allows supplier comparison:** especially important if you are considering a scaled-up future state, so a supplier can be tested on a smaller less-critical function before promotion.
- **Reshape processes around the application:** technology is becoming more driven by function and application. A multisourced approach allows you to take quicker advantage of industry developments such as service-oriented architecture or open source.

Multisourcing is not a new concept, but its popularity has been growing fast. Even in technology outsourcing there are commentators, such as Leslie Willcocks of the London School of Economics, who have been writing about it for well over a decade now.[17] The strategy has been documented as a successful tool in a number of industries, but it has yet to be fully exploited in the outsourcing of IT services. Statistics are still thin on the ground, but increasingly major deals are being created using the multisourcing framework. For example, five different suppliers are delivering ABN AMRO's Strategic Banking Platform.

Thanks to the late and legendary economist John Kenneth Galbraith, modern executives are now aware that it can be dangerous to accept the conventional wisdom on a subject.[18] Conventional ideas are stable and predictable, but should not remain beyond question, and we therefore believe that multisourcing is a strategy that merits executive consideration and exploitation.

In a world of global competition only those with a truly strategic vision can hope to lead, and multisourcing can help you to achieve this. Multisourcing is clearly a more demanding strategy than single-supplier sourcing. It demands commitment and additional management time, but the benefits can far outweigh the additional effort required to create sourcing governance structures. The emphasis is on building a successful framework of partners. This really is the future for large-scale sourcing in corporations with a strategic view on how they purchase services. The benefits and difficulties of multisourcing are plain to see, but there are a number of decisions that need to be taken if this strategy is to be utilized effectively.

The most important questions a forward-thinking Chief Information Officer (CIO) should be asking are:

- How many suppliers should I use?
- How can a framework be created for the selection of suppliers? Multisourcing isn't an easy option and it isn't right for every corporate environment. What the first step of the execution of your multisourcing vision should be is a critical decision, and one that is made easier by experience.
- How should I decide which supplier performs which task, when some have equal competence?
- What form of ongoing governance framework is required to make it work?
- How can you divide tasks to make use of common characteristics and economies of scale?

Naturally, the answers to these questions vary depending on the size and scope of the outsourcing programme in question. The number of suppliers cannot be easily mapped to the size of an outsourcing programme; there are no easy solutions such as 'use two software maintenance suppliers per £100 million', but you should examine where the programme may feature individual slices of similar work.

> In a flat world clients can easily select from a pool of global service providers; therefore a premium can be placed on being the best of breed. No single supplier can offer competitive excellence across every possible specialised service, and so the future is a more complex and diverse supplier marketplace. TCS is advising on the governance models that allow our clients to exploit the creative opportunities presented by multisourcing.
>
> Arun Aggarwal, EMEA Head, TCS Global Consulting Practice, www.tcs.com

CONCLUSION

Basic cost-plus pricing has been around since business commenced. It continues to thrive as the most basic way to charge for services, even international business process outsourcing. However, the newer and more innovative pricing models outlined in this chapter are far from theoretical. Some suppliers are even offering services that can be priced in a very simple way, using a shared benefits model or a complete joint venture – they offer pricing models all the way along the continuum.

Even smaller service and technology companies are starting to consider the merits of offering their services to be paid based on value, rather than time. It can be a risky strategy, but there is no need to follow the exact models prescribed here. If a supplier offers a client a no-profit model where costs are paid as with a basic service and profits are only paid if the expected value is created then there is an interesting business model that works for both client and supplier.

Clearly for any of these more complex pricing models to work, the supplier needs a very good understanding of the business their client is in. Domain knowledge is vital to understand the risk involved in providing any particular service. Therefore the tendency to get involved at a more basic level and work up the continuum will remain, because even where an industry is understood, there can be many specificities within a company that need to be learned.

The client needs to have a good understanding of how much effort goes into delivering their service. If they are moving straight from the retained organizational model to an outsourced structure the basic prices can often be a shock, without entering into the territory of shared gains. Educate the client over time, however, and the relationship can grow towards a genuine partnership.

The future shape and size of the company is a completely different model to the one that has been used through most of the 20th century, even redefining the concept of employment. The change to a layered model with shifting service boundaries will be painful for those seeking a lifetime of stable employment, but for consumer society in general it creates immense value – locating efficiencies and reducing costs in a world that has become globally competitive.

Customers, especially global customers, understand that services can be provided from anywhere (as some of them are used to dealing with multiple geographies in their own company). They are already seeing that their business operations can be supported from remote locations with a high quality and availability. They are satisfied that risks can be managed very effectively and more importantly are also able to satisfy the regulators. Cost advantage and continuous improvements are the main drivers for customers. Strategically, they also see that the services can be aggregated or consolidated offshore, thereby bringing synergies across their own diverse regional

(Continued)

(Continued)

setup. Many leading firms have used this consolidation to fuel their global expansion and growth.

This next wave of BPO is not necessarily volume-driven but capability driven. The earlier wave of voice-based BPO and certain aspects of back-office transactions were very much volume-driven. An ability to appreciate and understand the operational risks and the capability to manage them are essential. TCS is addressing this for its customers by a combination of very strong domain expertise both onsite and offshore, ability to execute and manage operations from nearshore or onsite, a strong focus on process improvement and process management regime underpinned by automation and significant improvements and/or transformation to the underlying IT platforms.

A.S. Lakshminarayanan, Vice President and Country Manager, UK and Ireland, Tata Consultancy Services, www.tcs.com

4 The Development of Technology

The level playing field agenda: Technology architecture itself is changing in order to accommodate the acceleration of change. By adopting 'loose' structures and creating 'virtual' systems that can easily communicate, the hardware is no longer as restrictive as it used to be. As flexibility is created, users become key generators of the content they themselves consume.

SET TECHNOLOGY FREE

Perhaps the toughest lesson of the early phases of the IT revolution was that, whatever the promise of the technology, the promise had to be accessed on terms set by the technology. At the start, only the technically skilled could make the technology work but, although this remains true to a certain extent, things have definitely moved on.

The decades prior to the 1990s were an era of the corporate computer centre as the temple, with its own priesthood. Richard can recall being allowed to use, out of departmental hours, the experimental screen-based word processing software being developed at Yale University Department of Computing to draft the text of his doctoral thesis on a PDP11 machine serving as a remote terminal to the Yale mainframe. The sharp-witted Yale undergraduates of the time had already discovered the value of the facility for preparing multiple, but simply customized law and medical graduate school applications – all neat and apparently unique – but in a tenth of the time that the electric typewriter required.

This was in 1972, when Mark was just graduating from nappies to shorts. When Richard was later moved from business leadership into the role of Group Vice President of IT in the early 1990s, one defining issue of the time was the corporate over-investment in global data centres in the late 1980s. The 'escape of the desktop' from the control of the corporate monopoly fuelled a vigorous policy debate, even as much of the company's new investment in computing power was similarly escaping central control with a surging population of local business-specific servers, located in the proverbial 'broom cupboard down the corridor'.

As the capabilities of technology grow exponentially, the options and the means for their exploitation and management also grow and change. For the initial decades, certainly through to the 1990s, the technology specified both the scope of its application and the way business was required to exploit the benefits on offer – and the business then had to re-engineer itself to access any further gains.

The legacy of those years is literally termed 'legacy'. Major investments in legacy systems still define the operating economics of significant swathes of the economy. The banking industry has been, over the decades, a pacesetter in the exploitation of new technologies. Given the major scale of their operations, and the productivity gains possible in replacing clerical with computerized data processing, the banks were major investors in mainframe-based back-office data processing facilities (comprehensive and in-house crafted software systems run on/based on world-scale computing centres) designed to automate their core banking systems. Research prepared by technology consultants Tower Group in 2005/2006 looked at the consequences – an annual industry spend of over US$180 billion on core banking systems, of which over 85 per cent was absorbed in the endless maintenance of this legacy investment. Therefore only much smaller sums are available for their replacement (approximately 8 per cent of the total) or to create and invest in the 'new' (approximately 6 per cent of the total).[1]

The major legacy investments were based around mainframe computers connected by telecommunications networks. This dependence on the mainframe for raw computing power enshrined the reality of a bottom-up approach to systems design – start with the big and centralized data centre as the inevitable reality, and then consequently specify the design of the banking applications that will operate on the data centre. The technological realities of the pre-millennial era – restraints in computing power, computing capacity and network capacity – all required an approach to resource optimization that restricted any real ability to be end-user driven. In the present century, when the competitive language of the banking services marketplace turned to speedy innovation in the nature of the customer 'offer', to the need for competitive agility and speed in change, the tension between the banks' marketing arms and those charged with the operation of the massively integrated but very slow-and-expensive-to-change core back-office systems became serious and palpable.

The story since the millennium has been of an accumulating impact of innovative technological capabilities, mostly already in place in the year 2000, that are now turning the legacy inheritance on its head – in essence flipping it over. Even compared to the rapid timescales the IT industry operates along, the speed of this flipping over is impressive. And a flip over it is, because in enabling the inversion from the restraints of technology-specified application scope to the freedom of application-specified technology scope, the revolution is already fuelling the development of significantly more agile and market-responsive business operations, not only in banking. All of this is in full alignment with the shift of the IT industry into a more user-shaped, user-driven modus operandi that was outlined in Chapter 1.

The fundamental driver behind this revolution has been the continued impact of Moore's Law – the computing power that can be exploited per unit area of a chip doubles every 18 months (more accurately, it is the data density achievable on an integrated chip that doubles approximately every 18 months), thus raising computing capacity and processor speed, and driving down unit costs. Linked and parallel innovation in cabling and optical fibre technology has continually grown network capacity in step changes and focused hardware and software innovation has delivered increasingly sophisticated capabilities to exploit the radio-frequency spectra as an integral extension of 'the communications network' in its very broadest sense.

As described above, the banks' major investment in legacy systems enshrined the realities of a bottom-up approach – the structuring of the big, centralized data centre and its network telecoms connections that specified in turn the design of the banking applications that operated on these infrastructural underpinnings – design realities reflecting real restraints in computing power, computing capacity and network capacity. The convergence of computing and network technologies enabled by the move of both to digital data processing has speeded the emergence of a new diversity of computing and network capabilities and services of almost unlimited capacity at increasingly competitive prices. One benefit has been to break the old restraints of designing from the bottom up (first the data centre ...) and enable an inversion to a top-down, and thus user-driven, design ethic.

'Almost unlimited capacity at increasingly competitive prices' has enabled two key developments in the revolution: a fast growing diversity of specialized software systems to manage and run other software systems, and an accelerating capacity to communicate between all points with bandwidth sufficient to enable these systems to deliver. These software technologies (and associated families of new industry standards and protocols) are now made both possible and worthwhile because their immediate impact on operating costs is now so low that they can cost-effectively deliver major capabilities in four key dimensions – four virtualizations. These are described next.

THE FOUR VIRTUALIZATIONS

The first impact of the new diversity of specialized software systems has been to enable the virtualization of the server (and, in context, the mainframe). Classically a server has been run on one operating system – whether proprietary such as Windows, Mac OS X, or an open system such as Linux – and the applications running on them have been accordingly restricted. In practical terms virtualization means that different operating systems and the applications that run on them can now be managed on a single machine – or flexibly across a number of machines. The virtualization software manages the computing power available in a highly flexible fashion against operating rules designed to optimize the use of capacity.

A McKinsey study[2] published in January 2006 reported that distributed servers running a single operating system utilized only about 5 to 15 per cent of their full processing capacity – virtualization made it possible for companies to boost average server utilization rates to 40 per cent or higher, while still meeting peak demands. The study goes on to identify additional operating benefits that sharply raise asset productivity – the ability to consolidate servers and reduce the complexity of the operating environment, so reducing asset investment – raising reliability as well as utilization rates, as work can be quickly moved between machines – and the flexibility to set up and tear down test environments quickly to speed innovation and further operational improvements.

What is the essence of this first virtualization? It is basically the conversion of the computing engine from a rigid to a highly flexible resource, making it much more able to respond to a rapidly changing environment while still operating at high levels of asset productivity. The computing engine has grown since its initial invention in a design framework of tightly coupled processes. Virtualization has enabled a new design paradigm of loosely coupled processes, and the loose coupling allows the flexibility required to deliver both agility and asset productivity. The archetype of 'the server in the broom cupboard', tightly tailored to the delivery of a few specific local applications, has changed into a new archetype – a computing resource responding to a changing flow of requirements over time, fast and flexibly, an asset that is always being worked hard.

The second impact of the new diversity of specialized software systems has been to enable a similar virtualization of the design and structuring of the applications systems and the complex number of business processes that they underwrite in the operation of the contemporary corporation. This emergent software capability, known as business process management (BPM), is a framework of specialized software systems that enable business processes to be both monitored and managed – automatically or by manual intervention, as best required.

In the classic pre-millennial era of the IT industry, the rapid development of standardized business process application packages (the ERP or enterprise resource planning revolution, pioneered by SAP of Germany) risked the reinforcement of the well-established organizational model of the business into distinct functional domains, silos of distinct operational capacity that interlinked across the corporation with difficulty. The substantive exercise of business process re-engineering (BPR), the ongoing source of much value creation through the 1990s and into the new millennium, sought to refocus the corporation along processes (and their underpinning information flows) more naturally aligned with the purpose of the business – the supply of goods and services to the customer – breaking the silo structure to so do. BPR generally was (and remains) a tough exercise in corporate change management. While the silo operational realities undoubtedly need to be replaced by operating processes more suited to the purpose of the business, the risk inherent in even the most successful BPR exercises is that the new processes, more suited as it may be, is itself insufficiently flexible and responsive to the ever-changing competitive pressures on the business.

On the one hand BPM can enable the easy integration of business transactions across multiple application systems, delivering their end-to-end alignment as and when required. The important capability to deliver straight-through order processing, as one concrete example, can now be implemented with relative ease. On the other, as BPM introduces a rules-based modus operandi, it enables flexible and responsive operations that can quickly be adjusted to new priorities and new rules. Because process measurement lies at its heart, BPM can enable tools that can be used to raise process productivity (to ensure that business processes are executed efficiently) and to allow the identification of opportunities for continual improvement and innovation – and the implementation of the changes that will deliver the improvements and innovation so identified.

What is the essence of this second virtualization? The breaking of the rigidity of tightly coupled legacy business applications, creating in its place the flexibility of loosely coupled processes, able to respond to rapidly changing requirements while still operating at high levels of asset productivity. Once again, this is about the migration from the tightly coupled to the loosely coupled.

The third impact of the new diversity of specialized software systems has been to enable the virtualization of the architecting of the diversity of components that are assembled to create the contemporary IT infrastructure – processing power, data storage and network bandwidth. This emergent structure of industry standards is called service-oriented architecture (SOA) – sometimes 'systems' is used in place of 'service', but the acronym remains the same. It is in essence an application architecture, in which all functions are defined using a descriptive language, with interfaces that can be invoked, or activated, to create interconnecting applications delivering business processes. Each interaction (interface) between the functions is designed to be independent of each and every other interaction – and the interconnecting protocols for communicating devices are specified to be interface-independent and the interfaces themselves are platform-independent.

SOA really delivers the promise of focusing on the business solution and not the IT platform. Clearly it is a key enabler of the BPM promise – the former creating the means for the latter to be delivered. The working assumption of both is a move from tightly coupled to loosely coupled systems. More importantly, the combination of both creates the environment for the architecting of systems around the specific requirements of the business objectives to be delivered. Reiterating the paradigm shift outlined in the opening paragraphs of this chapter, SOA enables movement from the restraints of technology-specified application scope to the freedoms of application-specified technology scope, fuelling the development of significantly more agile and market-responsive business operations.

What is the essence of this third virtualization? Breaking the rigidity of legacy IT infrastructure that will only operate in certain specific ways – creating in its place a flexible IT infrastructure able to respond to changing requirements. SOA really enables the loosely coupled IT infrastructure.

The fourth impact of the new diversity of specialized software systems, combined with innovative and powerful new hardware, has been to enable the virtualization of data communication across a wide diversity of frequency spectra, whether across cabled (from copper to fibre optics) or wireless networks. The spectrum being tackled is already very wide – from 'wired' delivery of 0.01–0.1 megabits per second (Mbps) associated with the fixed telephone and the CD, through the 10 Mbps of Ethernet servicing the office environment, to the 100 Mbps of Fast Ethernet – and the parallel 'wireless' delivery ranging from the 1–10 Mbps of personal services provided locally by Bluetooth 1.2 and 2.0, to the developing wide broadcast spectra of mobile telephony standards of sub-0.1 Mbps of 2G to the greater than 1.0 Mbps of 3G – with WiFi capabilities essentially mimicking Ethernet capacities over both local area and metropolitan-sized footprints.

The speed of innovation and development here is shaped by a complex mix of hardware development, software development and the development of agreed industry standards and protocols and, in the wireless world, regulatory regimes around the exploitation of the radio-frequency spectrum. Exploitation of internet data transmission protocols and new software structures has brought to market the 'over IP' capabilities being exploited by recent business start-ups such as Skype and Vonage (voice over IP, or VOIP, services). These exploit the operational reality that digitization of voice as data packages to be switched and transmitted over the internet (loose coupling) is so much more efficient over the fixed telecoms network than classic open-line analogue telephony that it can competitively undercut established services by major margins. The telecommunication companies are responding with major programmes of reinvestment in new-generation digital networks based on the exploitation of virtualization to allow very much higher productivity operations.

The economics of virtualization directionally move charging models towards a 'fixed charge and always on' and away from 'charge per unit time used' paradigms. The consumer imperative is the major driver, pressing the development of consumer hardware from the mobile phone to the mobile laptop to the television in the home, to be able to access and interact with ever greater bandwidth to give access to an ever greater diversity and sophistication of services. The consumer imperative speeds the options available for take up and rapid exploitation by the corporate world: the now vital business tools of mobile phone, PDA (personal digital assistant) and laptop (and products that combine some or all of these) able to draw on an increasing variety of wireless-enabled bandwidth access. Plans to fully 'wireless enable' the whole of the City of London's square mile (already densely cabled with high-capacity optical fibre technology for wired commerce) through a partnership deal between the City and The Cloud underlines just how radical the post-millennial communications revolution is proving in practice.[3]

What is the essence of this fourth virtualization? Breaking the restraints of a specific location and hardware to conduct particular business operations. The availability of hand-held mobile devices that can operate with high bandwidth available from wireless services. The shift in paradigm from the tightly coupled to the loosely coupled applied to both the individual and the working team. The virtualization of the telecoms networks through digitization and agreed data transmission protocols (IP) allowing radical improvements in asset productivity.

These four virtualizations lie at the root of the new freedom from the restraints of applications specified by the technology on which they will be run. Freed of these restraints, it is the application that now specifies the technology required to run it to best advantage; a total inversion of the design process. The combination of BPM with SOA brings us into a world where business requirements can define and shape the underlying IT infrastructure to respond and align to its needs – liberating responsiveness and agility that the pre-flip/inversion realities denied. The communications revolution liberates the individual to operate to best advantage in both time and space. The shift from the paradigm of the tightly coupled to the loosely coupled not only enables this greater flexibility, agility and responsiveness, but also provides the means of working assets harder and to higher levels of effectiveness and efficiency.

THE SERVICES REVOLUTION: THE FIFTH VIRTUALIZATION

The four virtualizations have helped set the scene for the emergence and rapid development of business services made available over the web – labelled in two broad, overlapping categories as software as a service (SaaS), and as web services.

The web has matured as a robust public utility. The consumer imperative has been the prime driver. The prime enablers have included the development of increasingly reliable server farms and data centres whose costs of operation have plummeted (reflecting the first of the four virtualizations at work), and increasingly reliable network capabilities, capacities and asset productivity (the IP impact) that have sharply driven down bandwidth costs. The costs of providing managed data storage are also sharply down.

At the same time, the consumer imperative has speeded the development of broadband access to the web. Competition between the cable and telecommunications industries has accelerated the process. Broadband access has now become essentially free in the UK, with TV providers such as Sky bundling access to any TV subscriber or the Carphone Warehouse offering it to phone customers. The linking of internal corporate networks to the web (through protective firewalls) has moved in parallel.

Consumerization has speeded the demand for capacity through the endlessly growing bandwidth requirements for such things as simple text and emailing, then basic instant messaging services, then the downloading of music, then the accelerating growth in the distribution of video and film, and then the support of online video conferencing. In addition, the push to exploit the mobile phone with services requiring increasingly greater bandwidth, accelerated by the 'over IP' revolution setting new norms, has resulted in mobile-to-mobile video conferencing becoming a reality.

Whether access is by wired or wireless means, the web has emerged as a natural delivery highway for a diversity of relatively straightforward digital consumer services – the transmission of 'digital stuff' (from emails to music files to films and video) to the remote accessing of online services such as Google. This has in turn promoted and fostered a range of new industry standards and protocols designed to further improve and extend the web's operational flexibility in servicing a wider arena of more complex and sophisticated digital services – our fifth virtualization.

These new open standards and protocols have created a framework that allows web services to share business logic, data and processes (the structured core of business applications) through programmatic interfaces across the web – applications interfacing applications, rather than users. The standards and protocols ensure that different applications from different sources can communicate with each other without time-consuming custom coding, and because all communication is in the web language of eXtensible Markup Language (XML), web services are not tied to any one particular operating system or programming language. These open standards allow data to be tagged (XML), transferred through a messaging protocol that is operating-system independent (allowing transportation using a variety of internet protocols), and provide standard languages to describe and list the services available on central catalogues. So web services allow corporate organizations to inter-communicate business logic, data and processes without any requirement for a specific knowledge of what systems lie behind the protective firewalls. These same standards are in the process of being actively developed to provide security structures for web services, including encryption and digital signatures.

What is the essence of this fifth virtualization? Computers (in the broadest sense of the word) can talk to computers in a far easier and more open fashion. The new open standards allow computer applications to reach beyond the confines of specific hardware, operating systems and programming languages. Human access to web services can be through browser software on the laptop and desktop or through mobile telephones and PDAs (despite their very different screen shapes and sizes, and differing connection speeds); through application programmes (such as, for example, order entry systems that can now automatically access a web-delivered credit check service); and through web services that themselves access other web services (an airline booking service that draws on a third-party credit card payment service). The consumer revolution has brought the means to book a flight, rental car or hotel, and buy the necessary insurance, just by visiting one of many dedicated websites. The web service revolution enables such offerings to be brought to the user's desktop in a potentially integrated fashion.

A lead example of the potential for web services in the core corporate arena has been the success of Salesforce.com, who offer a family of integrated and fully customizable customer relationship management services that are available on demand – all delivered over the web. The core services include the range of capabilities required to support effective sales work, including sales force automation, customer service and support, analytics, offered within a framework that allows straightforward assembly and self-customization. The architecture of the computing platform that Salesforce.com utilizes ('AppExchange') has more recently been exploited to allow a widening range of third-party software vendors to both customize and integrate Salesforce.com's applications and to build, publish and share their own enterprise applications as services on the Salesforce.com platform. Compared to the more traditional options of the purchase of sales force automation software packages and their launch and operation on the corporate computing infrastructure, experience shows a much more rapid process to both implementation and moves to widespread use, a much reduced cost of ownership, and thus a shortened time before the business gains real value from the new capability. As the service is offered as on-demand and paid for accordingly, in corporate terms it is a far more flexible option.

Salesforce.com is a leading example of a web service – an example of software as a service offered over the internet. A mid 2006 survey by the Aberdeen Group[4] in the USA of 631 companies reported: 'SaaS is gaining traction in a number of enterprise application areas, and making quick believers of previous sceptics.' Application areas covered included customer relationship management, supply chain management, sourcing and procurement, financial management and product lifecycle management – with implementation times generally in the range 2–3 months, and ROI (Return on Investment) in the range of six months to a year.

In a slightly earlier (mid 2005) survey by McKinsey of 77 senior IT executives, [5] the trend to SaaS delivered over the internet was noted. By buying access to externally hosted services, the total cost of deployment of some classes of enterprise applications was cut by 30-40 per cent when compared to the total cost of purchase and in-house mainte-nance. Of the 77 interviewees, 38 per cent reported plans to use SaaS in the following 12 months. McKinsey reports that popular application areas include software for HR management (including payroll), billing and order entry, sales management and security services for protection against spam and viruses – but that few companies were using SaaS in those systems, such as production planning and forecasting, that were judged to require a lot of tailoring or customization.

In summary, this chapter has sketched the essential features of a major revolution in the making. The consumerization of IT since the late 1990s has speeded the development of the internet as a public utility – a plat-form for service access and delivery. The five virtualizations introduced in this chapter have been releasing the world of applied IT from historic con-straints that ensured that technology specified the scope of applications. This restricted the opportunity for business-shaped, business-responsive applications. The new freedoms allow the world of applied IT to deliver applications specified by business need and opportunity.

TOO MUCH OF A GOOD THING

The developments set out in this chapter forecast the rapid growth in the global commerce of business-to-business technology-enabled services – increasingly delivered, managed and maintained over the internet. They also forecast a world of loosely coupled systems replacing the tightly architected IT world of the last decades.

In the pre-millennia world of tightly architected IT (and thus tightly coupled applications and systems), the challenges of quality, operational reliability, risk management, security and continuity planning could be addressed within quite tightly defined system and operational envelopes. A very major focus was placed on the quality engineering of software, and standards were developed within the framework of the International Organization for Standardization's (ISO) ISO 9000 on quality management. In the UK, this lead to the development of the TickIT scheme designed to support the implementation of the ISO 9000 framework.[6]

Similarly, based on work originally initiated by the UK's Office of Government Commerce, ITIL (Information Technology Infrastructure Library) provides a cohesive set of best practices for service management processes and the help desk function – more recently developed into the

British Standard Institution's (BSI) BS 15000. The US Software Engineering Institute (SEI) at Carnegie Mellon University has created a fundamental capability maturity model (CMM), which is expressed in a series of business performance frameworks designed to provide organizations with the essential elements of methodical and measurable approaches to guiding process improvement across a project, or a business. The Indian offshoring majors have positively exploited independently audited performance ratings within the CMM frameworks to establish a clear quality face to their brands. The framework was essential for providing a guaranteed delivery from a remote location, but the Indian companies went from needing the framework to being the leaders in using it.

As the capabilities of IT became increasingly vital for the breadth of operations of the contemporary corporation, an additional focus developed on the issue of alignment – ensuring that there was a tight linkage between what the IT was delivering and delivery of the business performance objectives it was supposed to be underwriting. A technically strong IT department, focused on making the complexities of the technology function efficiently, could risk losing track of what the technology was actually intended to be used for. The ITIL/BS 15000 frameworks and standards addressed such issues in part – against the background of an IT department pretty much integral to a business or a government department – or latterly in the context of a tightly held outsourcing relationship. The US-created COBIT (Control Objectives for Information and related Technology), a joint initiative of the ISACA (Information Systems Audit and Control Association) and the ITGI (IT Governance Institute) launched in 1992, provides a strategic framework of best practices, processes and metrics designed to maximize business benefits from the use of technology. Further, more specialized standards have been evolved to encompass newer requirements – for example BS 7799 on information management security services.

Classic outsourcing, operating within the realms of the facilities management (FM) model, carries forward a sufficiently close supplier/customer relationship at the operating level to ensure the continuing applicability of these standards in an essentially tightly coupled environment.

However, the move away from the FM model of outsourcing to the model of more arm's-length sourcing of services (SaaS, web services etc.) – and the move to the world of the more loosely coupled – has given relevance to the issue of how to ensure quality assurance across a service chain drawing on the contributions of a diversity of suppliers.

Experience drawn from the more tightly coupled world sets out the issues that need to be addressed. From one point of view: quality assurance (service component by service component) of the underlying IT infrastructure, and of the software applications running on it; related process management (including change management, business continuity and security at the component service level); and, in addition, quality assurance and change management at the interfaces between all the service components. From another point of view, issues of security management, risk management, change management and business continuity along the length of the service chain are key.

In businesses where there is a strong regulatory framework, such as in the financial services industry, the requirement to be able to assure that a particular combination of external service provision will ensure a business demonstrably operates within its regulatory envelope is clearly vital.

The term 'assurance' is perhaps the key to mapping out the direction that the current universe of standards and frameworks will have to evolve in. In the tightly coupled world addressed by COBIT and ITIL/BS 15000, certification processes provided by independent auditors can address the service infrastructure as a whole. In a more loosely coupled world, the challenge is to identify the combination of separate certifications that, overall, will provide the required level of business assurance to the customer at the front of the service chain.

The logic of a more loosely coupled system is that each component should be free to be optimized in its own context. This suggests that those facets of established standards and frameworks that can be used to assure and certify each component in its own right should be used to so do. In this context, the family of CMM (capability maturity models – now developed into the more advanced CMMI or capability maturity models integrated set of frameworks) and the newer offering from the Carnegie Mellon stable of eSCM-SP (e-sourcing capability model for suppliers) are likely to be strongly relevant in the software application and process management contexts – and eSCM-SP and the ITIL/BS 15000 together with the security management BS 7799 in the context of infrastructure management.

Nonetheless, this is to identify certification frameworks that can assure the individual parts of the business, rather than the whole. There is no clear framework as yet that can positively address the range of issues inherent in assuring a complex service chain as a whole. The current frameworks are, in the main, significantly standalone and inwardly focused – in the world of the loosely coupled, a strong external orientation is required.

Consider this potential real life example. A London business in the financial services arena that draws significantly on the services of Salesforce.com for its customer relationship and sales management, is reliant on the Salesforce.com IT infrastructure in the USA and the infrastructure of the entire internet for service delivery. Creating a positive business assurance across the small diversity of services it thus draws on (and none of which it has any direct control of) lies at the heart of the issue that has been set out in the closing pages of this chapter.

Simply outsourcing your back-office processes may deliver a one-off benefit, but failing to link it with the underlying technology will ensure that it has a limited shelf-life and frequently leaves the client wondering where the future productivity gains will come from. Looking at the needs of our clients, we see them outsourcing to improve the efficiency of a process (do it at lower cost), improve its effectiveness (deliver a better end result) or reduce the level of management attention that is required on processes that provide little competitive advantage. In Xansa, we design solutions that simultaneously meet all these needs and we are able to do that by combining our expertise in process design and operations with our technology skills and our delivery capability both in the UK and in India.

We are able to bring immediate cost advantages to our client by utilising offshore resources. The actual transitioning of the business process from our client to ourselves allows us to re-engineer specific aspects of the process to make it more effective. Once the process has been outsourced, we are then able to future-proof the solution for the client via the use of technology. There is only so far you can go with process re-engineering, cost reduction and six sigma-style improvement programmes alone and, frankly, it is impossible to deliver that important next step without a deep and current understanding of how technology can be leveraged for mutual gain. This approach allows Xansa to more confidently align its goals with those of our clients by creating commercial structures that motivate the right behaviours across all parties and share risk and reward.

Technology is the key enabler for improving business outcomes and to ignore its future possibilities is madness. As a client, would you be comfortable knowing that your back-office processes are being delivered in a static environment where any performance improvement is derived simply via the management mantras of 'Work Hard, Work Smart' or 'Focus', or would you prefer an environment where people are constantly exploring ways that technology can be deployed to speed things up, cut out errors, pinpoint problems, analyse data and enable better, faster, more informed decision-making?

Alistair Cox, Chief Executive Officer, Xansa plc, www.xansa.com

5 The Real Matrix

The level playing field agenda: All the important changes in modern society are being enabled by technology – that's our industry and we need to take more of an interest in the way our technological ideas are affecting the world around us. Thomas Friedman believes that technology is almost entirely responsible for creating his 'flat world' and the opportunities that this creates.

In *The World is Flat*, *New York Times* columnist Thomas Friedman identified 10 forces that are redefining the way we live and do business in the 21st century.[1] Friedman called them 'the ten forces that flattened the world'. Take a look at our summary of his list and see if you agree:

1. 9 November 1989: the fall of the Berlin wall and subsequent spread of democracy throughout Europe.
2. 9 August 1995: the date Netscape became a public company.
3. Workflow software: disparate systems able to communicate and share information.
4. Open sourcing: the growth of the free software champions.
5. Outsourcing: the boom in working with partner companies since the 'millennium bug'.
6. Offshoring: the use of offshore teams to reduce cost and improve efficiency.
7. Supply-chaining: the 24 hours a day, 7 days a week, 365 days a year culture of Wal-Mart.
8. Insourcing: companies such as UPS doing a lot more than just delivering the mail.
9. Informing: web search and information services.
10. The steroids: digital, mobile, personal and virtual tools.

Friedman is not a technologist and his book was far more about the application of globalization than technology tools, but it is fascinating to see how central technology is placed as a critical component of his list. Some commentators have even gone so far as to call his observations simplistic and without value. These are surely the cries of a jealous academic community who can only dream of selling two million books on a subject such as globalization. Friedman's art is simplicity and to argue that this is a bad thing would be the same as claiming that BB King's music is too simple to be valuable. He is a writer who cuts to the heart of an argument with the typical directness of a *New York Times* columnist. Technology practically jumps off the page in his list of flatteners. Democracy in its classical form doesn't have much to do with technology, but look at how modern democracy functions. The bloggers often get it wrong and they dance around the edge of libel, but because they don't have the constraints of a major publisher or the fear of being seen as biased they can break stories that otherwise might be just swept under the carpet. The various presidential misdemeanors of the past half a century would have been less likely in the present environment of constant news on TV, blogs and podcasts.

- **Wiki:** a form of website that allows readers to add, remove and edit content easily with the effect of immediate publication. *Wikipedia* is the best-known public example.
- **Blog:** short for 'web-log', a type of online diary where dated entries are regularly added and updated. Can be used as a personal diary by a teenager or corporate updates to follow the activities of an executive.
- **Podcast:** formed from contracting the name of Apple's ubiquitous MP3-player, the 'iPod', and 'broadcast'; a method of distributing multimedia files by pushing the content to subscribers. Popular podcasts often feature content from TV or radio broadcasters, but the system is so simple, anyone can start broadcasting.
- **RSS:** Really Simple Syndication. A family of web formats that easily facilitate the syndication of content on blogs, podcasts or news websites allowing you to subscribe to information that matters to you.

In his book Friedman goes into his case for each of the flatteners in depth. Without repeating what he has written, these are our observations on the eight technology-enabled flatteners.

FLATTENER 2, 9 AUGUST 1995: THE DATE NETSCAPE BECAME A PUBLIC COMPANY

Can you remember the first time you browsed the web using Netscape? Wasn't it just like one of those epiphanies you read about in books, where the central character suddenly realizes he should be hand-rearing llamas in the Andes rather than trading equities on Wall Street? Maybe not, but those of us who were online prior to Netscape can only remember a very expensive world of bulletin board services such as CompuServe, which charged a fortune for some very basic services within a members-only gated community. Suddenly, everyone could access any page, so long as they were online.

Although the internet existed long before Netscape, this tool allowed everyone to start browsing pages built with HyperText Markup Language (HTML). It was the true birth of the internet because it was the point at which the internet was democratized – it was shifted away from academia and into the life of every adult and child with an ISP account. The fact that so much web traffic is now hardcore porn or live video feeds from the Big Brother house is another debate for the sociologists to worry about.

FLATTENER 3, WORKFLOW SOFTWARE: DISPARATE SYSTEMS ABLE TO COMMUNICATE AND SHARE INFORMATION

In the early 1990s, one of the authors was working on state-of-the-art banking technology in the City where data transfers from one system to another needed a text file dump to floppy disk, then a manual transfer to another server. No doubt those of more advanced years can describe how the same farce was tolerated in earlier times with other media, such as a stack of punched cards.

Now through various protocols and the rise of middleware, disparate systems can 'speak' to each other. This has been taken to its logical conclusion within the corporate IT world through the rise in popularity of enterprise resource planning (ERP) systems, which integrate the data and processes used by an organization into a single unified system. The ERP system will utilize various IT systems to connect internal departments and processes, ensuring visibility across the entire supply chain.

One of the key elements of ERP is the use of a single unified database that can be queried by all system modules, anywhere in the company. This unification and grand overview of company operations eliminates the 'spaghetti junction' of various departmental systems and processes, along with the multiple interfaces between systems.

However, a major ERP installation typically requires a large investment in technology, changes to operating procedures and employee retraining. It can be an extremely disruptive change to the way a company operates because the effect is so far-reaching, yet the benefits of streamlining the organization can be great.

The bottom line for this process streamlining is that the customer experience should be improved. When a customer calls a company and is ready to place an order, the employee taking the call should have at their fingertips all the information needed to serve the customer. The ERP system provides a path through the entire order fulfilment process, allowing real-time information from separate departments to improve the flow of that customer order through the organization.

Taking that order as an example of what ERP can do when the employee has a customer on the telephone, the system will be able to access the order history and credit rating of this customer from finance, check whether the item they want is in stock or on order, and determine an expected delivery time based on these factors. The flow of information is faster, has fewer errors, and the real-time nature of the order fulfilment process can improve the relationship with the customer by assuring them of your competence and control over the entire process. Customers don't care about process integration; they just want to receive what they ask for, when they expect it.

FLATTENER 4, OPEN SOURCING: THE GROWTH OF THE FREE SOFTWARE CHAMPIONS

Open-source software has become a very important phenomenon, particularly in the present century. Open-source software is free. The licence gives the user the right to use, modify and redistribute copies of the software without paying royalties to the software author or publisher.

The most well-known example of open-source software is the Linux operating system created by Linus Torvalds, and still overseen by Torvalds – though it has changed so much that his original work probably accounts for only a fraction of the present code. The army of developers prepared to give their creative expertise to an open-source project in return for little more than kudos continues to grow.

The free and open-source movement has in the past been accused of being little more than a radical anti-Microsoft organization, yet open-source software is now taken very seriously in both the public and private sector. Though the software itself is free, companies have been able to generate profits from their expertise in installing and maintaining open-source systems.

Open source runs the modern internet. Over 70 per cent of servers now run Apache web server software – an open-source tool.[2] The Mozilla Firefox web browser is increasingly taking market share away from the ubiquitous Microsoft Internet Explorer, not least because the Microsoft tool is under constant attack from spyware and other nasties. There is even a British browser, Deepnet Explorer, that aims to protect from phishing and other security attacks.[3] The Open Office suite of free office products – a direct rival to the Microsoft Office suite – claims 10 per cent of the market for these office tools.

The open-source movement is changing the world. The drive to provide better content from harnessing the global capabilities of millions of software developers together, rather than just the employees of a private company, will have an enormous effect on the way we utilize technology.

The implications for technology adoption in the developing world are immense. Hardware costs are already quite low; in India HCL technologies launched a sub-10,000 rupee computer in 2005.[4] The One Laptop Per Child programme run by Nicholas Negroponte at MIT Media Labs in the

USA has designed a laptop computer than can be distributed at a unit cost of \$100.[5] With hardware costs this low and software that can be pre-loaded with a free licence, the options for IT use in developing nations are far broader than just a few years ago.

FLATTENER 5, OUTSOURCING: THE BOOM IN WORKING WITH PARTNER COMPANIES

The main point related to globalization is the change in corporate strategy and growing acceptance of outsourcing. It has become normal to strip away services that are not 'core' and to pay experts to deliver those services. It has become possible for an organization to be little more than a trusted brand, with all production and related services outsourced to partners. Companies are generally becoming more global in their outlook on where to find customers and this is also changing the way they interact with each other.

First-generation outsourcing was all about the financially engineered transfer of assets and staff, with service delivery on a cost-plus basis. In other words, mortgaging your future for short-term gains. Not sustainable. So we learnt, or thought we did.

Second-generation outsourcing was all about wage arbitrage and low-cost locations, creating geographical concentrations. India for this, China for that, Estonia for them and Singapore for those. In other words, looking at cost rather than value, refusing to accept that comparative advantage is about talent and not cost alone. Not sustainable.

Third-generation outsourcing, the age we're in, has begun to recognize that sustainable value comes from a Yourdon-like High Cohesion and Loose Coupling. The game has changed, and we cannot afford to export silo activities as silos any more, a more holistic approach has to be taken. Talent can only contribute via innovation, and innovation mushrooms at the edges where well-bounded processes meet, e.g. Seely Brown and Hagel's Only Sustainable Edge.

Organizations that adapt to exploit these developments will succeed. Globally distributed workforces that use Porter-like 'national comparative advantage' talent, to create circles of competence that cover new families of processes rather than historical silos. Workforces that are partly on payroll, partly partnered and partly voluntary (e.g. the open-source community). Workforces that use

(Continued)

(Continued)

collaborative tools to defeat time and space and culture. Workforces that do the right thing because they are empowered to, and innovate because they can. Workforces that choose to work because they enjoy what they do, where they work, how they work and who they work with.

Utility models will emerge to reflect these trends, but the providers of the models will not be the ones we have today; industry participants will recognize the need to work together to derive new value from such service acquisition.

J.P. Rangaswami, CIO, BT Global Services, www.btglobalservices.com

FLATTENER 6, OFFSHORING: THE USE OF OFFSHORE TEAMS TO REDUCE COST AND IMPROVE EFFICIENCY

As outsourcing has become more acceptable, so has offshoring. Although a global corporation has offices and staff in many locations, what has changed is the willingness to source services from suppliers located in a remote region. India has been the clear winner in both the IT and IT-enabled service sectors, but many developing regions are now working hard to present themselves as having the required infrastructure (reliable electricity, educated people, roads, airports, internet etc.) to support organizations in the developed world.

Offshoring has been very closely linked to outsourcing, as the out-sourcing itself is often to an offshore location, but it is a little removed, as many companies are not working with partners at all. In the case of heavily regulated industries, such as financial services, it is more common for the company to just set up their own service centre in the new location – in business–speak, a 'captive'.

Studies show consistently that 70 to 80 per cent of the economic benefits of offshore outsourcing, or 'offshoring', accrue to the country doing it, for four main reasons.

The first and most obvious is in lower costs and, to the extent that there is a flow of jobs overseas, lower inflation. After allowing for relocation costs and productivity differences, most companies would reckon on a 20 to 30 per cent cost saving.

(Continued)

(Continued)

This leads to a second gain, in real incomes. These occur through lower prices as cost savings are passed on to consumers, and through the boost to corporate profits and dividends.

Third, even where countries have high levels of unemployment they often have shortages of specific types of labour. Overseas out-sourcing relieves such pressures. The tighter the labour market, the stronger is this argument.

Finally, and most importantly, it enables workers in the country doing the outsourcing to be shifted into higher value-added/higher productivity functions. In the end, that is how advanced economies will survive in the new era of global competition.

David Smith, Economics Editor, *The Sunday Times* and author of *Free Lunch: Easily Digestible Economics*,[6] www.economicsuk.com, www.sunday-times.co.uk

FLATTENER 7, SUPPLY-CHAINING: THE 24 HOURS A DAY, 7 DAYS A WEEK, 365 DAYS A YEAR CULTURE OF WAL-MART

The ability to capture and model the complete supply chain of an organ-ization is changing the way companies behave and operate. Wal-Mart is the standard-bearer for this radical approach where every aspect of what a company does can be modelled or tracked, allowing stock to be mini-mized and improving customer satisfaction. It has been said that Wal-Mart knows what you are going to buy before you even walk through the front of the store; what is a fact is that as you purchase a product it is not only reordered automatically from that store, but the ripple of informa-tion flows all the way to the actual supplier.

FLATTENER 9, INFORMING: WEB SEARCH AND INFORMATION SERVICES

Who needs a memory anymore? Google is the collective memory of all that is known about everything. Google co-founder Larry Page has even suggested the idea of a Google brain implant.[7] Searching the web has moved on since the days of stabbing in the dark at a search engine that returned thousands of pages as possible matches. Not only has Google changed the entire model for searching the internet, but Microsoft, Amazon and Yahoo! have all improved and are in a race to offer the best system for finding what you need.

Search as a tool is bleeding into other areas of life, with search compa-nies moving into the forefront of the advertising industry. It's a natural fit, as a company that knows you are searching for a particular product or service has a great advantage over a company that adopts the more traditional 'old media' advertising of TV adverts, or pages in a newspaper.

FLATTENER 10, THE STEROIDS: DIGITAL, MOBILE, PERSONAL AND VIRTUAL TOOLS

In many developed countries the adoption rate of mobile phones is greater than one per person – we have not just embraced mobile phones, we adore them. People use one phone handset for work and one for personal calls – or one phone for the wife and another for the girlfriend. Those of us who remember the birth of mobile telephony in the 1980s may need to stop and think for a moment about the generation that has been born since then. Kids graduating from university around about now don't even remember a world before mobile telephones and the internet. Doesn't that make you feel old?

There was a time when meeting a friend for dinner at a specific restaurant at a specific time meant just that. Now it's common to agree an approximate time to meet at an approximate place and to use the telephones like homing devices: 'Can you see me yet? I'm standing by Starbucks waving like a lunatic!'

The ability to contact anyone, anywhere at anytime is of more benefit – and possibly detriment – to society than just alliterative fun and references to Martini. Tools such as the Blackberry (from Canadian firm Research in Motion) allow the line between work and home to be blended, giving access to work email at anytime. Some users have even become so addicted to checking their email that the device has been dubbed the 'Crackberry'. Microsoft has promoted mobile devices using lines such as 'Live a little, work a little ...' demonstrating a new approach to work.

Having access to all the information on the internet from a Blackberry, Motorola or Nokia device opens a new world of connectivity. People are always 'on' and always have access to any information they need. A major implication is the inability to escape work, but this may well be a hangover from an older generation of workers and their insistence on a black and white definition of what is work and what is not. After all, who has never looked at their personal email while sitting in the office, or checked up on an eBay auction, or had a look at the weather? *Financial Times* columnist Lucy Kellaway even wrote an entire column about how she bought an item of clothing from eBay during office hours for £4 and was surprised to find that the seller was a high-powered City lawyer who probably spends more on a coffee – all buying and selling on eBay during the supposed working day.[8]

A note of caution should be sounded here. Although it may be great having access to all information at all times from anywhere, not everyone likes it that way. The US Congress passed a bill on 2 October 2006 cracking down on internet gambling. The bill was presented in terms of protecting US consumers from the scourge of online gaming, yet the US government has not mentioned closing Las Vegas. There was additional talk after the bill was passed of a technological solution that would prevent US gamers from accessing the British gaming sites, such as partygaming or 888. To prevent citizens from accessing certain parts of the internet in this way sounds very similar to the attitude taken by China when insisting on a censored version of Google for local consumption. Let's face it, it's highly probable that this bill was passed not because of any moral concern over gambling, but just because the gaming companies are based overseas.

ENTERPRISE RESOURCES

Within the corporate world all this knowledge and information can either create an immense opportunity or cause a complete loss of productivity as staff never focus on anything long enough to finish it. As mentioned earlier, the improved standards allow ERP systems to create better data flows and greater knowledge capture within the organization, but a lot of the data is random and ad hoc. Capturing ad hoc knowledge can create a key differentiator where your competitors are using structured methods alone.

Encouraging your staff to capture ad hoc information not only creates a new and rich seam of information on customers, it empowers your people at all levels of the organization – anyone can contribute. This is not business as usual.

Let's just think of a few simple tools from the wild west of the personal internet that might be applicable within the corporate world.

- The database of intent: the concept of archiving and analysing the search history of the internet as described by John Battelle in *The Search*[9] can be applied within the organization to ensure you are aware of what your customers are asking for, and why. Not through some formal customer relationship management (CRM) or ERP system, but by capturing every tiny piece of information, even those that don't fit within the strict format of the supply chain. When Eddie Murphy gave his famous advice to wait before buying pork belly futures in *Trading Places* it wasn't because he had analysed the detailed trading patterns, he just knew something would happen.
- Using a wiki as a central information store encourages project collaboration and reduces email. You know all the emails that get sent around your office to update others on projects? What is it like for your boss? They get copied in on everything, whether it is necessary or not. Sometimes they are copied in because people want authorization, but usually it is so that people appear to be busy, or

they want to invoke their authority – the recipient would usually ignore the sender, but if the boss is copied in then something might be done. How about ignoring all these games and the email flood altogether by using a wiki for each project and collaborating in teams to add content, updates and the latest information within the wiki. The poor email administrator would be out of a job if it wasn't for all the spam.

- Allowing employees to post to internal blogs can capture and formalize informal knowledge or information about customers, giving a strong boost to your structured CRM system. This is an exciting concept because it moves past the issue of 'knowledge is power'. Structured CRM aims to map the relationships that you have with your clients and prospects, but we all know that some people have information that they want to keep for themselves and some just don't realize the value of the information they have. Imagine the possibilities if employees could regularly write notes into a personal blog, which creates a corporate data source of unstructured information that can be used by sticking a tool such as Google on top.

Customer relationship management (CRM) is a subject so ingrained in corporate planning and spending that it might seem strange to ask such a basic question as 'where is the knowledge?' CRM is a mature branch of IT services, with a plethora of tools and expertise on the market. Along with the maturity of standard software packages and processes comes an implicit assurance that companies know how to 'do' CRM correctly.

The ultimate intention of any CRM system, whether it is a manual process of capturing customer behaviour or an expensive software package that is fully integrated into your supply chain, is to please the customer. You want to please the customer by identifying ways in which they behave and customizing your service to anticipate or meet those needs better than could be achieved without any form of CRM. Keeping the customer happy has a direct impact on the bottom line, whether it is remembering the meal preferences of a frequent airline traveller or warning a regular customer that their favourite product is about to go temporarily out of stock.

The internet has proven to be more than just a facilitator for our business. Though we are a technology company anyway, we rely a great deal on the possibilities and opportunities offered by the web. The foundation stone of Greynium was laid on the internet when I created mahesh.com, one of the first Indian portals, back in 1993.

(Continued)

95

(Continued)

Today we have leveraged our experience to build a versatile network of online portals serving varied interests with web-based applications serving specific users.

The internet is an essential and integral part of our business model. Internet technologies, such as email, VoIP, P2P telephony and webcams have enabled me to attend multiple meetings across the world from my office here in Bangalore. With the help of these technologies, communication between Greynium and our clients has been greatly enhanced. Our travel costs have become minimal, as we are able to provide real-time project updates, demonstrations, synchronized implementation and troubleshooting over the internet. I strongly believe that without the Internet our ideas, strategies and business objectives would have had very limited avenues to explore.

B.G. Mahesh, CEO, Greynium, www.greynium.com

This knowledge about customer preferences and behaviour patterns are what changes in a CRM-centric organization. Once the philosophy of the organization changes to put the customer's needs at the forefront of the service offering then this anticipation of their needs becomes natural.

The knowledge about your customers that will create new unmined seams of value lie just outside the present supply chain focus – within the world of unstructured interactions, search terms, thoughts, and conversations.

As mentioned earlier, John Battelle, co-founding editor of *Wired* magazine and author of *The Search* believes in a concept he terms the 'database of intentions'.

Billions of queries stream across the servers of these internet services [Google, Yahoo, MSN, AOL, Ask ...] – the aggregate thoughtstream of humankind, online. What are we creating, intention by single intention, when we tell the world what we want? Link by link, click by click, search is building possibly the most lasting, ponderous, and significant cultural artefact in the history of humankind: the Database of Intentions.[10]

Battelle's concept is applied mainly to the knowledge we could gather from the entire internet, if the series of clicks (the 'clicksteam') from every search on every search engine could be aggregated. This ambition would capture everything that every internet user has ever searched for, creating an extremely valuable database of consumer behaviour. Until Battelle's vision becomes a reality (it won't be long) there are lessons to be learned from his focus on capturing seemingly ad hoc information. This can be applied within the corporation, or within society in general.

There are infinitely more ways for customers and suppliers to interact than there were even five years ago. It will be up to organizations, be they public or private, to proactively embrace new technologies and methods of pushing information on their products/services to clients in an efficient and non-intrusive fashion. Making use of channels such as email, the web, mobile technology and streaming media will be paramount to this task. Those that are able to use these methods to maintain and gain clients will realize the benefits, while those that do not will be left behind.

Peter Ryan, Call Centre and CRM Analyst, Datamonitor, www.datamonitor.com

Although corporate tools such as customer relationship management are more of an ethos than a technology, there are various tools that allow you to capture information about what customers need. There are only two areas in which ad hoc information about your customers and prospects can be captured, from within and outside your organization.

Let's start by considering the external options. Battelle's database of intentions is a good starting point; though Battelle is referring to every search made anywhere on the web it can be scaled down to your corporate website. Most customers will indicate what they want from you by running a search on your website, if the topic is not obviously located from the home page. The 'clickstream' (the record of your internet activity) of what people search for and how they navigate through your site is of immense value. This data must be captured and used to create structured business intelligence around why customers are visiting your website, what they are looking for, and whether they can ever find what they are looking for.

Capturing detailed and structured information from the website is one source of ad hoc customer activity, but the fact is that this information already exists; it's just that the information is often left unexamined, beyond counting page impressions. Enabling collaboration between your own employees on a many-to-many basis can unlock entirely new views on customer interactions. Structured analysis of this internal data rarely allows the views, thoughts and unsubstantiated feelings and opinions – the all-important gut feeling – of your employees to be captured and shared, yet there are a number of standard tools that can facilitate this type of interaction.

Of course, there is also a lot of useless information circulated within organizations. The viral email pictures promoted by *The Sun* newspaper probably clog up countless corporate networks along with emails such as the famous 'Lucy Gao – birthday party at the Ritz', forwarded millions of times across the world after the Citigroup intern made the mistake of sounding like a class-conscious snob in her birthday invitation.[11]

However, there is a lot of useful information that is never captured or analysed at all because the processes don't exist to capture information that does not fit in the formal 'boxes' of information. Most employees will collaborate on projects and share information on your customers using a combination of the telephone, email and probably some form of instant messaging software to facilitate team conversations. The use of these tools encourages a one-to-one or one-to-many approach – and the information about customer interactions is not available to those outside the immediate team.

The water cooler remains pre-eminent as the place where gossip and information on projects and customers is shared most often, yet if all this informal information on clients and prospects could be tapped and utilized in addition to the normal structured CRM or ERP systems giving a formal view on internal processes then the result would be a formidable competitive advantage.

> Everyone is aware of the issues and limitations that exist with current standard communications technologies. Email works best as a point-to-point means of communication or a one-to-many, but as a many-to-many tool it is inefficient and in many ways counter-productive. Any attempt at one-to-many communications results in 10 conversations occurring at one time and email loses the ability to build trust in an environment where trust is essential.
>
> J.P. Rangaswami, CIO, BT Global Services, writing in *Computing Business*, June 2006[12]

Creating a corporate wiki is simple, but the effect can be astonishing, as your employees fill the wiki with information about clients, prospects, news and industry developments. Project materials can even be hosted, edited and updated on the wiki – creating a measurable improvement in efficiency by reducing the need for email to multiple recipients.

Allowing employees to publish their own thoughts via internal blogs is a very useful way to capture the ad hoc thoughts or concerns that might be rattling around the organization – though not necessarily in the right team to make a difference to the way the customer is treated. Imagine the information that could be captured if every employee was encouraged to take just 5-10 minutes every other day to type in some thoughts: the clients they recently met, ideas for who to approach, and any other unstructured thoughts beyond their actual role and responsibilities. All this data can then be searched using an internal search engine. The benefit to a sales director planning to meet an important client would be enormous; not only can they capture the history of the relationship from the structured CRM system, but they can gather the collected thoughts of the entire company by checking the blog for any views or recent encounters that might be useful. These might not even be formal meetings or encounters. The blog might contain opinions on latest results, on the behaviour of the CEO, or anything that in isolation may seem like a minor observation, but collected together as a pool of data constitutes more than the sum of its parts.

Really Simple Syndication (RSS) is the glue that can make all this hold together, making it possible for you to 'subscribe' to everything posted by particular individuals or teams on their corporate blogs or wiki. Podcasts can deliver audio or video files directly to those employees interested in a particular subject area – which could be triggered by a company name or industry vertical.

Managing the customer relationship is still about trying to examine the behaviour of customers and how they interact with your supply chain, but there is a new opportunity with these modern collaboration tools. It has never been so easy to capture and analyse ad hoc views, comments, and thoughts from the people at the front line – your employees. The best thing of all is the sense of empowerment. By capturing information from the very top to the bottom of the organization you encourage collaboration and empower teams at all levels – even those who might not normally engage with the customer. Customer satisfaction should be improved as internal teams feel more valued – a genuine win–win situation.

> Increasingly, search is our mechanism for how we understand ourselves, our world, and our place within it. It's how we navigate the one infinite resource that drives human culture: knowledge. Perfect search – every single possible bit of information at our fingertips, perfectly contextualised, perfectly personalised–may never be realised. But the journey to find out if it might just be is certainly going to be fun.
>
> John Battelle, *The Search* [13]

SNAKES ON A PLANE

All this business about the flat world and capturing ad hoc data within the organization is all very well, but how is the level playing field combination of information and globalization changing the way society consumes the products companies produce?

The year 2006 produced a classic example of how email, corporate websites, personal websites, blogs, myspace.com and youtube.com could all blend into an unstoppable viral network of promotion for the Samuel L. Jackson movie *Snakes on a Plane*.[14] SoaP, as fans know it, was lined up to be a fairly minor 2006 release for production company New Line. When Jackson was signed up to take the lead role and screenwriter Josh Friedman mentioned the script on his blog fans started debating the content of the film before shooting was even complete.

The fans rebelled when the working title was changed to 'Pacific Air Flight 121' – though that is hardly a surprise as it's instantly forgettable. The studio switched back to the original draft title because of the online fan pressure and Jackson even stoked the fire by saying: 'We're totally changing that back. That's the only reason I took the job: I read the title.'

Fans uploaded T-shirt designs, spoof versions of SoaP and their own trailers to sites such as youtube. The buzz became so strong that some of the fans' content was actually included in the movie itself. Principal photography had been completed in September 2005, but the studio arranged five more days of photography in March 2006 where changes were added – mainly based on the anticipation of the fans. One particular addition was a line for Jackson's character, which was originally an online spoof and yet became a part of the movie itself and changed the rating of the film, due to the swearing. When the production company added the line 'Enough is enough! I have had it with these muthafuckin' snakes on this muthafuckin' plane!' they knew it would change the rating, but the buzz was so strong and the line is so funny (almost as good as the Sam Jackon wallet scene in *Pulp Fiction*). It's just a shame the critics panned the movie once it was actually released.

Myspace has become a phenomenon, using the concept of social networking to do little more than connect people together and give a forum for users to post photos, comments and create a database of friends. It has become a useful forum for bands to upload songs for free download, creating a fanbase who in turn send emails about the band and link through to the demo songs.

The Arctic Monkeys from Sheffield in the UK are a classic example. The Yorkshire teenagers started posting free demo songs on their myspace page and found that people liked the music. The word grew across the internet. The band posted concert dates on myspace and found that even though they had not released a record in the conventional sense, the fans could sing along at every show. When they finally released their debut album in January 2006 it became the fastest-ever selling album in British history, shifting 360,000 copies in the first week alone.[15]

But the issue of allowing any old unedited tat to appear on the internet also means that the music channels and blogs will be largely full of rubbish. Every schoolchild with a guitar will think he can lay claim to be an axe-wielding guitar hero because he has a page on myspace or bebo. We have always relied on traditional music publishers, editors or Artists and Repertoire (A&R) men to make the decision about who is good and who is bad. If there is no longer any control over quality and anyone can post songs about their pet budgie online then who controls what is worth listening to? The market does, of course – that's you, the listening public. Though a lot of people would debate the quality of Lily Allen's music, she also bubbled up through myspace to find chart success. A lot of people are now hoping she bubbles down again, David Beckham being first in the queue after Lily insulted his wife Victoria on her blog.

The Arctic Monkeys made it because they are good. Listen to their first album – it's almost impossible to believe that a bunch of 19 year olds could write such great music. The *New Musical Express* placed it into their top 10 British albums of all time, elevated to rub shoulders with The Beatles, Oasis, Blur, Pulp, The Smiths, The Sex Pistols and the Stone Roses – and all thanks to a social networking website.[16]

Chris Anderson's book *The Long Tail* talks about this phenomenon of letting the market decide what is good and what is not.[17] Anderson describes the situation we now find because of the internet where distribution costs are approaching zero. This allows minority interest music or books to be distributed where it may previously have been unfeasible. His observations are interesting and it is entirely because of the internet that this situation has evolved. A band uploading a song to myspace can see it downloaded by the lead singer's mother and her next-door neighbour, or it could be downloaded by tens of thousands of fans. It doesn't matter – it doesn't cost the band any more money or time.

The publishing website lulu.com, founded by former Red Hat executive Bob Young, is possibly the most important publisher of the century. Lulu lets the author design how their book should look, what paper should be used, what will be on the cover, how it should be distributed and so on – the author has complete control over the book and even earns an 80 per cent royalty on sales. Lulu does this through a sophisticated system of print-on-demand. They don't publish thousands of copies of single book and then hope it will sell; they print each copy as it is purchased. This allows a 24-hour delivery time to be honoured on book sites such as Amazon, Borders or Barnes & Noble, though of course it means less chance of a casual purchaser finding a copy in a bookstore – but then for most niche titles there is almost no impulse purchasing anyway.

THE REAL 'MATRIX'

Information is being collected together in a more coherent form today. The use of wikis as a way of collecting together information from a group of many people is a very strong force. The free and online system *Wikipedia* is now the world's leading encyclopedia.

The result of these changes in technology infrastructure and content generation is what is termed utility or on-demand computing, and has already been described in Chapters 3 and 4. In essence, this ensures that a company can draw sufficient computing power, at all times. The concept works in the same way that you don't need to tell the electricity company how many electric fans you are going to plug into their system, you just do it and pay for the electricity used. The managing director of THINKstrategies, Jeff Kaplan, summarizes the potential benefits of the utility model as:[18]

- higher system utilization and optimization;
- better application management and maintenance;
- more predictable operating costs;
- greater return on IT investment;
- renewed focus on core competencies.

The production and consumption of content is changing, with the podcast becoming a wildly popular way for broadcasters to reuse content and granting a platform to those with something to say to the world. The iTunes system lists hundreds of podcasts published by the BBC alone. You can catch the best bits from various radio and TV shows along with broadcasts such as a video summary of the *Ten O'clock News* in the past week – time-shifting so you absorb the content at a time that is convenient.

The change in content production is important for companies and consumers. Think about the difficulties involved in creating your own radio station for a moment. It must involve government licences for broadcasting spectrum, broadcasting equipment, a studio, and all kinds of hardware to record and mix the content. It sounds difficult, yet now with a single computer and a microphone you can easily record content and upload it to the web, it can even be published on iTunes as a podcast and listed alongside the BBC content. As with print-on-demand book publishing, it may be that nobody will ever download or subscribe to the podcast, but the ability to publish and distribute to a wide audience has been created – the quality of the content is up to the creator and quality content will find an audience.

There are consequences to this change in content consumption. When Google purchased the video-sharing site youtube in October 2006 for US$1.65 billion they must have factored in the risk of copyright holders taking the newly cash-rich company to the cleaners for copyright violation. Indeed, one of the first actions taken by Google was to start getting the major content producers such as film studios and music publishers to support the service as a legitimate platform for their material. Youtube is similar in many ways to myspace in that it uses a social network to decide what becomes popular. Users such as the British teenager cutiemish sing and dance in front of the camera at home and enjoy millions of global viewers for their efforts. In this particular example, her initial videos then spawned an entire subset of 'responses' critiquing her videos – with praise, but also some harshly critical questions such as 'why does she sound so English and yet look so Asian?' It could be argued that someone drawn to performance, as cutiemish clearly must be, would eventually be noticed in the normal way. Perhaps at drama school, or by forming a rock band, yet who can claim to have performed to millions of international video viewers by the age of 18? This wasn't possible even a decade ago. It's going to be an interesting addition to her CV in the same way that a 100% record on eBay over many years can give an impression of good character.

We asked cutiemish – her real name is Michelle Lam – about why she started posting videos on youtube in the first place. She said: 'I started doing it for fun. I didn't expect my videos to become so popular! I do love the different reactions to my videos. Some are quite nice and make me feel good that people recognise the effort I put into my videos, some comments are horrible, criticising me personally – saying my videos are a waste of space! It just makes me think how people can be so judgmental over such small things.'

Michelle then made an interesting observation that strikes right to the heart of Thomas Friedman's views on the flat world. Remember that Friedman had spoken of nations competing in the 19th century, followed by corporations in the 20th century and now individuals and their own personal talent in the 21st century, because the internet facilitates access to anyone with any skill, anywhere. On this theme, Michelle explained: 'I'm just doing my videos for fun, not a career, if anything I am doing my videos to show my ability to edit, so I can add them to my university media portfolio. So I guess you could say that I am creating my own style or personal brand. I think that creating a personal brand helps to identify the kind of person you are, and it would then attract the right audience for the videos.'[19]

PEER TO PEER

The concepts being used to democratize content production are also being applied to companies who trade with each other and consumers. The eBay auction site has demonstrated that supply chains can be effectively dismantled and reduced to just a buyer and a seller. If the network itself can connect those two actors then everything in the middle is not required – whether the distribution and logistics function or even the retailer.

This is an important concept to remember as many services could benefit from using the network effect of the internet to reach out to consumers directly. Some examples of businesses using the 'eBay' lesson are FXA World and Zopa. FXA World trades in foreign exchange. The consumer with cash in one currency, but wanting to change to another, can go to their website and it will locate someone else who has the opposite need. The traders can agree the price and everyone wins. The seller of one currency will find they can get a higher price than a bank would offer – because the bank uses a 'spread' to make a profit on foreign exchange transactions. This spread is the difference between what a bank will buy currency from you for and what they will sell it to you for. A simple way to understand this is to imagine you are going on a holiday and you just arrived at the airport. You go to the bank and try changing £100 into US dollars. Then the flight is cancelled, so you return to the bank with your dollars, but the bank won't return £100 for the dollars that are now in your pocket because there is a difference between their buy and sell rates. This website aims to connect the buyer and the seller directly so one can get a higher sales price and the other a lower purchase price – at the same time! FXA World even encourages their customers to use the Skype free internet telephony system, so they can talk about the trade, or just to plan future business.

Zopa works in much the same way to connect those with spare cash to invest, with an expectation of an interest return, to those who want to borrow money. So on one side a lender will commit their own personal money into the Zopa system, which will be transferred to another customer who needs to borrow. The borrowing customer will pay interest and the lender is happy to earn and help out a borrower. For both lender and borrower there should be a better price than working with a normal high street bank. The Zopa model sounds just like the old 'buildings and loan' type business depicted in Capra's classic movie *It's a Wonderful Life* and, in a way, it is. Zopa focuses on taking money from investors and spreading that investment across many borrowers to minimize the risk of default, and utilizes the internet to do all of this so that the expensive overheads of a regular bank are removed from the equation.

Now think about this peer-to-peer model for just a moment. Imagine if more services were available where you could tap into the talent of individuals or teams directly without paying fees in the middle. Any kind of agency work could be easily transferred to this type of environment, with the only requirement being enough traffic to the website to make it viable.

In both the consumer and corporate world it is truer than ever that content is king. Web 2.0 is really about user-generated content – sites that are built and maintained by their users. There is a lot more rubbish being published, but the ability to connect consumers to your business, or to publish without the might of a corporate machine, means that new opportunities are everywhere – you just need to find them. Some sites are going beyond just offering a service; they have ambitions of creating a new world. Take a look at secondlife.com for an example of a new world. This is not a game, like those multiplayer games where you pretend to be a troll and fight orcs all day in a world similar to Tolkien's imagination. This is a world in which you can adopt a new persona, take up a job, earn money, buy land or build a house. The BBC has even bought an entire island in Second Life where they hold virtual music festivals for the residents within this new world. Some companies are now advertising within Second Life. How does that shift the goalposts of reality? If virtual land and advertising now has a real value (where people pay rent to virtual landlords) then have we already reached the point at which younger people are no longer interested in watching the endless repeats of *Only Fools and Horses* on TV and are out there actively generating their own world and all its content?

6 The Globalization of Services

The level playing field agenda: The man versus machine debate goes beyond science fiction. In a world in which we can now choose to purchase services from regions offering cheaper labour, there is an exploration required that considers where a service should be performed by a human, regardless of cost.

A LEVEL PLAYING FIELD

In previous chapters, we have argued that the ICT industry is maturing into a purveyor of technology-enabled services, rather than technology. We have argued that the internet is evolving into a powerful global utility over which services can be offered for sale and consumed across the globe and that the impact of the new Indian majors has been to bring a genuine globalization to the world ICT industry in the services arena. In this chapter we look to the developing globalization of this (technology-enabled) services economy and explore the factors that will influence its commercial development.

World trade in services (roughly US$1.8 trillion in 2003) is only about 20 per cent of the trade in manufacturing and while approximately 50 per cent of global manufacturing is traded internationally, the equivalent figure for services is approximately 10 per cent. Yet, in the most developed economies, services account for some 70 per cent of gross domestic product (GDP).[1]

In Chapter 1, we explained how the offshoring debate within the ICT industry has focused on what UK government statistics capture and label as IT computer services ('software consulting, data processing and database activities, hardware consultancy, maintenance and repair of computing machinery, other computer services'). Offshoring has grown particularly in software and systems development and maintenance. Two countries lead the international trade in these services: Ireland (the earlier starter) and India (the later entrant, but now the largest player). Contrary to what some alarmists might say, the UK is in fact a net exporter of these services, growing its exports strongly as offshoring results in a strong growth in imports. This is something we cannot emphasize strongly enough. In fact, let's say that once more in larger type:

The UK is a net exporter of IT computer services

We also introduced the larger category of IT-enabled business services, incorporating a much wider range of professional services that are already significantly technology-enabled – including legal services, architectural services and so on, as well as the fast-growing business of business process outsourcing (BPO). This is – significantly – the home of the application professionalism also introduced in Chapter 1. Because many of these services are in fact in the territory of the IT industry clients (law practices, architectural practices, architectural engineering firms etc.) they are not included within the offshoring debate. However, they are major consumers of applied technology – and here the two strongest players internationally in terms of their net trade surpluses are the UK and the USA – well ahead of Ireland and India. Yes, that's correct – the UK and USA are also exporting technology services (and actually leading the world), but you don't see Indians wearing clothes proclaiming 'my job was Cambridged and all I got was this T-shirt!'

The major part of these services, technology-enabled as they are, are likely at this stage to be more classic professional services now significantly automated by technology, for example the architect moving from drawing board to screen. These services exploit increasing network capacity and email to move work to and from clients, including internationally, as electronic files, and exploiting websites to work interactively with clients. This is the significant early stage in the growing trade in technology-enabled services.

All of this demonstrates that, although international trade in services is still a relative youngster, it is a large and vigorous youngster. What factors will help and hinder its development?

Services come in many shapes and sizes. Many are not easily tradable – even though mobile executives may well have a choice of favourite hairdressers in different towns, cities or countries, the haircut still has to be delivered locally! Physical location, plus skill, reputation, cost and quality of service all still rule. A commercially astute hairdresser may well build a brand – even an international brand – that through investment in a chain of hairdressers, or through a franchising operation, offers the mobile executive a geographically responsive service – but not really a tradable one.

In contrast, an email service accessed over the internet is about as close to the virtual as it is possible to find – it need have no physical location or national affiliation as far as the user is concerned. Accessibility, reliability, security, compatibility with other email services, brand/reputation and cost are amongst the deciding factors, but not geography. In practical terms, the mail servers could as well be in Cape Town, Mumbai, Philadelphia, Milton Keynes or Ho Chi Minh City providing there is full interoperability with the internet, and full assurance of such key aspects of the service as security and reliability – the telecoms networks and hubs over which the email service flows will, in literal terms, cover most of the globe.

The hairdresser's service sits at one extreme of the services 'tradability' spectrum, and the email service at the other. Decades of experience with local, non-tradable service businesses like the hairdresser's make it relatively easy to spot the factors that will make the business a success or a failure. In contrast, the development of the global trade in technology-enabled services is still young, and the factors that will lead to success or failure are still open for exploration and debate. The one certainty is that a great diversity of entrepreneurs will create and test, with as much failure as success, a great diversity of business models. So let's face the truth, global services are still in their infancy and most companies are scratching around in the dark and hoping their 'global delivery models' are going to work – and not blow up spectacularly in the face of the client.

An email service as an internationally traded good is an ephemeral reality when compared to a Swiss watch. Yet the comparison is informative, though it is likely that we would all prefer a nice new Rolex to yet another '419' email from Nigeria.

In the experience of the customer, the email service has quite concrete aspects – emails must get to their destinations and arrive from their originators promptly, securely and reliably. The interfaces with the great diversity of alternative email systems and services must be enabled without failure: the service must be protected from infiltration by viruses and spam that will seek to exploit the access opportunities presented. The customer seeks both cost competitive quality of service and assurance that key factors such as security are integral to the service.

In the business model of the email service supplier, the email service will be one technology-enabled service nested in or interlinked with others – such as the operation of a server farm or a mainframe data centre, the provision of back-up capabilities, the integration with wider network services, the interfacing with other email services over the internet, the provision of firewalls and other protective filters, and so on. No technology-enabled service operates in isolation. The supplier will both seek cost competitive quality of service and assurance for the services he integrates with his own – and shape his business model to allow him to offer the cost competitive quality of service and assurances that the customer seeks.

The customer of the Swiss watch expects the quality and reliability that the brand promises, and the assurance of the design, materials and manufacturing qualities that justify money spent. The supplier, even if he runs an integrated manufacturing and assembly operation, will depend on materials (e.g. steel, glass, speciality lubricants, seals etc.) sourcing for which he will seek cost competitive quality of supply service and materials quality assurance – and shape his business model to allow him to offer, profitably, the cost competitive quality and reliability, the assurances that the customer seeks.

Traded (technology-enabled) services may thus have a strong element of the ephemeral, but certainly have concrete realities when it comes to building businesses around them. To explore and seek to scope the factors that will influence the development of the commerce in these services – and thus the international commerce and trade in them – we need to go back to some basics.

DOES IT MATTER?

In May 2003 the *Harvard Business Review* published a seminal article by Nicholas Carr that challenged the established vision by the IT industry – that adoption of the best new innovative technological offers of the industry was the surest route to competitive success.[2] Ever since time began, IT companies have always sold the latest technological developments by promising that better/faster equipment would help your company. His argument, developed further in a book,[3] was that there might well be a passing first mover advantage, but that would soon be competed out over time.

As with other key new technologies of the previous two centuries, from the railway to electricity, the 'new' soon became the 'utility' – available to all, exploited by all, an undoubted contributor to the overall productivity of the firm and the wider economy – but not a source of sustainable competitive advantage to the firm. Carr basically argued that IT is no longer something special that creates competitive advantage itself – it is a baseline requirement for a company to operate, like having electricity and water delivered to the office.

Much academic work has sought to statistically demonstrate that corporate investment in IT can be linked to improvements in business performance. In the main, the thrust of the conclusions to date has been to gather evidence that the US economy has been benefiting from a sustained productivity improvement that can be linked to its stronger investment in technology – and that the less focused and determined investment in technology in the European economies has been to their relative disadvantage. This tends to support the Carr thesis, in so far as the benefits of technological investment may be competed out between American companies in America, but because they invest more heavily than their European competitors, the US economy as a whole benefits relatively.

The Carr thesis nonetheless bears a closer examination – and a challenge. In 2005 McKinsey surveyed 37 European retail and wholesale banks 'to understand how they manage technology and to identify the IT-management practices of the top performers' by evaluating some 70 variables of management practice.[4] The survey identified a wide range of IT spending: from 10–30 per cent of operating costs, or 4–18 per cent of operating income. However, higher levels of IT spending did not increase the effectiveness or efficiency of the business – those banks that appeared to get the most business value from IT spent up to 40 per cent less than the weakest performers.

The McKinsey researchers concluded that two broad groupings of management practice correlated best with high performance: the quality of the bank's IT management, and the ways that the bank used IT to support the needs of the business. Their essential observation – 'it is not how much you spend, it is how you spend it' – is perhaps the right starting point to take our analysis forward.

In the final analysis, technology is a tool, and no more. A very sophisticated tool can, in the hands of an expert, be exploited to do amazing things. But a tool is a tool is a tool – without the human intervention, the human contribution, it represents potential for action but no more. The Fender electric guitar in someone's spare room is a tool for creating music, albeit a little rough in the owner's hands, but with the potential to sound like Eric Clapton. In the case of the 37 banks surveyed by McKinsey, the performance benefits flowed from management that knew what it was doing – this focus is what really supported the needs of the business. Interestingly, the banks that did the best in their use of IT were the banks whose circumstances required them to be the most penny-pinching and so the money they were spending was vital to their future.

The capabilities of some new technology can, given time, be readily copied – and any competitive edge they promise competed out. But the human contribution (management knowing what they are doing) is a lot more difficult to copy. And while time allows a new technology to be copied, time also allows the human contribution to build learning and experience, deeply embedded in the doing – and that is very difficult to copy.

So we perhaps best start by challenging the frequently articulated ICT industry concept of technology drivers by observing that technology does not, and cannot, drive – technology enables, and people drive. In the case of ICT, the human contribution may impact in many ways – innovating and designing a new aspect of a technology, creating a new application based on it, operating and maintaining that application, exploiting the application to ends that are beneficial to business and so on – but at every step it is the human contribution that is vital – the technology enables, but what it enables is in human hands to deliver.

SO WHAT ARE HUMANS USEFUL FOR ANYMORE?

Services are not created and delivered in isolation – services depend on services, just as good front-of-house service in a restaurant ultimately rests on the quality of the back-of-house services that underpin it. Just as the contemporary manufacture, distribution and retailing of goods relies on well-integrated physical logistics chains, contemporary technology-enabled services rely on well-integrated chains of services – service chains – to support and enable their delivery.

A practical and intuitively clear example is the electronic point of sale (EPOS) capability in a retail store. The EPOS capabilities at the till are a distinct technology-enabled service, and they form part of a service chain that includes other technology-enabled services such network services, data processing and analytical services, and data handling, interfacing with other systems and services such as stock control and goods ordering, and storage services, without which the EPOS service could not work. This analysis holds whether the EPOS capability is provided by the internal IT team, or sourced from or outsourced to a third-party supplier. However integrated an in-house 'IT shop' the retailer owning the store runs, at some point there will be interfaces with external technology-enabled capabilities and services, such as suppliers or logistics services.

So our basic view is that technology enables, but what it enables is in human hands to deliver. Each layer of the EPOS service chain described above has specific blends of technologies to enable it – both hardware and software. One distinct human contribution is therefore in the professionalism, skills and experience required to deliver the operations of each blend of technologies. Along the service chain may be requirements for some very distinct technical skills and professionalism – that in the data processing and analytical arena compared to those in the operation of the till-side EPOS kit as one example. The ability to ensure that the whole service chain integrates and operates as a whole is another.

The skills, professionalism and experience described above are clearly of the technical variety. The quality, cost-efficiency and cost-effectiveness of the operations of the service chain will depend heavily not just on technical skills and professionalism, but also on how familiar the operators are with the service operations being managed – their 'experiential intimacy' with that service. Experience is key – and deep experience (or intimacy) with the specific operations at stake is what really counts.

But the EPOS service is there for a purpose – to enhance the customer service offered by the store at the checkout – and to enhance the competitiveness of the business model of the store in different ways – a tighter control on shelf-loading, in-store stocks, ordering and delivery logistics – greater insight into the buying patterns of the individual store customer, and so on. At the point the EPOS service is exploited, there is a very different dimension of skills, professionalism and experience at work – that of the professional retailer, and more specifically the professional retailer with a deep intimacy of the exploitation of the EPOS service as a competitive tool. The skills, professionalism and experience described here are clearly of the application variety, and likely to be very different to those developed normally in an ICT company. Clearly, retailing professionalism has a contrasting competency profile to that for IT professionalism. It's obvious really. When you visit Tesco's, do you ever stop to think about the till and its functionality? You might be thinking that the till operators seem to get younger and younger, or why they never have those two-litre bottles of Scottish water anymore, or how they finance all those buy-one-get-one-free deals, but it is unlikely that you are thinking about your technological experience at the till. It's the retail experience, not the IT experience that you should notice.

To the store, it is vital that the EPOS service adds to the competitive edge of its business model. It relies on the competitiveness of the overall service chain that the EPOS service fronts (a chain is only as strong as its weakest point). That competitiveness is underwritten by a blend of technical skills, professionalism and experiential intimacy that aligns tightly with the operation of the service chain (in its parts and as a whole) with application skills, professionalism and experiential intimacy with the exploitation of the EPOS service in the heart of the retail environment.

This takes us back to the analysis in Chapter 1, where we introduced the importance of the growing impact and business exploitation of application professionalism in the development of the ICT industry 'offer'. We observed above that (technology-enabled) services might have a strong element of the ephemeral, but certainly have concrete realities when it comes to building businesses around them. We also observed that to explore and explain the factors that would influence the development of the commerce in such services we needed to go back to some basics.

In the EPOS service example the underlying network services required are likely to be able to be sourced as commodities, as technology-enabled network services. The immediate human contribution to these services will be primarily on the technical side – technical skills, professionalism and deep experiential intimacy in the management of network operations. The commercial sourcing parameters are likely to be cost, quality of customer service and service reliability. The need for an actual physical telecoms network connection into the store may restrict competition to some degree – otherwise this is a straight tradable commodity proposition – a commoditized infrastructural telecoms service. The winning supplier will be highly focused on making their network services the most competitive there are – and at the same time the most profitable.

In contrast, the actual till-side EPOS service, the front end of the service chain, requires a strong blend of technical professionalism with application professionalism. An external supplier whose technology works well, but who lacks a real intimacy with how the technology will be exploited in the specific retail environment, will rapidly become the weakest link in the chain. It is in the store, where the till is in use, where the real business benefits of the EPOS capabilities are garnered – it is till side that the EPOS 'rubber hits the road'. And this is where the application professionalism in the service blend is vital. It is still a tradable (technology-enabled) service, but is most likely to be in the hands of a specialized supplier with a strong understanding of retailing. The need for till-side equipment (with an integral EPOS capability) means that the service has to have a geographic dimension to it.

The intermediate services in the overall EPOS service chain may also require significant blends of the application professionalism in retailing embedded. The data processing and analytical services may require some highly retail-focused analytics – perhaps very innovative analytics – to be integral to the service. These services have no geographical restraint and could be remotely sourced. The sourcing parameters will likely be on the quality and relevance of the embedded retailing expertise, in addition to cost, quality of customer service and service reliability. A candidate for global trading – the retailing expertise will be the key – as will, in the very competitive retailing industry, effective assurance on security and IP protection.

This introduction to the EPOS service has surveyed some of the parameters that will influence the development of the commerce of technology-enabled services – and their global trade.

STANDING ON THE SHOULDERS OF GIANTS

We opened this chapter by observing that world trade in services is only about 20 per cent of that in manufacturing, and that while approximately 50 per cent of global manufacturing is traded internationally, the equivalent figure for services is approximately 10 per cent. As the youngster on the global trading block, what lessons can the technology-enabled services industry potentially take from the manufacturing sector?

By the time you read this, Toyota will have probably overtaken General Motors in sales volumes, having for many years been the more profitable of the two companies. The auto industry has long been global. It usually makes sense to manufacture vehicles close to their market, hence all the Japanese manufacturers producing cars in the UK – and sometimes even exporting from here back to Japan. While it is economically viable to shift vehicles around the world, the strategic steps taken by the majors have involved foreign investment to allow for local supply into major markets. Thus Toyota has a major manufacturing facility in southern USA, originally a green-field investment in North Carolina. One key element in its competitive edge over the Detroit-based General Motors is that Toyota's Greenboro site is a green-field one, designed from the start for modern manufacturing processes using as much automation as possible. Old brown-field sites, and major legacy investments that are costly to bring into the modern age, are a major restraint to General Motors. Automation at Greenboro not only improves the plant's daily operating economics, but also speeds the process of model change, improving business agility.

A key element in the steady rise to global scale and competitiveness of the post-war Japanese motor manufacturers, including Toyota, has been their total commitment to product quality. Seen strategically, this commitment to quality has benefited them in two major ways: very cost-competitive production economics through the sharp reduction in manufacturing waste, and a positive contribution to their product brand with the consumer in the marketplace.

The pioneer of the industry, Henry Ford, championed the concept of the integration under one corporate roof of the whole auto value chain – from iron ore mining, steel manufacture and rubber plantation management to the manufacture of the actual car. However, the steady development of the industry since then has been towards a distributed, layered industry structure, with tightly organized supply chains ensuring the just-in-time sourcing of components (some of which are themselves fully assembled systems, such as seats or dashboards) into the auto factory for final assembly. This has allowed for specialization and business focus at each level of the supply chain – and the development of the manufacturing scale for cost-efficient production of key components through their supply to more than one manufacturer. Again, a positive benefit of the Greenboro site is that it has encouraged, over time, the development of a network of local component suppliers able to operate closely with the assembly plant and respond more flexibly to its needs.

The auto industry is of course a lead user of technology-based services to enable the efficient operation and integration of its supply chains. Competition in the auto industry is also not solely about manufacturing economics – it is also about design and the ability to catch and respond to consumer taste. Another element in the Toyota versus General Motors competitive battle in the US market has been the move of US public preference towards the higher fuel efficiency of the Japanese cars as compared to the traditional US gas-guzzlers. Auto design in the fullest sense is highly technology-enabled now – a prime example of deep application professionalism blending effectively with some highly innovative technical professionalism.

There is, we think, some important learning here for the nascent technology-enabled services industry. After all, the manufacturers have had about a century to work out their own global strategies, whereas the technology-enabled service companies have only really had the past decade – with most growth since the millennium.

From the start, the young Indian companies that have powered into the market since the 1990s have put a strong emphasis on quality – for example, climbing the ladder of the Software Engineering Institute's CMM (capability maturity model) framework to levels 4 and 5, well ahead of their American and European competitors. Strategically this was an important part of their brand building – fighting any image that 'lower cost meant lower quality'. In terms of the productivity and effectiveness of their human assets, this same approach ensures a culture of continual improvement that will help keep their business models globally competitive even as their cost advantage erodes. Remember that the next time sometime suggests it is all over for India because of escalating salaries.

The Henry Ford Fort Dearborn model of 'all ICT capabilities under one corporate roof' that certain American majors (EDS and IBM in particular) initially appeared to be following is now being replaced by increasing signs of an industry moving towards a focus on key competencies – a 'layering' analogous to what happened with the auto industry. On occasion this involves significant steps – IBM's divestment of its personal computer (PC) business to the Chinese company Lenovo is one significant example.

Competition drives companies to focus on their real strengths. The business of technology-enabled services may not require such obviously major investment as demanded of a global auto company expanding its manufacturing operations. Nonetheless, expansion in the supply of services requires substantial investment in infrastructure – for example, Google is now reckoned to manage the world's largest estate of server capacity to underwrite its business. The ability to manage these assets, and to do so efficiently and effectively, with high security and effective backup to ensure that the services are delivered, requires a high quality of focused technical skills, professionalism and experience. This is the factory end of the industry, a place where what in essence are manufacturing skills rule.

This suggests that new companies will develop whose business is in the emergent large-volume technology-enabled services – the infrastructural services (computing power, high-capacity network services and large-capacity data storage and manipulation) and commoditized transactional services (such as payroll processing) where demand for essentially standardized services can be aggregated across many sectors of the economy. As already noted, the factory end of the industry, a place where manufacturing skills rule, and the human contribution is focused on the delivery of (through a very high level of automation) high asset productivity, tightly controlled costs, and a high reliability of quality and security assured services. The human contribution is in strong manufacturing technical skills, professionalism and experiential intimacy.

In contrast, the auto industry model suggests that other companies will develop whose business is more highly focused in delivering services tightly tailored to the special requirements of particular sectors of the economy – examples are specialist educational services in schools, or derivatives trading services in the financial community. Here the focus is on the ability to exploit the professionalism and experience developed through a long intimacy with the workings of the chosen sector. The business of these companies will be front-end services that their clients rely on for delivering key elements of their business models. Here the human contribution is in application professionalism, skills and experiential intimacy in the chosen sector, and it is around this human contribution that the company builds its business model and competitive margins.

This concept that low-level IT services and high-level IT-enabled services will diverge does rather fly in the face of some IT service suppliers who consider that they can deliver every possible technology service, whether it really needs technical or application knowledge. Let's just say that history favours the specialized solution provider. Think for a moment about delivering a service, such as a Magnetic Resonance Imaging (MRI) scan reading service where scans are taken locally, but analysed remotely. Those making a diagnosis when reading the scans need to be offering an expert service. This service provider lives or dies on the quality of its expertise, not the IT network it uses – providing the network is sufficient to deliver the scans as needed.

THE EMERGENT MODEL

We opened this chapter by observing that world trade in services stands at about one fifth of that in manufacturing even though, in the world's developed economies, services now represent about 70 per cent of GDP. With the ICT industry maturing into a purveyor of (technology-enabled) services, rather than technology, and with the internet evolving into a powerful global utility over which services can be offered for sale and consumed across the globe, we set out to explore the factors that would be likely to influence the commercial development of the global (technology-enabled) services economy.

We have explored some of the factors that make such services tradable, and identified that some geographical restraints will always remain. As long as we use office buildings, there will be the need for local infrastructural installation and physical maintenance, even if much of the rest of the systems maintenance and upgrading is carried out remotely over the network. We have emphasized the importance of the human contribution ('technology enables, but what it enables is in human hands to deliver'), the roots of value-add that lie in people's professionalism, skills and experience and built on the differentiation between technological professionalism and application professionalism.

Finally we have suggested that the nascent international technology-enabled services industry will, over time, 'layer' with some companies focusing on the big volume infrastructural and (back-office) transactional services (the commodity end of the marketplace) and other companies focusing on more specialized services for particular business sectors and niches.

The first insight that this prospective analysis suggests is that the global services playing field is perhaps a more open one than some currently fear. Service jobs will not all vanish to India. The commodity end of the marketplace is potentially so automated that exploitation of lower-cost professional resources in a country such as India is less of an issue – the real factors determining location will be real-estate costs, security and business continuity considerations, access to major bandwidth network capacity, and access to highly experienced technical 'manufacturing' professionals. Competitive triage between the USA, Europe, the Indian subcontinent and China becomes a very much more open process.

Equally, at the more specialist end of the service spectrum, the focus falls more on the importance of application professionalism – a deep intimacy with how a particular sector or niche of the economy operates, experience that is currently more available in those developed economies where the whole breadth of the economy is well developed. Again this suggests that competitive triage between the USA, Europe, the Indian subcontinent and China becomes a very much more open process.

In this context the current debate in the UK on what needs to be done to secure the future of its ICT industry in the face of the perceived threat from offshoring is perhaps instructive. The UK (and London in particular) is the home to a range of major globally competitive industries that are rich in knowledge-intensive and experience-intensive businesses: banking, financial services, insurance and the creative industries (media, publishing, education, design etc.). These are all purveyors of services that can be seen as both professionally and technologically rich. They currently thrive globally because they are competitively proven best-of-breed in their industry sectors. They draw to London some of the worlds brightest and best in their sectors. According to Hamish Mcrae: 'Within London's orbital road, the M25 motorway, is the world's highest proportion of non-UK national professionals. That puts London ahead of New York, which ranks second.'[5] In the context of the analysis we have developed in this chapter, a high concentration of 'best-of-breed' application professionalism.

We believe that if you take a long-term view, the opportunity of global sourcing goes far beyond labour arbitrage. There are quality implications and speed-to-market implications, and these will end up being just as powerful, if not more powerful, than the simple labour arbitrage. Ultimately it's how to engage the best brains in the world to work on your particular problem, so that you can build a stronger business.

When looking for an outsourcing partner that is really what companies have to focus on. It's more than whether the company is able to save you money, it's about them bringing the best brains in the world to solve your business problem – the 'intellectual arbitrage'. Intellectual arbitrage is the idea that in knowledge or service-intensive industries there's an opportunity to apply intellect at a cost not previously possible, to achieve dramatic business outcomes.

The winners of the future are going to be the organizations that can tap into the global talent pool and take advantage of that intellectual

(Continued)

117

(Continued)

arbitrage. If you can figure out how to gain a competitive advantage by tapping the best brains in the world for the particular problem that you have, then you're going to achieve success as a business.

Sanjiv Gossain, Vice President and UK Country Manager, Cognizant, www.cognizant.com

What is it that builds, encourages and nurtures this 'best-of-breed'? In knowledge-intensive, experience-intensive service businesses, being best-of-breed starts with the human dimension, and builds through the positive, virtuous cycle of the best attracting the best. This tight networking of the best-of-breed then feeds on the shared experiences built from continuous learning and innovation forged in the fire of the battle in the marketplace. The paradigm is that 'together we win, together we learn and innovate, and together we will win again'.

These knowledge-intensive, experience-intensive service businesses are, as already noted, strongly technologically enabled. Without contemporary IT capabilities, they could not operate as competitively as they do. So an equally apt description of them, as already noted, would be as technologically and professionally rich services. Being best-of-breed in this universe builds on the blend of both dimensions – the blend of technological professionalism with application professionalism.

Seen from one angle, the technological and professional capabilities the ICT industry provides to the City and the creative industries are vital to their ability to operate globally, and operate competitively. Seen from another angle, it is the ICT industries close involvement with those highly professional customers that feeds their ability to remain globally competitive themselves. The City is undoubtedly about being best-of-breed, and demands that its suppliers are best-of-breed – and in turn this symbiotic customer–supplier relationship feeds the ability of the technology supplier companies to be best-of-breed. Without a competitively vigorous IT supply side, the City would be weakened; without a competitively vigorous City, IT suppliers would be weakened. Symbiotically each is in hock to the other – with a mutual commitment to being best-of-breed they can together conquer the world.

The issue at the core of the offshoring debate in the UK is therefore not the competitiveness of 'UK plc' in any ownership sense – corporate ownership across these sectors is not all British by any means (and in the context of the ICT supply side, the Indian majors are now investing alongside their more established American and continental competitors as demonstrated by the acquisition of steel producer Corus by India's Tata group in early 2007). Nor is it any dimension of local institutional competitiveness – much of the business discussed above is in any case virtual, conducted globally in real time to rhythms set by the practice of the business and the 24-hour rotation of the earth.

It is rather the competitiveness of the UK as a hub, a major focus of activity, a preferred centre for action in this global virtuality. It is about the importance of close relationships between supplier and customer. And it is about a UK competitiveness that is currently rooted in broad swathes of world-class application professionalism integral to the world-class businesses and firms operating out of the UK.

So, in the context of the development of international trade in more specialist technology-enabled services, where the application professionalism and a deep intimacy with how a particular sector or niche of the economy operates, experience that is more available in the developed economies, competitive triage between the US, Europe, the Indian subcontinent and China becomes a very much more open process.

There are many parallels between the globalization of services and the historical path of manufacturing. Services globalization, however, has a much greater impact on the standard of living of the world's educated workforce, which in turn creates a much larger consumer market within the global economy. Countries and companies alike are working hard to position themselves to compete. Countries with a sizable college-educated, high-quality labour pool, reliable law enforcement and a modern technology infrastructure have a clear advantage. For the educated worker, the standard of living is improving, with decreasing dependence on the country or location of residence. Information technology outsourcing has led the way by providing a delivery model, but other services like accounting, research, human resources, marketing and consulting – as well as industry-specific business processes – will become global, creating opportunities for both global consumers and workers. The globalization of services will not only improve economies and expand consumer markets, but also speed innovation, reduce costs and improve the standard of living for the world's educated workforce.

Cliff Justice, Multishore Practice Leader, EquaTerra, www.equaterra.com

BROADER FACTORS

The increasing virtualization of so much business that can be done online argues for fast growth in the international trade of technology-enabled services. This trade will require supporting and formal structures to underwrite its growth.

In the broadest sense, there is a need is for assurance – assurance of service quality, assurance of service security, assurance of service risk management. The ICT industry has developed a comprehensive and structured approach to quality, 'operational excellence' and security management that is embedded in agreed standards, including ISO and BSI standards, and associated certification processes. The family of capability maturity models (CMM), six sigma, Customer Operations Performance Inc. (COPC Inc.) (for call centre services), and BS 7799 for information security management provide the potential for assurance services. One widely accepted methodology for assuring IT service management is ITIL (Information Technology Infrastructure Library) and the associated BS 15000 standard.

As set out in Chapter 4, however, the context within which these standards have been developed and matured is not necessarily well aligned to the emerging environment of more loosely coupled virtual services. ITIL is structured around an integrated set of management processes that relate to the classic IT service organization at the heart of a business or a government department. Once such a tightly business-integrated IT department is replaced by the external sourcing of services that may be provided by a small variety of service providers (thus an online accounting service from one supplier and an online HR service from another, both accessed over the internet through a local network service supplied by a third), then new factors come into play. ITIL was designed before multisourcing and multishoring became commonplace.

Equally, standalone certifications under schema such as the CMM family may give confidence in one key element in a service chain in isolation, but do not easily 'align' along the entire service chain, and the important interlinks that must run along it. The most obvious example of this is the problems faced by a non-CMM compliant client who employs a technology company assessed at CMM level 5 to provide services. The mismatch in operating procedures between the two organizations can make it almost impossible for the service provider to deliver and remain within its own audited framework.

Contractual and legal practice has developed to a great extent in the construction and management of classic outsourcing deals, including those that have major international dimensions and ramifications. However, the evolution of the virtual, with businesses relying on the sourcing of a portfolio of services, mainly sourced over the internet, presents new challenges to legal practice.

The protection of Internet Protocol (IP) within the framework of a closely held outsourcing deal can present a challenge, but one that can usually be scoped and managed. The protection of IP within the context of sourced services, and over-the-internet sourced services, again presents new challenges.

The ability of sourced services to operate within the legal protections that may be specific to certain countries, such as UK Data Protection and Privacy laws, broadens the issues faced. A fully commoditized offer of transactional HR services may in practice result in personal data being held in offshore locations. Current tightly structured outsourcing arrangements are providing the opportunity to develop constructive practices to meet legal and regulatory requirements – and may thus provide the learning necessary to provide frameworks relevant to the more virtual as it develops.

Finally, companies often work in regulatory environments that impose very specific rules, regulations and registration requirements. Substantial experience has been developed in the structuring of outsourcing arrangements that respond to this reality – in the move to the more virtual, the ability to demonstrably operate within, or the inability to so do, will become a vital factor in the development of some international trade in some services.

A TEST CASE

Imagine a banking investment venture that requires setting up shop in London – assume about a hundred staff at the start. It is not so virtual an operation as to not require any office space, although some of the staff will be essentially on the road most of their life, as with most 'consulting' type operations. It is most likely to lease contemporary office space that has the necessary managed services – including WiFi. Therefore equipment (desktop computers, printers, laptops, mobile telephones and PDAs) can be ordered and will arrive already loaded with the necessary standard software and inbuilt wireless modems. Once unboxed and plugged into the mains (or, in the case of portable equipment, charged up) it requires little local skill to switch on – and from that point onwards the total service management can be virtual and remote.

Almost all the services classically provided by the local IT team can now be managed over the internet – from the maintenance of the software, integration of new releases, management of the necessary firewalls, provision of backup, and continuity protection, helpdesk services and so on.

The question is – what parameters will now shape the company's (technology-enabled) services sourcing policies? Some ideas are outlined below.

- **Basic services:** the routine stuff required to ensure that equipment is running well, being backed up, software maintained, memory expanded in good time, printer not about to give up and so on can all be done remotely. In reality, however, some maintenance will require a human visit, so the choice is between either a very remotely managed service in collaboration with more local equipment specialists (perhaps the office management company) or a more local business that blends remote management with mobile hands-on technical services.

- **Back-office stuff:** this is most likely to be sourced over the internet as commoditized transactional services (most HR services including payroll and tax, core accounting plus cash management, banking and so on), which could well be serviced out of the USA, India or wherever.

- **Front-office stuff:** to the degree that this is relative standard and routine banking systems, it is likely to be sourced as an over-the-internet service from a supplier who is specialized in the banking sector, and who can offer 'on demand' a number of more specialized service suites to be used when required. The supplier will have offices in the City (and in Mumbai, New York, Shanghai and Tokyo) to keep a close watch over their extensive customer base, but will have their main delivery operations split between two major sites, one in India and one in Brazil, while considering a third 'major' in China because of the special requirements of that market (not the least, language) and the very fast growth in demand there. A satellite operation would be located in the City to provide certain services that fall within specific FSA regulatory parameters.

- **Derivatives trading:** very specialized, probably sourced from a specialist supplier over the internal network rather than the internet, with added security – but more importantly the supplier has the ability to systems innovate rapidly when the traders design a new model. The service comes with all the necessary data processing, storage etc. integrated down to the network level.

- **The development team:** this is the in-house 'secret weapon', able to rapidly identify and specify new systems requirements. The team would have a development contract with a small, quality team of software developers in Bangladesh – the new telecoms cable to Dhaka ensures that there are now quality internet connections, which allows 'over IP' combined voice-video-data conferencing at very low cost, resulting in very close team working.

CONCLUSION

The global stage is undoubtedly set for the strong development of the international trade in technology-enabled services. The internet holds great promise as the global and public utility that can potentially enable a level playing field in terms of access to that technology.

The range of factors that will influence competitive differentiation between the great diversity of suppliers, old and new, who will battle for market space is far more significant than the cost of professional IT resources. The human contribution (remember Carr) is more important than the technological. The importance of technical professionalism plays against the importance of application professionalism; the depth of the experiential plays against raw skills; the need for close intimacy in supplier–customer relationships plays against the remoteness that the virtual may deliver.

Stating that what you know is more important than the technology used to deliver that knowledge as a service flies in the face of the service provider trying to offer every possible service under the sun. Remember the old saying that a 'jack-of-all-trades is a master of none'. The global stage may provide a very much more level and competitive battlefield than people think and fear.

We live in an increasingly interconnected world in which the barriers to trade and the flow of information are being broken down at an ever-faster rate. News instantly races around cyberspace and services can be bought from almost anywhere in the global marketplace.

This process is full of potential for rich and poor alike. It empowers consumers with greater choice, equips internationally minded companies with the ability to sell to a far bigger market and it gives us all access to more information than at any other time in history. Globalization has also brought huge benefits to some of the world's poorest people as the walls of economic apartheid have started to crumble.

But the process of globalization also brings challenges. Some of these challenges are to do with the process of change that globalization inevitably brings – change of any kind can be unsettling – but much also to do with the process of building trust between people operating in different countries. Customers and suppliers all need to be able to have full confidence in their international partners.

At NASSCOM, we are spearheading a wide range of initiatives to ensure that the Indian IT and BPO sector can continue to command the full confidence of international customers. Fundamental to this is the need to always demonstrate the very highest standards in data security and customer confidentiality.

In India we have won much praise for our robust approach to data security issues. But no country can afford to be complacent. Criminals – be they in Delhi, Dundee or Denver – never stand still and so the sector has to ensure that it always remains at least one step ahead. This is a challenge to which NASSCOM and the Indian IT and BPO sector is utterly committed.

Sunil Mehta, Vice President, Indian National Association of Software and Service Companies (NASSCOM), www.nasscom.org

Sadly, Sunil passed away in December 2006.

7 Skills Needed for a Future Economy

The level playing field agenda: Global services mean that offshore outsourcing, education policy and immigration policy are all interlinked. A company can import labour, hire local skilled people or outsource tasks to an offshore location – these options are becoming more interchangeable as immigration of skilled labour increases and outsourcing becomes easier to manage. What skills should a developed economy prepare for the next generation?

In August 2003 the McKinsey Global Institute (MGI) published their much-quoted report *Offshoring: Is it a Win-Win Game?*[1] This report made the claim that every dollar spent on offshoring by US companies would create US$1.45–1.47 of value to the global economy, with the USA capturing US$1.12–1.14 and the receiving country capturing on average 33 cents. In other words, the USA captures 78 per cent of the total value, generating more for the US than the initial dollar spent.

This report was a watershed in the argument for offshoring, as politicians, economists and business leaders all argued that further engagement with the wider global economy could only be a good thing for any society. What was missing though was a similar – more independent – study that examined the types of jobs that could potentially be offshored and whether the consequence of a rise in offshoring really would be a flight of skilled jobs from the ICT sector. While the positive reports continued to be from the ranks of major consulting firms there would always be those who could doubt the independence of the data. As the primary data used for commercial analysis often is not available, this lends further doubts as to its independence.

This doubt is not directed wholly at McKinsey – many other commercial research and consulting firms have written analysis that proposes the view of offshoring and its positive net contribution to an economy. McKinsey just had the fortune to write the most-quoted study.

Therefore, new analysis from the OECD, led by Desirée van Welsum and Xavier Reif and published in February 2006, was very welcome.[2] What is most important is the researchers have analysed jobs and assessed their potential for offshoring, finding that one in five could be delivered remotely. Some of the the report's key points are repeated below.

- Almost 20 per cent of all employment could potentially be delivered remotely through the use of technology-enabled offshoring. (It is important to note that this does not mean 20 per cent of UK jobs will be lost, as there is the potential for the UK to deliver services remotely to other locations.)

- There is no discernible correlation between the use of offshoring and the levels of employment in those sectors that could potentially be offshored. Offshoring cannot be proven to have created job losses in the IT and IT-enabled sectors.
- ICT standardization, advancement and automation are responsible for rendering many roles redundant, not offshoring.
- Offshoring does not necessarily result in a decline in services employment; rapid growth in countries such as India and China should increase exports to those regions from OECD countries.
- Low-cost locations for offshored services activities (e.g. India, China and Brazil, and also eastern European countries such as Latvia, Lithuania and Estonia) have experienced rapid growth of business, computer and information exports (1995–2003), which may confirm their emergence as offshoring locations in recent years.
- Over the same period, the UK has grown its exports by approximately 12 per cent every year – considerable growth and not 'the end of IT as we know it'.
- The countries with the most consistent growth in exports are those who are also purchasing services from offshore, leading to the conclusion that a free and open service sector encourages far better growth and performance than one sheltered by protectionist measures.

THE SKILLS IMPERATIVE

Growth in this market is inevitable. The world is changing in a number of ways and the potential that existed 20 years ago to create multinational flexible companies has been realized by the birth of the internet and its widespread adoption since 1994.

Companies are looking at global services as a way of tapping into resource pools from across the world. Often particular expertise exists only in certain markets. A further attraction is the potential for creating new markets for products and services, but by far the greatest driver of the use in international services has been to reduce costs in expensive developed economies.

In June 2005, the McKinsey Global Institute (MGI) published a research paper that analyses the emerging global labour market and how demand for talent in offshore locations is growing.[3] Clearly the demand for offshore resources is a good indicator of how the entire offshore services industry as a whole is growing. What is interesting to note about the MGI analysis is where they start from. First they want to demonstrate how much of the entire services market can potentially be delivered from offshore. Clearly there are many services that must be delivered locally, so the stampede of services jobs to offshore locations is not quite the rush it seems from the breathless newspaper headlines. MGI calculate that it is theoretically possible to remotely deliver about 11 per cent of services. They estimate that the size of the global service industry in 2008 will be about 1.46 billion jobs, which means that the maximum number of services jobs that may ever be delivered offshore should be in the region of 160 million.

It is important to note that the MGI research indicates that 89 per cent of service jobs could never be delivered offshore; it's an interesting statistic that helps to assuage some of the fear of offshoring.

As the opponents of offshore contact centres will tell you, customer-facing functions often don't work well when delivered from a remote location. The more customer-facing work an industry sector has, the lower the potential to offshore many functions. For this reason MGI has determined that the retail sector, with the vast majority of employment tied to stores, has the lowest such potential: 3 per cent of all retail jobs could be performed remotely. Because retail is a huge employer of people, however, the small percentage translates into a large absolute number of people and jobs – potentially 4.9 million of the world's retail jobs in 2008. In contrast, almost half of all employment in the packaged software industry could be offshored. Yet this fraction only represents a potential 340,000 jobs by 2008, because that sector employs far fewer people than retail worldwide.

Just like industries and business sectors, some occupations are easier to deliver from remote locations. Engineering, and finance and accounting are the most amenable to offshore delivery, with support roles as the most difficult to deliver remotely. MGI predicts that actual offshore employment will reach 4.1 million jobs worldwide by 2008.

> The McKinsey Global Institute predicts that just 2.5 per cent of the work that can possibly be delivered remotely will be offshored by 2008.

As this book is written, there are about half a million service industry jobs offshored from developed regions to lower-cost developing countries. To move from half a million to 4 million by 2008 will be a dramatic shift in the way services are delivered globally, and implies that the IT and IT-enabled service sectors will be very busy for the next few years.

However, as analysed earlier in the book, countries such as the UK export more services than they import. For developed economies to adapt they must develop two key areas of skills related to IT: high-value business skills where IT is a tool used to solve business issues, and entrepreneurialism – to devise and adapt lower-level services for the local market.

As this concept of remote delivery becomes more prevalent, especially in particular industries or for individuals with specific skills, there is an accompanying important societal change. Commentators on offshoring often identify a need to consider how the citizens of developed and sophisticated economies need to consider retraining. The labour unions argue that governments should be responsible for retraining those in professions that are most amenable to offshoring, so these individuals can compete in a labour market where their skills have become useless. It might be worth pondering what happened to all the public gas-lighters once electricity allowed streetlights to operate without a daily lighting round.

In the UK, the government has accepted the idea that people need more education to compete within a knowledge society. The stated objective is for at least half of all school-leavers to earn a university degree by 2010, which by present standards seems like a pledge that cannot be achieved. In the 2005 university entrance process, some 511,669 potential students applied for university courses – over 107,000 of them could not find a place. Some believe that demand in the UK for university places was artificially high in 2005 as the fees for university courses tripled in 2006, but even the costs from 2006 remain reasonable compared to regions where education is paid for as a free-market service.

It is our belief that the debate about offshoring should be more strongly connected to the debate on immigration and education. Education policy determines the skills possessed by present and future citizens. In the future environment of an economically developed society where knowledge and intellectual skills are valued above physical labour there needs to be a managed process to keep improving those skills – as valuable 'knowledge' skills will change throughout a person's life. Consider the difference in career between a plumber who learns the career once in youth and can then apply it throughout life, to a computer programmer who must constantly be abreast of new technology and improved computer languages. Lifelong learning is an essential part of life within a knowledge society. (We are aware that the plumbing industry itself is becoming more high-tech and there is a requirement to learn about new pumps and heating management systems – the industry is used for illustration only.)

Offshoring can be used as a reaction to a skills shortage or a workforce that is uncompetitive. In many cases the use of offshoring is applied as a combination of labour availability and cost. Where skills are not available in a region, or where those skills cannot be secured without paying an intolerable premium, then offshoring can be a valid strategy for a company to complete tasks.

Immigration can be used to gain skills lacking within a society. However, there are many issues with the use of immigration and even a mention of the term can cause minds to close. Economic migration has been the powerhouse that created the modern USA. Immigration is now fairly common where particular skills are required, but it is also increasingly common for low-value tasks such as cleaning, domestic services, and bar or hospitality work.

127

Each component is connected to the others and will influence the other members of this 'trinity'. For example:

- a skills shortage can stimulate an increase in offshoring; conversely an abundant supply of well-qualified individuals can reduce the need to consider the use of immigrant labour or offshoring;
- an increase in the migration of skilled workers can reduce the need for offshoring and can influence the skills local people will attempt to gain;
- an increase in offshoring can reduce the need for skilled migrants in particular industry sectors and can directly influence the skills local people will attempt to gain.

The outcome of the present growth in global services will be for all three sections of the 'trinity' to be affected:

- skills need to be upgraded and replenished more frequently, or a new focus for skills development is required;
- migration will increase as the jobs' market extends to be truly global – at the low end of the job market as much as the senior level;
- offshoring will increase as specific industries use it to drive growth.

THE EFFECT ON THE UK ECONOMY

As the BPO industry grows globally, nations in the developed west will feel a change to the way their economy operates. We were very interested in a 2004 report published by the research analysts Evalueserve where the changing nature of global services and its effect on the UK economy were analysed.[4]

The Evalueserve report demonstrates that the UK economy should gain substantially from the global sourcing of services. UK firms will benefit from lower cost structures, access to high-skill talent pools and increased flexibility. The utilization of offshore firms and the resulting growth of local economies will lead to an expansion of global markets for goods and services from the UK.

> Many project management skills were lost from Royal Mail during their successful outsourcing programme. This included the outsourcing of 'Business Systems', Royal Mail's internal IT provider that was home to much of Royal Mail's skilled project management resource.
>
> Royal Mail's 'Deploying Effective People and Projects' programme (DEPP) was set up to fill the skills gap and has an objective to
>
> *(Continued)*

(Continued)

develop a 'Technology Professional Community'. In 2005/06 the programme had two main projects. One project was to procure, config-
ure and implement a skills database that would allow us to harness
the skills of our people, to understand the skills gaps and to fill them,
and to create development plans for our people.

The second project was called 'Harmony' and started with an
objective 'to design and implement a delivery lifecycle methodology'. It soon became clear that a delivery lifecycle in splendid isolation would have a limited impact. Instead the challenge was to
design and implement a 'project delivery tool kit' that could be used
on projects of all types and size, including IT projects.

In November 2005 IT Directors from across the Royal Mail Group
and the CIO, endorsed Harmony to be used on all IT projects, or
the IT component of business projects from 1 April 2006. The tool
kit includes the original requirement of a comprehensive delivery
lifecycle. In addition the launch of the tool kit has effectively
included the return of Prince 2 [a popular project management
methodology] as Royal Mail's preferred project management
method.

Other processes that are not well covered by Prince 2 have been,
or are, under development.

Irvine Caplan, Director, Commercial Management of Outsource, Technology &
Purchasing, Royal Mail Group plc, www.royalmail.com

Evalueserve observed that the impact of offshoring on the UK workforce
is real and will lead to the displacement of workers, but that the UK labour
market is flexible and capable of dealing with this impact. To limit the
impact and to ensure optimal reallocation of workers, however, the UK
will need to upgrade its retraining infrastructure and provide displaced
workers with additional assistance (such as additional insurance) until
they find new jobs.

In the 1990s the UK experienced its longest period of uninterrupted
growth since the Second World War. During 1993–2002, its real
GDP grew by 2.89 per cent annually, driven primarily by an annual
1.87 per cent improvement in labour productivity. Average wages also
witnessed a healthy annual increase of 4.12 per cent (compounded
average growth rate). Productivity gains came primarily from improvements in technology and processes, and growth was further accelerated by changes in government policy and privatizations in public
sector undertakings.

The UK economy added more than 2.3 million new jobs during the period 1993–2002. The unemployment rate declined from 11 per cent in 1993 to 6.2 per cent in 1998 and then to 4.9 per cent in 2001, and then rose slightly to 5.2 per cent in 2002. At the time of writing this book, UK unemployment is at pretty much the lowest recorded level for about 30 years.

The creation of new jobs during the 1990s and a fall in the unemployment rate has resulted in a large number of vacancies. These vacancies were attributed to the unavailability of sufficiently skilled workers – this skill shortage existed across several industries and occupations. Some employers even reported an increase in operational costs and a fall in quality because of these skill shortages. UK firms, therefore, resorted to global sourcing by hiring immigrant workers and later by offshoring.

During the next few years, the UK economy is expected to continue its robust growth pattern of the 1990s. Evalueserve predicts that the real GDP will grow by 2.49 per cent annually and productivity will improve by 2.0 per cent annually during the period 2003–2010. Rapid economic growth during the next few years will lead to the creation of new jobs. However, slow population growth and the effect of an aging population will lead to a shortfall in the supply of domestic labour in the UK. Evalueserve estimates that the gap between supply and demand in the UK will reach 714,000 jobs by 2010. Industries that will face the maximum shortfall are likely to be health care, information technology and education.

> The supply and demand gap for jobs in the UK will rise to 714,000 by 2010 – jobs without local workers and therefore requiring offshoring or immigration to fulfil the tasks.
>
> Evalueserve[5]

If this labour shortfall is not addressed, the UK economy will have to bear a loss in its potential output. During 2003–2010 the annual GDP growth may fall from the projected rate of 2.49 per cent to 2.08 per cent. This would translate into a cumulative loss of £113 billion in potential output.

Global sourcing provides a means of addressing at least some of this shortfall. During 2003–2010 immigration is likely to provide approximately 372,000 workers. The remaining shortfall of 342,000 will still need to be taken care of. Evalueserve estimates that about 272,000 jobs in the services sector will move offshore during the period 2003–2010 and a total of 303,100 jobs would have been offshored from the UK by the year 2010.

The war for talent has been talked about for many years, but now the reality is starting to catch up with the hype. Where a business requires intellectual input from employees rather than physical services, those people could really be based anywhere. Our company is the first peer-to-peer currency exchange in the world; it's a bit like eBay for foreign currency. We don't manufacture cars or need people to serve in shops. We have a local contact centre in the UK so the customer-facing team is local, but the technology and technical analysis of derivative products that drives our exchange can be delivered from anywhere – in our case, India. It's not that India is cheaper – we worked with local IT people in the UK for a long time, but because there is so much expertise available in India we find it a lot easier to get what we need, at a reasonable price.

Vijay Kumar, Managing Director, FXA World, www.fxaworld.com

It is important to stress that independent government data, from the UK Office of National Statistics (ONS), does verify the Evalueserve predictions. More importantly for the critics of offshoring, the ONS data in 2005 demonstrates that the UK is creating more jobs even as more are offshored in specific industries where critics have feared huge job losses, such as call centres.

The *Labour Market Trends* report published by the ONS in September 2005 shows that employment growth in occupations related to call centres in the UK has been nearly three times the overall growth in employment, while redundancy levels have also consistently fallen since 2001.[6]

The employment data calculated by region is also in line with that growth trend and, according to the ONS, this suggests offshoring has had minimal effect on the employment prospects of IT-enabled occupations across the UK.

THE OVUM/DTI ANALYSIS

In June 2006 the telecoms and technology analyst group Ovum (since purchased in October 2006 by Datamonitor) published a report titled *The Impact of Global Sourcing on the UK Software and IT Services Sector*.[7] The report was commissioned by the UK government Department of Trade and Industry and is a detailed analysis of what may happen to the software industry in the UK as a result of global sourcing of services.

The Ovum analysis is focused specifically on the software and IT services market and paints a gloomy picture, in particular for smaller companies with fairly commoditized technical skills. According to the report:

In summary, while we often hear talk of a 'backlash' against global sourcing and it is easy to find counter-examples (such as some UK banks rejecting offshored call-centre operations), our research under-lines the fact that the tide of change continues to move in one direc-tion. Moreover, we must accept that the requirement for IT workers located in the UK will drop as a result of these unstoppable trends and we should not be distracted by the current growth and high-profile onshore hiring activity of some of the larger players in the market.[8]

The Ovum prediction is that the absolute numbers of people employed within the British IT industry will decline:

Our analysis shows that the size of the workforce employed by the software and IT services industry in the UK is set to drop by a total of 15,500 employees in the three years to the end of 2008. This total represents 6% of the current UK S/ITS [Software and IT Services] headcount of 249,000. Over the same timeframe, the total number of UK-facing staff employed offshore will double to 131,000.[9]

We would not want to dispute the Ovum analysis – this is a detailed study involving some detailed quantitative and qualitative analysis with extensive input directly from the industry – but it's worth commenting on the points we raised in Chapter 1 about application professionalism. It's clear that the need for fairly basic technical skills will reduce in a region such as the UK, when the end result of those skills can be easily transferred across the inter-net – or the skills can be imported on a temporary basis. A clear analogy can be drawn with professions that no longer exist because they were replaced by some form of technological advancement – where did all the gas lamp-lighters go, or the chap with the red flag who would walk in front of a car?

As we outlined earlier, however, the growth in a need for application professionalism means that the developed economies of the west will not collapse into a mire of joblessness and existential angst. It is the use of technology by an entire swath of industries – not just the technology itself – that creates the value added for these economies and so we believe that the outlook is not as gloomy as the Ovum figures suggest.

THE CENTRAL ARGUMENT

Clearly the change to the career is central to this debate. We are not only considering a change to the life and career of those within the IT indus-try, but those with any industry skills. In the UK, the term 'Polish plumber' has become commonly used to describe the skilled East

Europeans arriving and offering their services – although it's generally used as a disparaging term. Since the European Union expanded in 2004 workers from across the former Soviet Bloc nations have been free to arrive in the UK and work and many have taken advantage of this freedom, as can be observed by the number of white vans bearing Polish registration plates.

Is it good or bad to allow this free movement of labour? It's true that the UK was more progressive than most other European nations in allowing the new EU entrants open access to their labour market. Only Sweden and Ireland joined the UK in offering an open-door policy, with every other member state claiming they needed 'more time' to work out how to deal with the projected flood of low-cost workers. In fact, the UK government hopelessly miscalculated the potential for European migration. Official estimates by the British government in advance of EU expansion in 2004 projected that 5,000 to 13,000 workers from across the 10 new member states might migrate to the UK seeking work. In fact, over 175,000 came in the first year alone and over half a million had arrived by 2006. Not surprisingly, the British government has announced restrictive measures on job seekers from the most recent additions to the European Union, Romania and Bulgaria.

What is a fact is that the immigrants are not all plumbers. There are plenty of Polish programmers as well. The Polish plumber is a metaphor for the change everyone in any job is experiencing. There was a time when a plumber would be able to find a role as an apprentice to an established tradesman. They could learn the trade and then work through the rest of their career using the same tools they used to learn the trade.

That's never been true of IT. The capabilities of the technology have always moved forward at such a rate that anyone within the industry has to engage in constant learning, just to remain employable. Cast your mind back to the early 1990s. It doesn't seem to be all that long ago that Guns 'n' Roses were topping the charts and a 100 Mb hard disk was astonishing. At the time it would not have been unusual to be programming in BASIC or COBOL on a monochrome monitor. Yet, today those skills are next to useless – IT has moved on.

Just because technology is becoming an increasingly commoditized utility that is either automated or outsourced to Bangalore doesn't mean that IT doesn't matter. On the contrary, that allows a business to devote more energy and resources to the core areas where technology can deliver genuine strategic and competitive advantage.

Now, more than ever before, technology is a mission-critical and strategic part of every business, and that represents a real

(Continued)

(Continued)

> opportunity for the modern IT professional to be a valued member of the boardroom leadership team and the agent of change who sets an organization apart from its competitors.
>
> But that demands the IT professional of the future to be a much more hard-nosed businessperson capable of providing input into business strategy issues, holding their own in the boardroom. If they can't, then other executives will take their place at the top table, and so the question is whether IT professionals can rise to the business challenge?
>
> Andy McCue, Chief reporter, *silicon.com*, www.silicon.com

So the world is changing and the career has changed with it. Thomas Friedman has argued that it is 'every person for themselves'[10] in a modern society where individuals will need to create their own personal brand. The personal brand analogy makes sense on paper. We have moved from the competition between states to the competition between companies to a situation where global competition between individuals is now possible – see RentACoder for an example.[11] The only problem is that the world is still primarily designed around companies that hire employees, not maverick individuals.

Of course, a further distraction is that not everyone can be truly great. For those in Britain suffering the scourge of the Polish plumber, comfort can be drawn from the fact that the rest of the European Union (EU) needs to be as welcoming as the UK was earlier, from 2007. So it may be that the UK has witnessed the peak of European migration over the past few years – and yet the economy continued to grow and new jobs were created during that time.

Detractors of the offshore outsourcing model argue that the market cannot always be correct. Their key objections are discussed next.

> If jobs go offshore then we lose our competitive edge in the global market. Eventually everyone with technical skills will be replaced by offshore resources and we will have nothing but hairdressers and tourist guides left

This statement just over-eggs the potential for everything to be remotely delivered. It is true that many large corporations have the management expertise and bureaucracy required to manage international divisions and suppliers, yet most people in the UK are employed by small and medium-sized enterprises (SMEs). Although SMEs are exploring the idea of offshoring, we won't all be running for jobs as Windsor Castle guides soon – for a number of reasons. First, just because remote delivery is technically feasible does not mean that it is the best or most desirable way of delivering a project. Second, most projects need some local or domain knowledge that cannot be found in an offshore location. We should accept that offshoring will grow as a strategic business solution for reducing cost, or finding new skilled resources, but it won't be the end of skilled employment as we know it. Developed countries such as the UK are also exporting their skills to others; just take a look at the first chapter of this book for reassurance of that.

> Those who get displaced by offshoring end up in low-paid 'McJobs' and cannot use their skills effectively

This is generally an issue of geographic availability. The UK IT industry is generating new jobs at a rate that is much faster than the general economy – so jobs are out there. However, it's clear that in some local situations an employer of skilled people may close in the UK and off-shore work to another location, affecting their employees. It can happen, but then it can happen in any industry.

The bigger picture is that IT delivery is changing generally. Companies today are far more likely to see IT as a commodity purchase and to use an IT supplier rather than employing internal employees. Most supplier teams will be employed locally, to be near the client, but some may be off-shore, as some tasks can be delivered remotely. The change is more in the nature of how IT is purchased by companies, rather than how offshoring is changing the industry – offshoring remains a relatively small part of the entire IT delivery equation.

> Workers and society should be considered, not just the profit of multinational corporations. Creating local jobs is of more value to society than delivering a better than expected dividend to fat-cat shareholders

The debate should actually be focused on whether companies should be allowed to get on with whatever they need to do to perform well for their various stakeholders. Companies perform better when their corporate social responsibility policy is defined alongside their strategy for success and profit. If the company doesn't generate a profit then it won't be around for long anyway. In the case of public companies with tradable shares there is further cause to help them perform well. Most of us have some savings or investments, or contribute to a pension fund. The fund manager will invest these funds in the stock market and so your own future pension provision depends on the share price performance of major corporations.

Supporting a vibrant and flexible economy by allowing companies to use outsourcing as a strategic tool when needed is essential and to consider prescribing approved or unapproved strategies to private companies is almost ridiculous.

The OECD analysis mentioned earlier in this chapter[12] does compare the performance of the IT services sector in various European countries and there is a clear correlation between less restrictive control from the government and more success, including more job creation.

THE ROAD AHEAD

Amongst all the fear, uncertainty and doubt one key point can easily be forgotten. The offshoring of services is itself just a transitory step. If a company employs 1,000 in London then it is naturally cheaper to have 1,000 people performing the same tasks in India or China. However, what would be even better for the company is to have only 500 people in India or China, but for them to be just as productive as the 1,000. So one could view the present wave of offshoring as just an exploration of the global possibilities for services, with the ultimate aim being an immense improvement in efficiency.

In both 2004 and 2006, the BCS reported on the effect of offshoring on the British IT industry.[13] The findings and suggestions from this research can be applied across any other industry; the focus on IT was because the BCS conducted the research and technology is naturally one of the first areas where globalization and offshoring will affect. IT organizations are spoiled for choice when seeking an offshore partner and if they have the scale then they can easily set up their own offshore operation.

> The world of IT has changed out of all recognition over the last eight years. The old 'fill a room' mainframes are now generally considered passé for most businesses; PCs have become the mainframes of today. But over the next ten years, we will see even more fundamental changes in the way IT evolves. Today, an IT professional needs to be very business aware if he (or she) is to succeed. Many consider the best IT professional is primarily a businessperson, with IT as a secondary skill. Ten years ago, the very opposite held true. And change remains the order of the day. Those that endeavour to stand still and build on the skills of the past will lose out.
>
> Roger Ellis, Chairman of the IT Directors Network and former IT Director of Blue Circle Industries PLC, www.itdirectorsnetwork.co.uk

The BCS research did analyse the question of skills required within the IT industry. Though we have paraphrased the comments to fit this context, the summary of the BCS research in 2006[14] is discussed next.

THE IMPACT OF GLOBALIZATION

We cannot be certain how many jobs will be affected by offshoring, or indeed how many new jobs the global market may create. Although the numbers of estimated job losses look large, they represent only a small percentage of the total IT workforce in the UK. Some IT projects would be uneconomical in the UK and will only be progressed overseas where wage rates are lower (but where IT professionals are well paid compared with other sectors). This can be demonstrated within a country such as India, where the labour market for skilled employees is so dynamic that employers need to take great care of their employees, or else they will leave quickly. This market situation encourages good conditions for employees, as the supplier companies desperately need them, and is quite the opposite of the 'modern slave labour' talked of by the labour unions when arguing for a utopian single global minimum wage.

The numbers of jobs moved offshore will probably be sufficient to make it harder for IT professionals with limited skills to find work. As more routine work is moved overseas, it may become difficult for new recruits to get good basic experience in IT work. This has started to become an issue in the UK already, as the letters page of magazines such as *Computing* can attest. However, the heavy social burden of labour legislation in countries such as Sweden and France has made the situation far worse for young inexperienced people in those areas. Young French students took to the streets to protest against the insecurity of modern life and work in 2006. Specifically they were protesting against a proposal by the government to allow more flexibility in hiring young people; the employer would have the right to let the employee go within the first couple of years of employment without needing to go through the normal onerous process. Paradoxically, the less 'protection' there is from government, the easier it is for younger people to find work, and as a result the labour market is naturally more dynamic and creative. To anyone outside France the idea that you can graduate with a university degree and expect a job for life is more than a little bizarre.

Think about this logically now. The employers told the government that they didn't want to hire young people because the 'job for life' type employment contract used in France means that it is almost impossible to get rid of someone who is not suitable for the job. This issue really applies to all employees, but the young were particularly targeted because they generally have no track record to demonstrate their ability. The government responded by proposing to ease restrictions on younger workers, making it possible to hire someone, see if they are suitable, and easily fire them if they are not. This should have led to a huge increase in job availability for young people as employers would be prepared to take a chance on them, yet the French youth chose to riot in protest and this ensured that the new proposals never hit the statute book. How could the French prime minister have been made such a scapegoat for a measure that would almost certainly have created jobs for French youth?

Free trade, without protectionist measures, is beneficial for all countries. It exposes companies to international competition and this leads to greater productivity and more effective use of new technology and encourages innovation. The UK has been a beneficiary of global trade in IT services for many years; US-based companies like IBM and Microsoft have established research centres in the UK and created UK-based jobs. Many high-wage countries, like the UK, have ageing populations. Labour shortages in future years will need to be tackled through a combination of immigration, offshoring and longer working lives. The UK is reforming its creaking immigration system around a points-based system, not least to stop the public confusion of economic migrants with asylum seekers or refugees. Countries such as the UK and USA are likely to suffer less from the ageing indigenous population because of the genuine welcome they offer to skilled tax-paying immigrants. Japan is possibly the most developed nation that has yet to tackle the issue in a comprehensive way, choosing to promote reproduction through blunt measures such as cash bonuses. Japan has a very homogenous population that is not exactly welcoming to foreigners. Even if they settle in Japan, they are always considered to be outsiders – as was demonstrated when a hopelessly lost bearded Arctic seal appeared in the Tama River in 2003. 'Tama-chan' became an immediate celebrity and was even granted an official resident's permit by the Nishi ward in Yokohama, an honour not even granted to long-term resident migrants. Many of those human residents chose to disguise themselves as seals for their next visit to the Nishi ward office, in case they might also win the honour of a resident's permit. The Japanese really need to ask questions such as 'when did any parent decide to enter the lifelong commitment of child-rearing because their government gave a bonus equivalent to the price of a luxury pram?'

The demographic issue is critical and not just a philosophical debate over migrating cultures. The UK economy is regularly creating new jobs through continued growth. Those jobs need to be filled if economic expansion is to continue uninterrupted. So migrants need to join the UK workforce, or knowledge-based work can be offshored, or the expansion has to cool down to a sustainable level. Jobs are created while unemployment also exists due to the availability of people not always being in the same location as the vacancies. It may appear to be an oversimplification of the entire labour market, but job creation is often overlooked in favour of monitoring unemployment alone.

THE COMPETITIVE STRENGTH OF IT IN THE UK

Globalization has opened up opportunities for British IT professionals to work overseas and to provide services from the UK to world markets.

But we need to compare our performance objectively with the best in the world – whether we work in IT or any other knowledge-based profession. To think otherwise would risk underestimating the competition we face and the capacity of overseas workers to provide high-quality, cost-effective services. We need to nurture our strengths and make the most of new opportunities.

In assessing which jobs will remain in the UK, we need to identify areas where UK IT professionals add value and can offer more than offshore workers. UK-based professionals have a good understanding of British and international business processes, they can offer a combination of business knowledge and IT skills, and they have good problem-solving and analytical skills. Our business culture also encourages creativity: we regularly question the way things are done and seek out improvements; and we have a diverse society and are used to working with professionals drawn from different ethnic backgrounds. The large freelance contractor workforce in the UK provides mobile and temporary resources where and when they are needed.

These are not just 'wise words' aimed at ameliorating the nastiness of offshoring. British professionals will always be able to work better with other British professionals because contracts between companies are always signed between people, not the companies. This cultural dimension is always likely to exist and can be a real issue for overseas companies once a contract has been awarded, but for those who work in the UK anyway it should be remembered that having a strong cultural understanding of the company and people you are working for is of immense value by itself.

Those of us who interact with the offshore outsourcing community have seen many examples of how this can go wrong, and examples continue to come in. Skilled workers who fear for their job really shouldn't worry too much, because it is hard to get global sourcing right. It can be done and it has been proven, but offshore companies often don't help themselves.

CAREER DEVELOPMENT

The challenge for British professionals now is to gear up for the globalization of the IT services industry. Everyone today needs to consider where their career and the industry they work within will go in the next decade. Cast your mind back to the mid 1990s. Those of us who were using the web or email back then were considered a little strange. Who can remember seeing a URL on an advert for the first time? The world has changed so much since we were all choosing to support Blur or Oasis – why was it always considered so strange to like them both?

Traditional IT skills such as software development have become globally ubiquitous and a narrow focus on technical skills and their application will not help tomorrow's professionals. Think about skills that can be global and skills that need to be local. Knowledge of C++ or Java is something that can be purchased from anywhere. Detailed knowledge of how a technology system improves the business it serves is much harder to combine with the technical knowledge. Quite often, techies underestimate their own business knowledge. There is a often a mindset of career progression through learning new technical languages of architectures, rather than progression within the business environment.

The report by the BCS working party on offshoring described a new career model in which professionals move on from foundation IT training to developing additional skills such as project and relationship management expertise, business skills and knowledge of specialized technologies.[15] This would open up a wider career path, including the possibility for IT professionals to work in other business functions. The ultimate aim is to create an environment in which IT can be a career where longevity is valued and IT know-how is transferred into the business arena. Lifelong learning will become more important for all IT professionals, making full use of services such as BCS's Career Builder.[16]

We have managed technical teams where people have built up immense business knowledge, within areas such as investment banking, only to discard that in favour of a new job that offers the chance to try out some new technology or language. This approach has to be doomed in the long term as technical skills become even more commoditized. The technologists of the future in countries such as the UK must be able to prove a business case for the technology they are supporting – not just be able to develop in the basement surrounded by posters of Jeff Minter and Syd Barrett.

HELPING PROFESSIONALS DISPLACED BY OFFSHORING

However beneficial offshoring may be for companies and the economy at large, individuals can suffer as they see work transfer overseas and are forced to tackle the task of finding new employment. This is the fear of every professional – being 'Bangalored'. The BCS identified the major challenge as being how to protect the interests of IT professionals rather then trying to protect specific jobs.[17]

Corporate social responsibility (CSR) principles provide a useful framework for handling job losses caused by restructuring and can be applied to offshoring initiatives. Agreements between some UK companies and their trade unions help protect the interests of IT professionals at the same time as recognizing that some work will transfer overseas and deliver corporate benefits. This assistance is funded from the initial corporate benefits derived from offshoring projects.

There has to be an acceptance of change by individuals though. We no longer live in an age where a job is for life and the only competition is with our immediate neighbour. Individual IT professionals need to take personal responsibility for their own career development. We all need to raise our professional standards to maximize our job prospects and develop our careers.

Steps you can take to increase your opportunities for future employment include:

- developing business skills and knowledge and focusing on how IT can interact with the business you are focused on;
- focusing on roles that will remain in your region, such as jobs requiring close interaction with users and jobs where agility and innovation are more important than cost;
- training in new and emerging technologies;
- monitoring sectors where new jobs are being created;
- avoiding becoming locked into areas that are more likely to be offshored.

This is particularly relevant for freelance contractors who cannot look to a corporate employer for training and development support.

For all UK-based IT staff, maintaining professional standards will become even more important. The BCS is uniquely and ideally placed to help and offers a range of services for IT professionals, including internationally recognized qualifications, chartered status, continuing professional development and web-based information.

ENABLING THE ECONOMY TO BENEFIT FROM OFFSHORING

Offshoring is a reality of business life today. The capability to source globally is a growing competitive differentiator for companies (and countries). Successful offshoring depends on strategy, skills, quality processes, management effort and governance:

- companies need to devise a strategy that determines which services can profitably be offshored;
- skills are needed to support technical design, project management, supplier management, data protection and transition management functions – so new skills are needed just to manage the offshoring process;
- quality processes within the company need to be sufficient to be able to work alongside an offshore supplier that may have achieved a high level of compliance with internationally recognized standards;
- appropriate procedures and governance structures need to be in place.

It is clear that some activities are never going to be offshored. For various reasons they are just not suitable for remote delivery. The four factors that determine this are:

- activities for which distance or proximity is crucially important;
- services for which the value of the activity far outweighs the cost;
- functions that require employee agility;
- activities that form a sustainable centre of expertise.

EMBRACING THE SKILLS CHALLENGE

It should be remembered that price is not the only factor of importance in the global market. Singapore is a good example of a country with a highly successful IT industry in which average salary levels, quality of life measures, and infrastructure far exceed those of neighbouring countries. The UK economy will benefit from openness to trade if a business-friendly environment and a flexible, skilled workforce support it.

For many years there has been a debate amongst educators about the concept of learning as a process. The 'old-fashioned' system of learning by rote, or repeating and memorizing facts, has been discredited and replaced by teaching children how to learn. So the old memorization of tables has been replaced with lessons in how to perform mental arithmetic more effectively. This is analogous to the situation regarding the level playing field and global services. To protect the current way of doing things is not pragmatic – we know that employment is changing and that labour will ebb and flow throughout the world. Some services may be better sourced remotely and so will no longer offer jobs in the UK, but others will be created in their place. The main skill for anyone in the labour market is to learn about this flexibility, focusing on how to consider what may change and what skills will be important in future. By ensuring you are flexible and not chained to a specific way of working you can guarantee a lifetime of valuable employment.

Microsoft, the BCS, and Lancaster University have joined forces to create a new working party for 'developing the future'. The working party produced an initial report in July 2006 focused on the challenges and opportunities facing the software industry in the UK.[18] Some of their final conclusions address the challenges that lay ahead for professionals in this industry as they face competition from others across the globe. The key questions raised by the working party were:

1. How can the UK meet the opportunities and challenges for globalization?
2. How can the industry attract new skills and talent for the future?
3. What can be achieved to create a modern image for sustainable competitive advantage?

4. What strategic initiatives, policies and data are required to develop a leading-edge industry?

5. How can we ensure that the UK is at the centre for European software development and innovation?

For our purposes the obvious focus is on question 1, 'How can the UK meet the opportunities and challenges for globalization?' The working party made these recommendations in response to the challenges of globalization:

1. Develop more rigorous certification at every level for software developers to increase the professional image of the industry (not just at the graduate/postgraduate level).

2. Address the wide variation in quality of tertiary education courses in computer science and affiliated subjects.

3. Develop initiatives that closely align software development with the career aspirations that young people have.

4. Institute an education programme amongst young people that tells them about the realities and opportunities of a career in software development.

5. The Department for Education and Science and other stakeholders should help to devise a strategy that reverses the current decline in popularity of the 'at risk' subjects within secondary and tertiary education.

Clearly if these recommendations are followed and initiatives such as the Skills Framework for the Information Age are developed further,[19] then the British IT industry can remain vibrant, even in the face of offshore competition from the east.

For many years IT professionals have been aware of the need to develop new technical skills in the fast moving world of IT. In today's world, however, as more routine technical work is moved overseas, IT professionals need to focus on developing those skills that continue to be needed here in the UK. Employers regularly report a shortage of skilled IT workers who combine a knowledge of technology with an understanding of how IT can be exploited to bring business benefits or who can effectively manage projects to deliver IT-enabled business change. IT professionals need to branch out, especially into other business functions, to develop a more rounded skills-set and to integrate key technical and analytical skills into mainstream business functions.

Extract from *Embracing the Challenge, Exploiting the Opportunities: Building a World Class IT Profession in the Era of Global Sourcing* – the second report by the BCS Working Party on Offshoring (May 2006),[20] www.bcs.org.uk

8 The New Globalization

The level playing field agenda: Manufacturing eventually went global several decades ago, allowing access to skills and labour in remote locations. We are now witnessing the same change to high-end intellectual services, along with an automation of some tasks we might expect to remain a part of the service economy – such as contact centres. This industry is defining the politics of the world and there cannot be a more exciting time to observe how work and industry adapts to the new possibilities.

In his book *The World is Flat* the *New York Times* columnist Thomas Friedman explains that in his view there are three major historical eras of globalization.[1] Globalization 1.0 lasted from 1492 to about 1800. Basically, when Columbus set sail for the New World an era was created where the world started shrinking. Globalization 2.0 lasted from about 1800 to 2000. During this period the human perception of the world shrank to today's relatively very small size. The key agent of change was the multinational company doing business across the world and falling transportation and communication costs, with inventions such as electricity, the railways and the internet. Globalization 3.0 is from 2000 to the present. What is different now is that this period of globalization is no longer driven by Europe and the USA. This century will be driven forward by non-western nations, especially China and India. The emphasis has also shifted from the large company to the personal, empowering individuals to collaborate and compete globally. Individuals must ask 'where do I fit in to the global competition and opportunities of the day and how can I, on my own, collaborate with others globally?'

Friedman makes an excellent observation on the way the world is changing, both for business and individuals. According to Friedman, we already have the telecommunications technology and internet connectivity that allow intellectual services to be delivered from anywhere. Airlines are charging less and less for air travel. The only fly in the ointment is the volatile oil price, causing uncertainty for many airlines and their passengers, as fuel costs are passed on in the ticket price.

This chapter explores the questions that surround the developing global delivery model (GDM) for services. First, it is important to analyse whether the company and country they are operating from is compatible with your own intentions. It's also important to have an appreciation of global services and how delivery of services is morphing into a new industry where the players can deliver from very remote locations. Outsourcing has moved far beyond the earlier models of 'body-shopping' and global delivery now offers a way to work with service companies from across the world, for delivery in almost any location.

As stated, one of the most important questions when considering a partner for an offshore outsourcing contract, or when examining a country as a potential location for a captive centre, is whether this is the right country for your service. India is a country that often hits the headlines for its expertise in both IT and business processes, but there are many lower-cost environments across the world now with the maturity of business processes to be able to cope with whatever you ask of them.

INTERNATIONAL SELECTION CRITERIA

Political stability

This is one of the most important criteria for any manager considering a country as a potential location for their business processes. One thing to remember is that all business processes are important and fit into the supply chain somewhere. The discussion on offshoring does tend to focus on low rather than high-value tasks, but even low-value tasks can play a highly important role in the competitive economics of the supply chain of your organization. Now imagine taking those tasks and placing them in the country you are researching. Does it feel comfortable? What is the record of free and fair democratic elections in that region? There is no need to sit on high and judge the country while quoting selected paragraphs of Thomas Paine, but you still need to be comfortable that this is a stable country without the possibility of a coup or martial law to cause an interruption to those essential business processes.

Stability can often be a judgement that you will need to be advised on. India still suffers somewhat because of the chequered relationship with neighbouring Pakistan and the dispute over Kashmir that has simmered for decades. In 2002 the two countries became ever more belligerent and more than a million troops lined the border, awaiting orders to attack. The situation eventually cooled, but commentators in the west were on edge due to the nuclear-strike capability of both nations. Most people we spoke to in the Bangalore IT supplier community were hardly aware of the tense political situation, not through ignorance, but through a belief that the war just would not happen (and as a result of most political worrying being conducted in Delhi). Many Indians blamed foreign news media, such as the BBC, for presenting nuclear war as a likely outcome to the situation.

The India and Pakistan relationship is now better than ever. However, there are other popular regions with offshore outsourcing expertise where it would be advisable to seek expert local knowledge on the genuine risk, rather than the perception. One rule of thumb is to make a personal visit, rather than just relying on news reports about the business support offered in any particular location. The difference between reality and perception can be astonishing.

Government support

Strong backing from the government is essential for an industry to succeed, particularly where it is a nascent industry that is counting on a partnership between new service companies and the government. In addition to the government itself, there should be a strong industry association that can act as a single voice for the industry when interacting with the government.

India stands out because of its long experience in the software and services market. The National Association of Software and Service Companies (NASSCOM) was founded in 1988 and has wide-ranging support as the voice of IT and technology-enabled services in India. Other nations have widely copied the NASSCOM model as an example of best practice in lobbying and industry research.

Areas of importance where governments need to take action include the following:

- **A general support for international services:** a willingness to promote the service industry of their nation to other regions and to provide the infrastructure required for the industry to flourish.
- **Minimal tariffs on the trade in services,** especially for services that are traded with overseas destinations.
- **Tax benefits for foreign direct investment:** any company looking to open an office and invest substantial capital into a region, along with the associated job creation, should expect some help with local taxes – potentially a complete holiday for a specified time.
- **A keen interest in the emerging issues** of data protection, identity theft and economic crime: criminals will always be a step ahead of legislators, but it is not acceptable to have the IT services industry governed by a framework of rules that were written in the pre-internet era.

This may sometimes seem too much to ask of the political classes, but we are not indicating that ministers should be blogging on myspace.com, just that they support the international trade in services and accept that the industry is rather different to many others.

Labour pool and education

The attractiveness of the labour pool is, again, an absolutely critical issue. Not only do the right people need to be available in the location where you are proposing to do business, but there also has to be enough of them to make the business viable and to allow for future expansion.

Ireland is one of the best locations in the world for offshoring IT services. The Irish have no cultural problems integrating with an American or British workforce; in fact their own culture is increasingly exported to those countries! However, there are only about 4 million Irish people in the entire country and about 5,000 new technology graduates each year. This might be fine if your plan is to set up a facility with a hundred or so people and a slow but steady expansion, but what if you needed to quickly become an offshore centre with a couple of thousand staff? Of course it might be feasible for some skills, but it is unlikely that you would consider Ireland for high-volume services.

This is where countries with very large populations can have a distinct advantage. The BRIC region of Brazil, Russia, India and China accounts for a total population of around 2.5 billion people, a considerable proportion of the 6.4 billion people on the entire planet.

The people need to be available in the right numbers. They need to use the language of your business, which is presumably English if you are reading this book in its original language. They need to be educated to the required level, which may mean you need a steady stream of graduates, or possibly you need more specific skills. Finally, they also need to be culturally aligned so that teams from both your home base and from offshore can work together easily enough.

Infrastructure

The level of required infrastructure can vary depending on the type of service needed at the offshore location. The monsoon of 2005 in Mumbai caused a loss of power, the road network, telecommunications and the internet to most of the city. For a software development function this would just mean a delay of a few days until things returned to normal. However, if you were running a customer service function with guaranteed response times for phone calls and emails then the situation would be more serious.

Mumbai can be forgiven in a sense – almost a metre of rain fell on the city in a single day, which would wipe out services in any city. The 2006 monsoon also caused chaos, however. Customers are not very forgiving, so these issues do need to be considered.

In this regard, the major difference between business process outsourcing and IT outsourcing is the need for service to be 'always on'. Business process outsourcing (BPO) really is a 24-hour-a-day, 7-day-a-week, 365-day-a-year service, where employees need to be able to contact their office at any time of the day or night. The taxi rota at some service companies is a feat of logistical planning that has to be admired, as cars shuttle across cities collecting people from their home and returning elsewhere with those ending their shift.

Good airports, serviced roads, reliable electricity, clean water and safe food, high-class office facilities, fast internet access, cheap and reliable telecommunications – all of these are the most basic infrastructural requirements for a business facility anywhere in the world. However, for a new office back at home you would not usually need to consider how people might get to the office if the rains are harder than usual.

Even the BPO industry leader India cannot boast a perfect score in this section of the requirements, and not only because of the annual deluge. The international airports in India are atrocious. Film crews looking to shoot historic documentaries need stray no further than the arrivals lounge in almost any major airport, the décor is usually worse than the horrific flock wallpaper found in any cheap Indian restaurant.

Cost

Clearly this is a key issue for almost every major offshoring contract. Although there are many strategic reasons for offshoring, such as the ability to access new pools of talent and the abundance of the desired intellectual talent, cost reduction is almost always the primary driver for the move. In a way, this is only natural as finance is the one part of business that no executive can avoid – everyone will naturally keep on doing the same thing as yesterday if it works.

Many popular locations – Ireland and Canada for example – are not really all that cheap. They offer a slight cost advantage over their neighbours, but not really enough to justify the risk of moving a service from a nearby location. They win contracts by blending a strong performance in all the other areas listed in this section with a small cost reduction. India has long promoted itself as a cheap location that offers low cost combined with intelligent and well-trained citizens. Now other countries are stepping in and undercutting India, particularly for some of the easier functions such as transcription.

You need to consider the cost of the ongoing service in each location as well as regular travel to that location, and local expenses such as hotels and cars. To get the real picture you need to add together all the costs of doing business with the region as well as the basic salary costs of staff in that country. It is worth remembering that the full cost of paying a service provider a daily rate for a person should not be compared to local average salaries – the service provider will have significant ancillary costs – and a profit margin – to add in. It may seem obvious, but many newspaper articles talk of offshore staff costing 'one-tenth' of European employees, without bothering to explain that the figure for salaries doesn't include the cost of finding, training and retaining those people.

Cultural compatibility

For the British, working with Kiwis from New Zealand is a joy. They just understand us and laugh at our jokes. They even like to go out to the pub after work for a 'brew'. This cultural connectivity makes it nice to do business with the Kiwis, but it has a serious side too because any contracts with those companies are likely to run more smoothly due to the good communications process. Miscommunication can be generally avoided and mistakes smoothed over by understanding exactly how to deal with a problem.

Where a common culture and heritage is shared in some way then it will be easier to get along than where those connections are more limited. This is not a reason to not engage with companies from outside your personal comfort zone, but it should ensure that additional measures and controls are engaged, especially around the progress-checking procedures.

One of the authors spent some time working in India and found it initially quite difficult. When he worked in London and Paris, the team hated interference from a manager, they wanted to be steered in the right direction and then just left alone to get on with their work. In Bangalore he found that the same tactic created a group of disgruntled colleagues who felt that their manager was distant and uninterested.

China is emerging as a serious force in the global IT and services outsourcing industry. It is a nation with excellent infrastructure and a huge labour pool of educated people. Even though the government is working on an immense programme of education in English, themed around the Beijing Olympics in 2008 and the ability of China to welcome the world to its shores using English, there is a problem with cultural alignment. It can't be escaped, because national cultures prevent the world descending just yet into a homogenous mass of coffee-swilling Anglo-Saxons, but in terms of business relationships it pays to be aware of the differences and to care. At the most basic level, make sure you understand when yes really means yes and no means no.

Data/IP security

In June 2005 Indian Prime Minister Manmohan Singh urgently asked for changes in national cyber-security laws to protect the data in foreign work handled by Indian companies. The Prime Minister directed the Department of Information Technology to hasten the process of amending the Indian IT Act to ensure that any breach of secrecy and any illegal transfer of commercial or privileged information was made a punishable offence, an area where the current IT Act is sorely lacking.

The Prime Minister said: 'Indian professionals have built for themselves an enviable global reputation through hard work, dedication and commitment, and the occasional misguided acts of some individuals should not be allowed to damage the high reputation of all professionals.'[2]

This urgent review was brought about by the June 2005 case where customer data was sold by an Indian call centre employee to an undercover reporter from British newspaper *The Sun*.[3] Prime Minister Singh said at the time that the sting operation may have been directed to give Indian industry a bad name in light of its growing competitiveness – a genuine fear in India.

Infinity e-search, the company at the centre of the story, fired Karan Bahree, the call centre worker who sold the personal data, but to date no formal charges have been placed by the Indian police. NASSCOM started building a database of every single employee in the Indian BPO industry as a security measure after this episode.

While the story from India may be concerning, it is from a region that is used to handing data under strict security standards. Many regions – including China for example – have a lower regard for data security and intellectual property and identity theft is pretty common in countries such as the UK and USA too, with dangers such as card skimmers creating a need to remain alert at all times.

Quality

One of the great benefits of working with a services company through an outsourcing process is the business process reengineering that can take place. By employing an expert in a particular process, you can gain access to world-class resources and new frameworks that help to improve efficiency.

Because offshore services do have to work with distance between the client and vendor, quality frameworks have become very common. This has allowed a framework to be placed on the entire service, increasing quality in general and creating a situation where some of the offshore vendors have become leading quality advocates. Every serious vendor you speak to will be using an internationally recognized quality benchmark, such as ISO 9000, to show that their process management is second to none.

In the software development vendor community it is increasingly normal for the companies to be assessed for the Software Engineering Institute's capability maturity model (CMM). The CMM rating runs from 1 to 5, with 5 being the highest attainable quality rating. CMM Level 5 is extremely difficult to attain and demonstrates not only that the company provides exceptionally high quality software, but also that they are constantly improving the quality.

India has more companies ranked at CMM level 5 than any other. No other country comes remotely close. Many offshore vendors use this focus on quality as a sales tool by claiming that clients come to them for cost, but stay for quality.

These quality frameworks were basically forced upon the industry because offshore suppliers needed a way of making sure that they always delivered what the client expected. However, the ability to apply process quality control to services has become a differentiating factor for many service providers.

Be aware though that the quality standards have become something of a hygiene factor in environments like India, where every company seems to be certified. It's a lot harder to find a quality partner when everyone appears to have certificates pasted on every wall of the office. Think about what kind of quality you need. If your own procedures are fairly ad hoc then it will be a nightmare to work with a highly certified company – they will expect reports and standards from your team that you are not ready to commit to, and you are paying the bills!

COUNTRIES TO WATCH

We felt that an exhaustive list of countries and their specialist skills within the BPO market was not appropriate, as many authors have already included these lists in their own books on sourcing. In addition the situation is constantly changing, so the best approach is to use the guidelines already listed and to then research the regions from live sources, most likely the internet.

If you want to look at a list then the two best lists in book form (that we have seen to date) are published by Elizabeth Sparrow in her book *A Guide to Global Sourcing* and Atul Vashistha and Avinash Vashistha in their book *The Offshore Nation*.[4] *The Offshore Nation* lists the following countries as the leaders for offshore services: India, the Philippines, Russia, China, Canada and Ireland. It then lists the following as strong contenders, with up-and-coming services: the Czech Republic, Poland, Hungary, Mexico and Malaysia.

The following countries are listed as later starters who are now growing their service offering quickly: Vietnam, Singapore, Brazil, Israel and South Africa. Sparrow does not differentiate in the same way; rather she goes into detail on 18 of the most popular destinations for offshore outsourcing, providing information on leading service companies in those regions and resources for further reading.

We would add that although Poland, Hungary and the Czech Republic are clearly the service leaders in eastern Europe at present and new members of the European Union since 2004; there were another seven new member states admitted to the European Union that year: Estonia, Cyprus, Latvia, Lithuania, Malta, Slovakia and Slovenia. Romania and Bulgaria joined the union in 2007, therefore benefiting from the protective legislative framework of the EU.

Other regions worth mentioning include New Zealand, which is reinventing itself as a hi-tech research and development destination, and Ghana, which is potentially the place where the African offshoring industry will take hold and boom – after South Africa, which is focusing on the contact-centre market.

THE COMMONWEALTH FACTOR

The Commonwealth (or Commonwealth of Nations) was informally formed in 1926, with the modern Commonwealth dating from 1949. The Commonwealth is an association of independent sovereign states, almost all of which are former colonies once governed by the United Kingdom as part of the British Empire.

The Commonwealth is primarily a non-political organization in which countries with diverse economic backgrounds have an opportunity for close and equal interaction. The primary activities of the Commonwealth are designed to create an atmosphere of economic cooperation between member nations, as well as the promotion of democracy, human rights and good governance in them.

What is of interest to the manager interested in global services is that the Commonwealth region of 53 countries includes most of the key players offering English-language services. Because of the historic Commonwealth bonds these countries share common ties such as the rule of law, the English language and very similar accounting and legal structures. This makes global outsourcing far easier and creates a stronger cultural tie.

Dr Mohan Kaul – formerly Dean of possibly the most prestigious business school in India, the Indian Institute of Management, Ahmedabad – has been director general of the Commonwealth Business Council (CBC) since it was created in 1997. The CBC focuses on connecting government with the private sector and trying to encourage trade flows to the less developed of the 53 Commonwealth nations. The CBC is worth approaching for help as they can use the Commonwealth muscle to encourage wealthier countries to help those with less, within this friendly 'club' of English-speaking nations.

Historically, regional development has been associated with formal inter-state economic and strategic institutions. However, given globalization and associated novel relationships, regional development is increasingly non as well as/rather than inter-state. It is becoming more concerned with logistics and franchises rather than macroeconomic trade and investment let alone orthodox 'national' defence rather than 'human' security. Such alternative perspectives are increasingly recognized and analysed by 'new regionalisms' approaches which focus on the non-state and [in]formal.[5] This note suggests that the rather abstract and academic 'new regionalism' approach might be compatible with BPO and outsourcing which derives from a business orientation.

Such innovative conceptual analysis could then come to also recognize and embrace corporate communications which increasingly entail regional hubs and spokes, as are apparent in, say, the place of Nairobi, Lagos and/or Dakar in middle Africa. But the heartland of such continent-wide regional arrangements is Gauteng. And post-apartheid South Africa has been able to take advantage of its relative technological sophistication to advance a range of services throughout much of the continent: cell-phones

(Continued)

(Continued)

and satellite TV, financial services, hotels and air travel, fast food, supermarkets etc.[6]

The succession of Indian and other 'anglophone' diasporas are a function of the British empire or 'raj'. One unanticipated/unintended consequence of the language of British imperialism becoming the lingua franca of globalization is that Commonwealth connections facilitate contemporary economic exchange as in the days of the global Royal Navy and Cable & Wireless. Whereas other imperial languages tended to dissipate after decolonization and independence in the post-war world, English remained resilient, in part because of US dominance and in part because of 'globalization'. The Commonwealth is in many ways an inter-regional arrangement which brings together a set of primarily Anglophone regions – Australasia, Caribbean and South Pacific islands, East, Southern and West Africa, and South Asia – with a few geographic outliers like Britain and Canada.

Professor Timothy M. Shaw, Professor of Human Security and Peacebuilding, Royal Roads University, Canada, www.royalroads.ca

GLOBALIZATION

So, after analysing the various regions of the world where you could consider remote delivery, it is worth examining what is happening to create this global delivery model environment. Everyone has a favourite definition of globalization. Some think it is the work of the devil and is a process designed to rid honest hard-working folk of their jobs. Think of all those Bruce Springsteen songs like 'My Hometown' about grimy, muscled workers struggling with a changing world. Then there are all the economists and their eloquent defence of free markets, often preaching from the best-seller lists. For the purpose of this book we want to assume that globalization refers to the way in which national economies are becoming increasingly interconnected with one another.

World trade has been increasing for centuries as explorers have discovered trade routes and transport has improved. The great voyages of Christopher Columbus to the Americas in 1492 and Vasco da Gama to India in 1498 are dramatic examples of this long-running process of globalization and, as mentioned earlier, present-day commentators are still citing these events as being of immense significance. While these heroic journeys opened up new trading opportunities, however, the trade tended to be in high-value-added items that played a relatively small role in the economy. If trade is substantial, then prices for the same commodities should be similar in each location. A large price differential can only persist if traders cannot buy commodities in the cheap location (which pushes up prices) and sell them in the more expensive location (which depresses prices). Trade forces prices to converge because of the basic rule of supply and demand.

As Thomas Friedman has indicated with his 1.0, 2.0, 3.0 analogy, the first really big wave of globalization began in the early 19th century as transport costs fell. By the early 20th century, this globalization process had led to high levels of integration, reflected by economist John Maynard Keynes in his book *The Economic Consequence of the Peace*: 'What an extraordinary episode in the economic progress of man that age was which came to an end in August 1914 ... The inhabitant of London could order by telephone, sipping his morning tea in bed, the various products of the whole earth, in such quantity as he might see fit, and reasonably expect their early delivery upon his doorstep.'[7]

But the glory of regular newspaper deliveries described by Keynes came to an end as the First World War broke out and caused a subsequent increase in trade restrictions. After the Second World War, national governments coordinated to create transnational institutions such as the International Monetary Fund (IMF), the World Bank, and the General Agreement on Tariffs and Trade (GATT, the forerunner of the present World Trade Organization). The resulting decline in trade tariffs initiated a new wave of globalization that accelerated in the 1980s and 1990s as an increasing number of emerging markets adopted trade-oriented policies.

Advocates of globalization argue that it brings many benefits – from world peace through the static gains of comparative advantage to beneficial effects on long-run growth. Thomas Friedman is considered the present 'bermensch' of globalization and his 'Golden Arches' theory neatly captures his views on the benefits of global trade:

> 'Globalization won't end geopolitics. Countries will still want to go to war with each other at times. But this new system will increase the costs of such adventures. That's why I have my McDonald's theory in which I pointed out that – the current exception of Yugoslavia aside – no two countries that both have McDonald's have ever gone to war against each other since they each got their McDonald's.'[8]

While economists tend to look favourably at globalization, there is vocal criticism of the concept for a number of reasons including the loss of national sovereignty and cultural diversity, rising world inequality and poverty, the abuse of international institutions by multinational enterprises, and environmental concerns. Outsourcing is no exception. The idea that services can now be purchased from any location across the world has united many in opposition to what is seen as a destroyer of employment in the west.

The driving forces behind the first age of globalization were the dramatic declines in transportation costs. The driving force behind the second wave of globalization has been falling trade tariffs as the global economy becomes more interconnected. In recent decades, world trade has increased faster than world gross domestic product (GDP), with the majority of this trade in manufactured goods. Global sourcing in manufactured goods is already a mature market and is very familiar to anyone who has ever bought almost any manufactured product – 'made in China' is a ubiquitous stamp on the bottom of most products these days. Products are no longer manufactured and sold in the same small village. We can buy Nokia phones, Ford vehicles, Pink shirts or toys consisting of thousands of components from across the world. Last century, most manufacturers tended to do 'everything' in-house. The automotive industry is a classic example, with the example of Henry Ford building or owning everything he needed to produce a car being a business-school favourite.

GLOBAL SOURCING IN SERVICES

Not so long ago, a student of economics would have learned that goods can be traded across borders, whilst services need to be produced and con-sumed at the same location. Those same students might have been con-fused by the concept of services that can be outsourced to a remote location; to quote the Nobel Laureate Paul Samuelson: 'You cannot export a hair cut'.[9]

Well, here we are now in this new era of globalization and remote serv-ices. This is an era in which many services can be disaggregated and deliv-ered from low-cost locations. This is a world in which the 24-hour-a-day, 7-day-a-week, 365-day-a-year global supply chain is already a reality for many service companies. The concept of global real-time collaboration is changing the way we live. This change has evolved over several decades, from the manufacturing sourcing of the 1980s to the IT services sourcing of the 1990s to the new wave of BPO, offering new opportunities for global services.

The offshore outsourcing of business and IT processes was really kicked off by companies such as American Express and General Electric (GE) using their own captive centres in low-cost regions in the 1980s. Former GE Chief Executive Jack Welch used a simple (and powerful) message to describe his views on offshore outsourcing – 70:70:70. Using this formula Mr Welch indi-cated that he would like GE to outsource at least 70 per cent of business processes, with 70 per cent of those processes going offshore and 70 per cent of that offshoring going to India. This is a good example of the early approach to services offshoring taken by large organizations such as GE.

Service providers soon launched their own offshore service offering, learning from the experience of the multinationals with offshore facilities. A boost came during the 1990s when IT departments across the world feared a system meltdown as legacy systems faced the fabled millennium bug. As any reader of this book should be aware, especially if you were paying attention back at the start, the millennium bug was the problem of software written during the 20th century with date processing limited to two bytes of information for the year, such as using '97' to represent 1997. The problem was that no one knew how many legacy systems would be affected once the year rolled over to 2000. Companies that would not normally have considered offshore IT outsourcing had to work with some of these vendors because they were offering great prices, they had the highly skilled labour, and the deadline for checking the systems could not be moved – unless a new calendar was going to be drawn up before 2000. As far as the offshore technology suppliers were concerned, the millennium bug was 'the goose that laid the golden egg'.

The multinational companies that did not have a deep understanding of local culture in these remote low-cost locations created partnerships with some of the more mature local vendors, often with an option to buy back shares in the joint venture after a few years. A good example is the creation of an Offshore Development Centre (ODC) by Dun & Bradstreet, who formed a partnership with the Indian technology services provider Satyam Software. The new entity was formed in 1994 as Dun & Bradstreet Satyam Software, with a technology centre in Chennai, the city in southern India formerly known as Madras. Dun & Bradstreet retained an option to buy back the shares, which they eventually exercised, creating one of the first build-operate-transfer (BOT) examples in the industry. This organization, which began life as a captive technology centre, was eventually sold off in 1998 as a separate entity and listed on the NASDAQ (National Association of Securities Dealers Automated Quotations) market as Cognizant Technology Solutions.

THE EMERGING GLOBAL DELIVERY MODEL

In March 2000 the dreams of millions of 'dot com' entrepreneurs were shattered as the rug was sharply pulled from under their feet. One side effect of the dot com crash was that the world was left with a legacy of immense excess capacity in global telecommunications infrastructure, because the telecoms companies had been installing as much bandwidth as they possibly could in the belief that the good times would last forever. This oversupply meant that the cost of communications became rapidly cheaper and these decreasing infrastructure costs made the option of executing processes in an offshore location a far more viable option.

The international software and services industry has never been slow to adopt new possibilities, so the present focus by most of the major companies on creating a genuine GDM comes as no surprise. This trend focuses more on solutions rather than specific capabilities and helps the companies to differentiate themselves and stay ahead in an increasingly competitive marketplace. The essence of the GDM approach is to deliver work from where it can be done with the best combination of quality resources and the lowest price, with an acceptable level of risk. The attraction of a GDM can be summarized as resource, rupees and risk.

THE GDM ROLLS INTO TOWN

While global players such as IBM, EDS and Accenture have already adopted a coordinated approach to global resource and delivery it is interesting to note that the major Indian service companies, such as TCS, Infosys and Wipro, are all keen to present themselves as global operators – i.e. less Indian and more international. In fact a neat little acronym for remembering the major Indian players (though not in order of revenue or size) is SWITCH:

S	Satyam
W	Wipro
I	Infosys
T	TCS
C	Cognizant
H	HCL Technologies

Information technology firms are rationalizing future corporate strategies in order to align themselves to this new method of solutions delivery. The global outsourcing giants have built a strong offshore presence, either through acquisition or organically. So a strange dynamic has been created where the major offshore suppliers are all rushing to create delivery capabilities closer to their customers at the same time as the local service companies are rushing to set up offshore delivery centres. For example, Accenture is hiring thousands of new employees in India as they increase the amount of work they attempt to deliver from offshore, while TCS and Infosys are hiring in Europe and the USA at a phenomenal rate – and paying local salaries.

HCL Technologies is now one of the largest foreign employers of British people, mainly thanks to their BPO facilities in Belfast that allow them to offer service delivery from Europe or Asia – depending on what the client wants from their supplier. In 2006 the Indian back-office service company Firstsource (formerly known as ICICI OneSource) opened a new contact centre in Northern Ireland that immediately created over 1,000 jobs in the UK.[10] It would seem that the Indians are now exporting their skills back to Europe.

This an important point to make. The expertise is flowing in both directions, removing the formal 'onshore' (here at home) and 'offshore' (far away in a lower-cost environment) distinctions. The traditional off-shore players are creating onshore delivery capability and also buying or working with local consulting resource. It cannot be long before companies from supposedly remote destinations engineer reverse takeovers, buying their way up the value chain from back-office services to offering front-line services to consumers in the west. And as this change takes place, all the traditional consulting and service companies are racing to open offshore delivery centres, in a desperate rush to reduce their cost base. This multilateral flow of business activity has helped to create what we call the global delivery model, creating centres of knowledge excellence around the globe.

The GDM is the natural evolution of the onsite-offshore model. The GDM advocates that pieces of work should be broken into their logical components and distributed to the appropriate location, performing the work where maximum value is created – rather than just focusing on the lowest-cost environment. In this next-generation sourcing model, an organization having benefited from cost arbitrage will focus on creating value. The GDM builds on the fundamental concept of modularization and applies this concept to business processes. This model helps organizations to think about the sourcing of services in a systemic and enterprise-wide way, and it helps in creating a strategic alignment of the business, operations and IT.

THE GDM EVOLUTION

The GDM allows organizations to be more adaptive to the ever-increasing pace of change that surrounds them. It could be considered a paradigm shift in global sourcing, as the entire model is changed from a focus on cost reduction to one of value creation. It defines a set of frameworks and real steps that business and IT decision makers can utilize to put the concepts into practice, and to therefore realize operational efficiencies and business innovation. The GDM model creates value in a number of ways, including:

- Companies in high-cost locations such as the USA and Europe are increasing their access to lower-cost operations and high-quality process-based labour.
- Service providers in lower-cost environments are using the GDM model to allow an increased focus on customer relationships, to take their service more upmarket, and to build industry expertise.

It is our opinion that only the largest global corporations will rely on a captive centre as a method of accessing a global labour pool; most enterprises will create a GDM through outsourcing because it allows the client to tap into the skills of a service provider.

In the GDM framework, companies use a globally dispersed team that works in unison, regardless of time difference or geographic distance. The global team needs to be well coordinated through excellent communication and well-defined guidelines for the delivery process. There are a number of key characteristics to a GDM beyond just being multinational, including the following:

- The model has more than just an onsite and offshore component. The work is distributed globally where it is performed at the best combination of quality and cost.
- The component that is closest to the customer consists of those activities that require end-user interaction, proximity to the market, quick turnaround time or testing infrastructure, and therefore have to be executed at the customer site or can be delivered more efficiently from that location.
- The activities done at the lower-cost location are those that do not require constant end-user interaction and can therefore be easily executed at a remote location.
- The distribution of activities between these multiple locations is engagement-specific. Some activities are done in tandem, with teams from both locations providing complementary skills.
- Activity distribution is also based on factors such as availability of skill sets, the level of control required by the customer, the amount of risk mitigation required and cost implications (the ability to locate some services or production in lower-cost environments).

BIGGEST BPO DEAL IN THE UK LIFE ASSURANCE MARKET: DILIGENTA SEALS £486M DEAL WITH PEARL GROUP

Tata Consultancy Services (TCS) subsidiary Diligenta today announces that it has entered the UK Business Process Outsourcing (BPO) Life Assurance market having secured a £486 million deal with Pearl, the Peterborough based closed fund group. Diligenta will provide BPO services over an initial 12 year period for Pearl Group Ltd in processing and administration.

Diligenta is a UK based, FSA regulated subsidiary of TCS, the world-leading information technology consulting, services, and business process outsourcing organization. It will offer similar services to other life companies, presenting it with an opportunity for significant future growth as BPO becomes increasingly prevalent in the UK Life Assurance industry.

David Power, Diligenta's CEO commented, 'We are delighted Pearl has chosen Diligenta. Diligenta is in a great position as it combines an in-depth knowledge of UK Life Assurance with the proven IT and delivery capability of one of the world's top IT service, consulting and BPO firms, TCS.'

(Continued)

(Continued)

Over the course of the 12 year deal, Diligenta will leverage TCS's IT expertise and consolidate 11 financial and administrative systems onto a single platform.

Jonathan Moss, Managing Director Life Services in Pearl Group, said, 'This is a start of a new chapter in Pearl's history and is good news all around for customers, shareholders and staff. The new arrangements provide certainty over a major portion of the cost base well into the future. This is very important protection for policyholders because over the long term the unit cost per policy will be maintained at competitive levels.'

Moss added: 'We went through a rigorous process to select Diligenta and are delighted that they will build a UK Centre of Excellence in Peterborough. The transfer process has been smooth and we look forward to working together.'

'Given the groundbreaking deal with Pearl, TCS is now a serious player in the insurance BPO space,' said Catherine Schmitt, senior analyst at research firm Celent. 'The launch of Diligenta highlights TCS's ability to deliver core back office services to the industry using local skill sets, which is key for the European markets. Diligenta places TCS firmly on the list of BPO providers to be considered for large complex insurance BPO deals.'

'TCS has created the Diligenta centre of excellence around the Pearl Group operation in Peterborough,' said Anders Maehre, Datamonitor. 'This initial deal sees TCS enter the UK Life Assurance BPO market with the single biggest outsourcing contract of its kind. Diligenta's business proposition of predominantly onshore operational capability combined with TCS' global transformational expertise aims to attract further open and closed book business.'

With circa one thousand staff, the Peterborough office will be a centre of excellence providing the foundation for the company's development and expansion.

David Power concluded, 'Winning the Pearl deal immediately gives Diligenta a major market share in the UK. Our aim is to grow the business and expand in this developing UK market to become the market leader within 3 years.'

TCS Press Release[11]

UNDERSTANDING THE GDM ADVANTAGE

Many service organizations are now adopting the concept of the GDM, and this demonstrates how companies are working within a challenging global business environment by adopting their approach. Table 8.1 describes how the GDM approach affects a number of business drivers.

TABLE 8.1   *How the GDM approach affects business drivers*

Business driver	Impact of GDM
Total cost of ownership reduction	The GDM creates an environment where client firms do not need to invest in a large delivery team. The GDM can be fine-tuned to suit emerging needs, allowing a delivery team to be scaled up or down, as required.
High quality and predictability	The GDM offers a variable cost for resource, depending on their location, allowing a solution to achieve the best combination of value and quality.
Reduced risk	The GDM creates an entirely networked environment with high and efficient recoverability. Services are delivered from multiple locations allowing one location to provide redundancy for others.
Time to market	The GDM utilizes multiple time zones to increase the length of the working day. Projects can be subdivided and worked on simultaneously in several regions.
Quality	Most suppliers now use internationally recognized process quality standards.

Cost arbitrage is just about at the bottom of the list when analysing the benefits of a GDM. Cost reduction is a primary driver in the onsite–offshore model of outsourcing, but the GDM is focused on doing things right, not at the lowest possible cost. A good example of this is the way Tata Consultancy Services (TCS), the largest Indian technology supplier, presents their own GDM to the market.

TCS aims to service customers using an optimum combination of onsite and remote delivery options. They call this the global network delivery model, a slight variation on the standard GDM nomenclature. With global delivery centres in the USA, Canada, Brazil, Uruguay, South Africa, the UK, China, Hungary, Australia and Japan, as well as India, TCS can genuinely claim to be able to deliver from many locations.

It is interesting to list the benefits for customers claimed by TCS in their own literature on their network delivery model:[12]

- **Optimum value:** customers benefit from unparalleled economies of scale and scope, lower costs, faster time to market and an innovative range of services and solutions.
- **Lower risk:** TCS's integrated project and quality management frameworks enable a reduction in errors and ensure operational and data security, leading to higher levels of productivity and

predictability. TCS sets the benchmark in quality standards, for example as the first company to be assessed enterprise-wide to CMM level 5.

- **Technological capabilities:** through a seamlessly integrated pool of high calibre, cross-functional local and global staff with technical skill sets, TCS can provide best in class services to multi-country operations of global companies, while ensuring the same high level of service delivery throughout. Substantial research and development (R&D) investments help us enhance and differentiate our services and strengthen delivery capabilities.

- **Domain experience:** while the value of IT as an efficiency-enhancing business tool remains constant, its application requires a thorough understanding of specific industries and business processes. TCS has deep intellectual assets and a proven track record in industries from banking through to retail and healthcare.

- **Scalability:** TCS has the ability and resource to deliver the capacity required, and the flexibility to scale up or scale down according to your project needs.

The benefits claimed do appear to be similar to those documented for any standard global delivery model. TCS is an Indian organization that has accepted that an offshore delivery centre in India may not always provide the best possible service to their clients if local support is based on sales and customer relationship management alone. Service often needs to be delivered far closer to the customer for particular reasons such as language or culture, but truly global delivery is not just about the haphazard scattering of delivery centres throughout multiple continents. So what is the difference between a GDM and a GNDM (global network delivery model)?

This is an interesting structure. TCS has created a four-layer network of delivery that allows them to achieve economies of scale, with low-cost, high-volume centres working in harmony with small-scale highly specialized research labs. Each of the four layers is connected to all of the other layers, creating a spider's web of delivery capability.

The TCS GNDM structure places India and China at the core of what they do. The global delivery centres in these two locations are very high scale with many tens of thousands of TCS people located there. All customers from any location can be serviced from the global delivery centres and the two centres have the key strengths of very deep process maturity and immense business domain knowledge. India has a reputation for process delivery at a large scale and TCS is now transferring their expertise to China to ensure a strong dual-sourcing capability (India/China) at the heart of the TCS GNDM.

The next part of the model is the regional delivery centres. These are 'centres of delivery excellence' established in countries such as Hungary,

Brazil and Uruguay. These are medium-scale delivery centres that are focused on specific skill sets and regional customers. These centres offer large-scale delivery for customers who need a strong language or cultural affinity with the delivery centre.

At the next level are the local delivery centres. These are smaller delivery centres located in the same country as the customer and offer a strong sense of customer comfort because of the local nature of delivery. TCS has local delivery centres functioning in many customer locations, including New Jersey and Arizona in the USA, Guildford in the UK, and Yokohama in Japan.

The final level is the TCS solution centres. These are small labs that focus on best practice and knowledge management for very specific topics. They may be small units, but they are globally leveraged because of the support structure of the entire GNDM. TCS has a media and entertainment centre in the heart of Hollywood, an automotive team in Detroit, an RFID team in Chicago, an engineering team in Minnesota, and a retail team in Chennai. These small solution centres are entirely focused on ensuring that TCS can lead research and development practice in these fields.

The GNDM is a strategic framework for global delivery and goes far beyond a simple onshore–offshore mix. Although the approach described above is specific to TCS, every service company is developing their own version. TCS's model is interesting, however. They can offer a client the best price by delivering the majority of a service from the core, but partner this with some local work where customer interaction is more critical, along with advice on new industry trends and best practice from the solution centres. It is a model that appears to work well and seems to offer an optimal mixture of industry thought-leadership and an economy of scale.

In all the excitement to promote these various models of global delivery, it should be noted that many CIOs have yet to see an example of seamless delivery 'at the coalface'. The model looks great, but the complexity can cause immense headaches.

India-based Firstsource is making its first entry into Europe with the opening of two new centres in Northern Ireland. The company has received backing from Invest Northern Ireland and is itself investing several million pounds in new bespoke outsourced service centres in Belfast and Londonderry. The Firstsource venture will create 1,000 new jobs in Northern Ireland over the next two years.

Northern Ireland has a developing contact centre industry, as several companies have already set up centres in the region. Satisfaction levels amongst companies setting up in Belfast tend to

(Continued)

(Continued)

be high. A recent report from OMIS Research showed that Belfast is one of the best places in the British Isles to run a call centre, with an excellent infrastructure and a well-educated labour force and competitive costs. The move is part of Firstsource's strategy to extend its global reach and offer a wider choice of outsourcing facilities to its clients. Some clients have made the strategic decision to outsource some of their business processes, but want the option of outsourcing in the UK rather than the overseas route.

The Indian outsourcing sector has in recent years moved beyond the cost-saving model and has developed well established processes and procedures for quality and process improvement, based on COPC and six sigma. Firstsource aims to bring its quality and process improvement procedures to the UK and is working in partnership with its clients to set up a 'best practice' operation.

Clients have seen how the company has implemented best practice in terms of six sigma and process optimization and wanted to bring this specialist expertise into the UK. As part of the quality practices, Firstsource will be training its new agents in the six sigma stages to ensure consistency with the processes implemented in India.

Firstsource's centres will initially provide inbound customer service and technical support for a number of clients in the telecommunications sector and going forward, will provide additional processes for other industries, in particular financial services.

Ananda Mukerji, Chief Executive Officer, Firstsource, www.firstsource.in

CONCLUSION

The concept of global delivery being an essential component of service delivery will continue to grow in importance. As predicted by industry bodies such as the National Outsourcing Association,[13] this really does create a global level playing field for services. India is leading the field in chasing the existing pack of global service companies because India has already established itself as a credible player in the global IT field. The question now is whether the major Indian companies such as TCS, Wipro and Infosys can grow large enough to worry the major international firms on their home territory.

There is some evidence that this is taking place. The creation of Diligenta by the Pearl Group in partnership with TCS showed that by working in partnership with an Indian IT firm a new industry model could be created. TCS has been able to demonstrate to the financial services community that they were the partners of choice, above and beyond any of the existing players in Europe. Other cases have been documented, such as the large Dixons technology maintenance contract awarded to HCL early in 2006. This £150 million deal went to HCL after LogicaCMG had been seriously considered for the contract.[14] At the time, a research analyst from Ovum claimed that the 'comfort-blanket' had just been snatched away, implying that the Indian firms were now ready to compete with the majors.

And why shouldn't they be? The IT and IT-enabled services market could do with a shake-up anyway. There is no reason why it should be dominated by a handful of US and European-based companies when these are the services that can be most easily delivered from any location. If the Indian majors can already match their rivals for quality of service then it won't be long before they can match them in size. TCS posted revenues of approximately US$3 billion in 2006, yet they have a very public target to achieve US$10 billion by 2010. Depending on when you read this book you can place that claim in context: either it is a phenomenal target that they will do well to achieve without purchasing a rival, or it may have already happened and the Indian juggernauts will be rolling into the sunset as Accenture and other rivals continue to work out how to reduce cost further.

Credible services groups with good revenues are springing up all over the world now, taking lessons from India. Companies in countries such as Brazil, Russia and China are trying to develop their own brands. Luxoft from Russia has a PR agency in London helping to develop awareness of the brand in the UK. If the Indian companies are starting to threaten the global players then the others are just a few years behind the Indians and have the advantage of a well-developed road map.

In the long term, companies such as IBM, Accenture or EDS will have to become more like TCS, Infosys or Wipro. They might continue to win business because of strong brand awareness and trust in that association (remember the old adage about never being fired for buying from IBM?), but eventually the awareness of others will grow. IBM cannot just invest in building a back office in India by purchasing Indian companies without someone asking why they don't just hire one of the Indian companies instead. In addition, the Indian companies that are taking the GDM seriously are hiring local faces at local prices, not shipping young MBAs into London or New York and hoping they might be able to compete with an experienced Accenture partner. Wipro CEO Azim Premji claims: 'Within three years you won't be able to tell the difference between a Wipro, Infosys, IBM or Accenture. We are copying their business model and they are copying ours.'[15] Your next invitation to watch the cricket at Lord's or to chat with Tom Friedman over breakfast is as likely to come from Infosys as it is from IBM.

There is one final point to make on the growth of the global delivery model. If you just graduated from university and you are looking for an exciting job where the opportunities for promotion are endless, bonuses are frequent, business travel allows you to see the world, and the next month is always different to the last then forget about the traditional companies that come to campus and recruit. Go and talk to the Indians, the Russians, the Chinese and the Brazilians. These are the world-class companies of the future and their growth is so fast you might even need to wear a seat belt at your desk. Why join a sinking ship just because your dad has heard of the company?

Over the last two decades, manufacturing around the globe has gone through a significant transformation. Low labour cost countries quickly gained a large market share, but, over time, we saw the emergence of other countries that became global leaders in manufacturing of the more complex and intellectual property related goods. While Japan and other places dominated early, Taiwan and China have become leaders in higher-value manufacturing, enabling smart manufacturing companies to pass the cost savings on to the customer. The global economy is full of better products that cost less as a direct result of the changes that occurred in how we manufacture and distribute goods.

These benefits seen in the manufacturing industry did not go unnoticed. The outsourcing of services began with GE and Xerox in the late 1980s and has continued to evolve and transform our global economy. Over the last decade, successful companies like American Express and Citicorp sought distant shores to build a strategic advantage through lower costs and higher service levels for IT and other back office processes. The resulting growth opportunities of the industry have led to the development of countries, locations and suppliers with critical mass and expertise. This move in services is now no longer about offshoring but is now about 'services globalization'. Leading firms are leveraging services globalization to grow their business, improve operations and reduce risks. This new model is seeing the complexity of processes moving offshore evolving from data entry to complex analysis, ITO and BPO converging and a significant increase in the scale of activities both in captive and third party centres. A leading manufacturing firm in the USA leverages its Philippines operations for customer service, Russia for industrial design, India for IT services, China for manufacturing and manages it all through its global program office in the USA. This is the new model for services. Go globalize!

Atul Vashistha, Chief Executive Officer, NeoIT, co-author of *The Offshore Nation*,[16] www.neoit.com

9 Conclusion

This book has taken quite a journey to reach you in its present form. The original intention was to examine the development of business process outsourcing (BPO) and its inexorable growth. Yet if there is a single theme running through the headlines about IT outsourcing, offshoring, BPO, immigration and globalization it is the sea change of delivery and expectations related to global services. Services run through all these issues from top to bottom, underpinning the entire concept of outsourcing and running through business like the words embedded within a stick of Brighton rock.

When Thomas Friedman sat down at his word processor and started creating the first draft of *The World is Flat*[1] he cannot have anticipated the stir it would create in the companies that utilize global services. That his book sold millions of copies is testament to the fact that most business services already include some international dimension, apart from the most obviously local ones. Think about business services such as information technology, back-office processing, human resources, logistics, public relations, research ... the list could go on, but more and more of these services involve the world outside your head office.

The world became used to globalization in manufacturing a long time ago. Container ships and airfreight shift products all across the world everyday, from factory to customer in a complex dance of logistics that spans the world. When you open the box on that beautiful new Apple computer the first words emblazoned on the wrapping paper are 'Designed by Apple in California', yet hidden away on the bottom of the box is the innocuous statement 'Assembled in China'. Apple can't hope to compete with other technology equipment manufacturers with a production line in the developed west.

Yet the Apple product is highly differentiated. It is a niche product, as most people still buy a PC that operates using Microsoft Windows – Apple purchasers are often from the creative industries or are PC-converts because of a positive experience with the iPod. Most corporate environments still function on the PC platform. So perhaps the Apple could be assembled locally? So why is Dell now opening a new production line in Tamil Nadu, a region in south India? After all, Dell has a reputation for 'writing the book' on production-line efficiency.

The answer is that a product would need to be manufactured on an extremely small scale for it to not be worth considering an offshore manufacturing plant. Countries such as India and China have abundant skilled labour and experience. The quality is as good as anywhere in the world and the price is lower than in highly developed regions. It doesn't make commercial sense to manufacture products at any scale without considering the offshore option.

This book has focused on the various issues surrounding the globalization of services and it is worth a final review of our message, because in this era of sound bites who has the time to scan through an entire book any more?

MILLENNIUM

The turn of the century changed the game for global services enabled using information technology. The immovable deadline and the immense task of checking every single computer system throughout the world to ensure that they could cope with the 'millennium bug' created an enormous opportunity for the offshore service providers – particularly in India. If it was not for the millennium bug then the Indian providers would not have been trusted so completely and so quickly – as it happened most companies just had to get their systems checked by the most credible provider around, and in stepped Infosys, TCS and Wipro. All had a good industry reputation and international revenues pre-millennium, but these companies saw explosive growth after 2000 thanks to them proving that offshoring really can work.

BUSINESS SERVICES

The internet is a natural delivery platform for consumer products and business services, so the edge between what is a personal service for a consumer and what is a business service is starting to blur.

Business services are business-to-business (B2B) services characterized by a significant professional content and generally enabled using IT. This IT area is a part of the white-collar sector of the general B2B services marketplace, distinguished from blue-collar B2B services such as catering, cleaning, building maintenance and security.

Sub-sectors such as IT services and IT-enabled services are the home for IT professionals as well as those who use IT to earn a living, but cannot be classed as IT experts. It is important to emphasize the reality that many services are as much as about applied IT as the services categorized under the IT-computer services rubric – which in turn are also characterized as professionally rich, technology-enabled services – with the emphasis of the professionalism perhaps more in the exploitation of the technology per se rather than its particular end application.

Such is the importance of the City to the UK economy that the statistics for financial services, which can in parallel also be characterized as professionally rich, technology-enabled services, are categorized and reported separately. The City, in its broadest sense (from banking to insurance, and incorporating its close links to other major UK geographical clusters of financial and insurance services such as Edinburgh and Leeds) delivers both B2B and B2C (business to consumer) technology-enabled services.

We can't emphasize enough the idea that many people are engaged in services using technology, but are not necessarily classed as working as within the IT industry. The importance of this point is clear when you consider the amount of services a country such as the UK or USA will export to others – once these professional services are included in the comparison. Let's just quickly review the 'business services' numbers provided by Professor Mari Sako of Oxford University again:[2]

- the sector employs 4 million people – one in seven jobs in the UK;
- it has generated 50 per cent of UK job growth over two decades;
- it provides a strong trade surplus (~£18 billion) – even as offshoring fuelled a fast growth in imports to ~£14 billion in 2004, exports grew even more rapidly to ~£32 billion;
- it is in trade surplus across all sub-sectors, both in IT-computer services and IT-enabled business services;
- it has rising sector productivity, broadly matching that of the US (the other major net exporter of business services amongst the OECD economies).

WEB 2.0

Though the nomenclature may be cringe inducing, Web 2.0 is more than marketing hype. The really important feature of this Web 2.0 revolution is that the service offerings are increasingly two-way in the fullest sense, with users contributing actively, rather than just consuming a service. Availability of services on the web enables full customer interaction with them – as with airline booking systems where search, enquiry and options development and evaluation are now the norm before the actual booking is made. The capabilities of the web allow remote management and servicing of equipment, including upgrading software, adding new software, troubleshooting, maintenance and backup.

The twin capabilities of interactivity with consumers and companies through Web 2.0 and high broadband availability fuel some interesting challenges:

- the internet is strengthened and becomes an essential public infrastructure through which web-enabled services can be delivered and accessed with increasing ease – globally;
- the power of contemporary software to capture human-based (intangible) Intellectual Property and commoditize it into a whole

range of services whose economics of production and delivery are highly competitive – where the delivery mechanism earlier made this impossible.

KNOWLEDGE PROCESS OUTSOURCING

Knowledge process outsourcing (KPO) is merely a continuation of business process outsourcing (BPO), though with rather more business complexity. The defining difference is that KPO is usually focused on knowledge-intensive business processes that require significant domain expertise. The offshore team servicing a KPO contract cannot be easily hired overnight as they will be highly educated and trained and trusted to take decisions on the behalf of the client

KPO delivers higher value to organizations that offshore their domain-based processes, thereby enhancing the traditional cost–quality paradigm of BPO. The central theme of KPO is to create value for the client by providing business expertise rather than process expertise. So KPO involves a shift from standardized processes to advanced analytical thinking, technical skills and decisive judgement based on experience.

The importance of KPO emerging as a known acronym and a standard and accepted strategy tool is the constant redefinition of the retained organization. If decisions can be outsourced and intelligent work requiring highly educated teams can be outsourced then where do the barriers between internal and external functions now lie?

CHANGING CORPORATE STRUCTURE

So how should a company structure itself if every service can be outsourced? This is a question that almost every organization now needs to ask. Companies are considering new models that move beyond the historic command and control from head office:

- **The team structure:** using product or service teams allows companies to break down the walls between departments, stimulating a fluidity of ideas and creativity by ensuring that staff with various skills can work together. Self-managed teams calling on the resources available within a bureaucratic structure are becoming relatively common.
- **Virtual organizations:** this is where the use of outsourcing can often come into play. The virtual organization can be best described by considering how a Hollywood movie is produced. A company is formed and every 'team' member is contracted to the company for a limited period of time while the movie is being produced, only to be let go once filming is complete. At that point other professionals, perhaps with marketing expertise, are needed

to sell the movie, but the actors, lighting and sound teams will have moved on to the next movie. The company ramps up and down as required and is extremely flexible, never wasting resources. The company structure is therefore entirely virtual and is reorganized as and when it is required.

- **Boundaryless organization:** Jack Welch, the former Chairman and Chief Executive of General Electric created the term 'boundaryless organization'. He was describing a vision where the department silos and team functions were entirely blended, with no borders. Status and rank are minimal within such an organization, as there is no chain of command. Employees need to be appraised by the range of fellow staff and management (including those more senior and those more junior) – the '360-degree approach'. Uniformity of privilege is also encouraged – so no corner office for line managers then.

Clearly these changes are painful. Jack Welch may have commented endlessly on the ideal way to run a company, and he is fondly remembered at GE, but humans are human – you try creating a genuine boundaryless organization without bruising egos.

SERVICE PRICING

Think about the traditional idea of cost-plus pricing, the most basic model for pricing products or services and where a lot of service sourcing remains at present. This model takes into account the cost of servicing the client and adds a margin on top, allowing the service provider to generate a profit. Quite often the profit might be a percentage of the cost, so the supplier may always try to charge a rate to customers that is cost plus 10 per cent – giving a 10 per cent profit on all income.

This model has naturally suited the offshore outsourcing market because it has been largely dominated by price and margins. Where competition for a particular service is very price-sensitive then it is likely that suppliers will cut their costs to the bone and then make a slim margin through a cost-plus strategy. This naturally works best for high-volume services, making a slim 1 per cent margin on revenues of several million pounds can support a service company. Making 1 per cent on small and sporadic contracts will rapidly lead to bankruptcy.

The service companies offering global services are making genuine efforts to present themselves as partners, not low-cost offshore labour. One of the key ways in which the claim can be presented as genuine is in the flexibility of the service company to price a service in a way that helps both parties – such as a project being delivered free, but the service company sharing in the benefit of that project.

THE 'VIRTUALIZATION' OF TECHNOLOGY

In our view technology itself is becoming less 'hard', visible, and inflexible and more virtual – allowing extreme flexibility that only encourages wider use and therefore more potential for global service delivery through the internet. We believe that the virtualization of information technology can be divided into four areas.

The first is basically the conversion of the computing engine from a rigid to highly flexible resource, making it much more able to respond to a rapidly changing environment while still operating at high levels of asset productivity. The computing engine has grown since its initial invention in a design framework of tightly coupled processes. Virtualization enables a new design paradigm of loosely coupled processes – the loose coupling allowing the flexibilities required to deliver both agility and asset productivity. The archetype of 'the server in the broom cupboard', tightly tailored to the delivery of a few specific local applications, has changed into a new archetype – a computing resource responding to a changing flow of requirements over time, fast and flexibly, an asset that is always being worked hard.

The second impact of the new diversity of specialized software systems has been to enable a similar virtualization of the design and structuring of the applications systems and the complex number of business processes that they underwrite in the operation of the contemporary corporation. This emergent software capability, known as business process management (BPM), is a framework of specialized software systems that enable business processes to be both monitored and managed – automatically or by manual intervention, as best required.

The third impact of the new diversity of specialized software systems has been to enable the virtualization of the architecting of the diversity of components that are assembled to create the contemporary IT infrastructure – processing power, data storage and network bandwidth. This emergent structure of industry standards is called service-oriented architecture (SOA) – sometimes 'systems' is used in place of 'service', but the acronym remains the same. It is in essence an application architecture, in which all functions are defined using a descriptive language, with interfaces that can be invoked, or activated, to create interconnecting applications delivering business processes. Each interaction (interface) between the functions is designed to be independent of each and every other interaction – and the interconnecting protocols for communicating devices are specified to be interface-independent and the interfaces themselves are platform-independent.

The fourth impact of the new diversity of specialized software systems, combined with innovative and powerful new hardware, has been to enable the virtualization of data communication across a wide diversity of frequency spectra, whether across cabled (from copper to fibre optics) or wireless networks. The spectrum being tackled is already very wide – from 'wired' delivery of 0.01–0.1 megabytes per second (Mbps) associated with the fixed telephone and the CD, through the 10 Mbps of Ethernet servicing the office environment, to the 100 Mbps of Fast Ethernet – and the parallel 'wireless' delivery ranging from the 1–10 Mbps of personal services provided locally by Bluetooth 1.2 and 2.0, to the developing wide broadcast spectra of mobile telephony standards of sub-0.1 Mbps of 2G to the greater than 1.0 Mbps of 3G – with WiFi capabilities essentially mimicking Ethernet capacities over both local area and metropolitan-sized footprints.

Entire US cities are wireless-enabled already. The Canary Wharf area of London is entirely enabled. The city of Norwich is completely enabled by the local authority, as a service to tax payers. Always-on internet in any location will change the devices used and the services provided.

The speed of innovation and development here is shaped by a complex mix of hardware development, software development and the development of agreed industry standards and protocols and, in the wireless world, regulatory regimes around the exploitation of the radio-frequency spectrum. Exploitation of internet data transmission protocols and new software structures has brought to market the 'over IP' capabilities being exploited by recent business start-ups such as Skype and Vonage (voice over IP, or VOIP, services). These exploit the operational reality that digitization of voice as data packages to be switched and transmitted over the internet (loose coupling) is so much more efficient over the fixed telecoms network than classic open-line analogue telephony that it can competitively undercut established services by major margins. The telecommunication companies are responding with major programmes of reinvestment in new-generation digital networks based on the exploitation of virtualization to allow very much higher productivity operations.

The economics of virtualization directionally move charging models towards a 'fixed charge and always on' and away from 'charge per unit time used' paradigms.

These four virtualizations lie at the root of the flipping, or inversion, from the restraints of technology-specified application scope to the freedoms of application-specified technology scope. The combination of BPM with SOA brings us into a world where business requirements can define and shape the underlying IT infrastructure to respond and align to its needs – liberating responsiveness and agility that the pre-flip/inversion realities denied. Think about how hard it used to be to change software – even with in-house programmers. The communications revolution liberates the individual to operate to best advantage in both time and space. The shift from the paradigm of the tightly coupled to the loosely coupled not only enables this greater flexibility, agility and responsiveness, but also provides the means of working assets harder and to higher levels of effectiveness and efficiency.

The four virtualizations have helped set the scene for the emergence and rapid development of business services made available over the web – labelled in two broad, overlapping categories as software as a service (SaaS), and as web services.

The web has matured as a robust public utility. The consumer imperative has been the prime driver. The prime enablers have included the development of increasingly reliable server farms and data centres whose costs of operation have plummeted (reflecting the first of the four virtualizations at work), and increasingly reliable network capabilities, capacities and asset productivity (the IP impact) that have sharply driven down bandwidth costs. The costs of providing managed data storage are also sharply down.

There are no longer any limits. If you can think of a service that can be done better because of the global scale of the online environment or has not even been delivered before then form your company – now!

THE REAL MATRIX

The consumerization of the internet as an outlet for global services and products that have become accepted as equal in quality to offline services is a seminal moment in modern society. Think about the kids who are at university today, probably born in the late 1980s. This generation of graduates are entering work without any knowledge of what life was like before everyone had a phone and all of human knowledge was easily available on the internet.

The music industry and Hollywood are rapidly embracing the online world as it offers a platform for their products to be easily delivered to a global audience, without any of the distribution issues of physical CDs or DVDs – though piracy is just as easy as legitimate distribution. Lily Allen became a summer sensation in the UK in 2006 thanks to her myspace page and cheeky songs about life in London. The Arctic Monkeys made it big not just because of a great myspace page, but because they are good. The *New Musical Express* elected their first album into their top ten British albums of all time, elevated to rub shoulders with The Beatles, Oasis, Blur, Pulp, The Smiths, The Sex Pistols and the Stone Roses – and all thanks to a social networking website.

Chris Anderson's book *The Long Tail*[3] talks about this phenomenon of letting the market decide what is good and what is not. Anderson describes the situation we now find because of the internet where distribution costs are approaching zero. This allows minority interest music or books to be distributed, where it may previously have been unfeasible. His observations are interesting and it is entirely through the internet that this situation has evolved. A band uploading a song to myspace could see it downloaded by a couple of people, or by tens of thousands. It doesn't matter – it doesn't cost the band any more money or time.

The publishing website lulu.com, founded by former Red Hat executive Bob Young, is possibly the most important publisher of the century. Lulu lets the author design how their book should look, what paper should be used, what will be on the cover, how it should be distributed, and so on. The author has complete control over the book and even earns an 80 per cent royalty on sales. Lulu does this through a sophisticated system of print-on-demand. They don't publish thousands of copies of single book and then hope it will sell; they print each copy as it is purchased. This allows a 24-hour delivery time to be honoured on book sites such as Amazon, though of course it means less chance of a casual purchaser finding a copy in a bookstore – but then for most niche titles there is almost no impulse purchasing anyway.

Services will never be the same again.

SPECIALIZATION

In his blog,[4] *Silicon.com* editor Tony Hallett, described his views on the service companies presently offering almost every type of service from banking to retail to utilities to regular IT: 'Right now, for the top Indian players, life is pretty sweet. Win those commodity contracts that are too low down the value chain or too mundane for companies in places like the UK but also sell on quality, expertise and a local, on-shore presence and knowledge in many cases. But that sweet life won't always be there.'

Hallett was commenting on some comments made by one of the authors at a British Computer Society event, where the argument was made that technology companies will eventually need to focus on technology services and non-tech service providers will come to the fore with their expertise. It's not rocket science, but it's almost heresy with the outsourcing community to declare such an idea. Think about it in a different way, do you buy your lunch from the company that delivers your electricity?

New companies will develop whose business is in the emergent large-volume technology-enabled services – infrastructural services (computing power, high capacity network services, major capacity data storage and manipulation) and commoditized transactional services (such as payroll processing) where demand for essentially standardized services can be aggregated across many sectors of the economy. As already noted, the factory end of the industry, a place where manufacturing skills rule, the human contribution is focused on the delivery of (through a very high level of automation) high asset productivity, tightly controlled costs, and a high reliability of quality and security assured services. The human contribution is in strong manufacturing technical skills, professionalism and experiential depth.

In contrast, the auto industry model suggests that other companies will develop whose business is more highly focused in delivering services tightly tailored to the special requirements of particular sectors of the economy – examples are specialist educational services in schools, or derivatives trading services in the financial community. Here the focus is on the ability to exploit deep application professionalisms and experience developed through a long intimacy with the workings of the chosen sector. The business of these companies will be front-end services that their clients rely on for delivering key elements of their business models. Here the human contribution is in application professionalism, skills and experiential depth in the chosen sector – and it is around this human contribution that the company builds its business model and competitive margins. As mentioned, this does rather fly in the face of some IT service suppliers who consider they can deliver every possible technology service, whether it really needs technical or application knowledge.

THE CHANGING CAREER

Clearly the change to the career is central to this debate. We are not only considering a change to the life and career of those within the IT industry, but those with any industry skills. In the UK, the term 'Polish plumber' has become commonly used to describe the skilled East Europeans arriving and offering their services – although it's generally used as a disparaging term. Since the European Union expanded in 2004 – and again in 2007 – workers from across the former Soviet Bloc nations have been free to arrive in the UK and work and many have taken advantage of this freedom, as can be observed by the number of white vans bearing Polish registration plates.

Is it good or bad to allow this free movement of labour? It's true that the UK was more progressive than most other European nations in allowing the new EU entrants open access to their labour market. Only Sweden and Ireland joined the UK in offering an open-door policy, with every other member state claiming they needed 'more time' to work out how to deal with the projected flood of low-cost workers. In fact, the UK government hopelessly miscalculated the potential for European migration. Official estimates by the British government in advance of EU expansion in 2004 projected that 5,000 to 13,000 workers from across the 10 new member states might migrate to the UK seeking work. In fact, over 175,000 came in the first year alone and over half a million had arrived by 2006.

What is a fact is that the immigrants are not all plumbers. There are plenty of Polish programmers as well. The Polish plumber is a metaphor for the change everyone in any job is experiencing. There was a time when a plumber would be able to find a role as an apprentice to an established tradesman. They could learn the trade and then work through the rest of their career using the same tools they used to learn the trade.

The career is now a rather different concept; possibly it no longer exists, because whatever skills one had at 21 are highly unlikely to be of much value at 61. The education sector needs to focus on creating an environment of easier lifelong learning with support from professional bodies such as the BCS.

THE GLOBAL DELIVERY MODEL

While global players such as IBM, EDS and Accenture have already adopted a coordinated approach to global resource and delivery it is interesting to note that the major Indian service companies, such as TCS, Infosys and Wipro, are all keen to present themselves as global operators – i.e. less Indian and more international. Others, such as the Russian Luxoft, are rapidly opening new facilities in Europe and the USA to help present a more international – rather than simply offshore – face.

Information technology firms are rationalizing future corporate strategies in order to align themselves to this new method of solutions delivery. The global outsourcing giants have built a strong offshore presence, either through acquisition or organically. So a dynamic has been created where the major offshore suppliers are all rushing to create delivery capabilities closer to their customers at the same time as the local service companies are rushing to set up offshore delivery centres. For example, Accenture is hiring thousands of new employees in India as they increase the amount of work they attempt to deliver from offshore, while TCS and Infosys are hiring in Europe and the USA at a phenomenal rate – and paying local salaries.

HCL Technologies is now one of the largest foreign employers of British people, mainly thanks to their BPO facilities in Belfast that allow them to offer service delivery from Europe or Asia – depending on what the client wants from their supplier. In 2006 the Indian back-office service company Firstsource opened a new contact centre in Northern Ireland that immediately created over 1,000 jobs in the UK. It would seem that the Indians are now exporting their skills back to Europe.

This an important point to make. The expertise is flowing in both directions, removing the formal 'onshore' (here at home) and 'offshore' (far away in a lower-cost environment) distinctions. The traditional offshore players are creating onshore delivery capability and also buying or working with local consultants. It cannot be long before companies from supposedly remote destinations engineer reverse takeovers, buying their way up the value chain from back-office services to offering front-line services to consumers in the west. And as this change takes place, all the traditional consulting and service companies are racing to open offshore delivery centres, in a desperate rush to reduce their cost base. This multilateral flow of business activity has helped to create what we call the global delivery model, creating centres of knowledge excellence around the globe.

THE WRITING ON THE WALL

So it has become apparent that services really are at an important crossroads. The robust platform and acceptance of the internet by consumers and business alike has changed the game for services – they really can be considered global.

The key points we have emphasized throughout this book are as follows:

- Companies presently offering IT as a service and then expanding to offer business processes will find that they need to focus on technology rather than try riding two horses.
- Service companies without any technology expertise will enter the global market, using the public internet as a delivery platform. Think for a moment and consider what could be delivered online, then ask why someone is not already doing it.
- Technology delivery itself is becoming virtual – loose coupling of systems is creating an entirely new and flexible environment.
- The global delivery model is encouraging offshore suppliers to be a regular part of the supply chain in highly developed markets.
- Skills and education need to be reconsidered in the face of increased automation and the availability of skilled resources via the internet.
- Countries such as the UK and USA are doing quite well really – there is no 'race to the bottom' as all jobs vanish offshore. The UK economy is growing and creating new jobs – and it is exporting more services than it is importing.
- With KPO the possibilities are endless. Once highly valuable skilled tasks requiring domain knowledge and decision making are out-sourced then we will know that almost anything can be.

Historians will judge this era on a par with the introduction of the railway, or of electricity, or of the printing press – and these really are valid comparisons. With narrow vision it is easy to look at the dot com crash of 2000 as a demonstration of how little the internet can deliver, despite the promises. Yet, we are standing on the edge of an entirely different world and it affects consumer and business alike. Services can be delivered globally using the internet as a platform and they are being accepted; the pace is accelerating.

The old cobbler who made and repaired shoes for others in the village could never have imagined that anyone would travel elsewhere to buy shoes. Now the internet offers you access to shoe producers in Milan, Maine or Manchester – at no additional cost. If you need a document translated, if you need a report to be written, if you need some research or analysis to be undertaken, if you need a patent to be written and filed, then you can now find the best person or company in the world to perform the service – at no additional cost.

Life moves pretty fast. Enjoy what you are doing now, because tomorrow the rules will change.

Notes

Chapter 1

1. Anthony Miller, Partner, Arete Research: Presentation at The Regent Conference, 8 February 2006, London.
2. CSC Leading Edge Forum/FT corporate survey made in Europe 2004. Diagram used with permission.
3. *silicon.com* placed Paul Ginsburgh, BP's VP Enterprise Architecture in its top 20 global Agenda Setters 2006 for this initiative. See their website at www.siliconagendasetters.com
4. Moholy-Nagy, L. trans. D.M. Hoffmann (2005 [1930]) *The New Vision: Fundamentals of Bauhaus Design, Painting, Sculpture, and Architecture.* Dover Publications, London.
5. Sako, M., Griffith, R. and Abrahamovsky, L. (2004) *Offshoring of Business Services and its Impact on the UK Economy.* AIM Research (Advanced Institute of Management Research), London Business School.
6. Conceptual diagram courtesy of CSC Leading Edge Forum 2006.
7. Corbett, M.F. (2004) *The Outsourcing Revolution: Why it Makes Sense and How to do it Right.* Dearborn Trade, Chicago, IL.

Chapter 2

1. The etymology of the acronym KPO is unclear and – as might be expected – there are a number of journals and industry 'gurus' claiming to be the inventor of this terminology. Ashish Gupta, the head of Evalueserve in India, appears to have the best claim to the ownership of this term as the first person we can remember hearing using it in conversation and writing about it. Let's just hope Ashish doesn't expect a royalty every time the term KPO is used.
2. Estimates from www.nasscom.org
3. Mr Roy purchased 40 per cent of Annik Technology Services (www.anniksystems.com) in September 2005 leading many commentators to suggest that the 'father of BPO' has now moved his attention to KPO.
4. Mitnick, K. (2003) *The Art of Deception.* Wiley, Inc., Indianapolis, IN.
5. Data taken from Evalueserve, 'From BPO to KPO', April 2004, available at www.evalueserve.com

6. Confederation of Indian Industry (2005) 'India in the new knowledge economy', available at www.ciionline.org

7. Many thanks to Mike Taylor in the UK and Alok Aggarwal in the USA for helping to arrange this update of the 2004 research.

8. Thanks to Hedda Pahlson-Moller of Evalueserve in Luxembourg for helping to produce these KPO examples.

9. Thanks to Carl Stadler and Rajiv Dey for help with the cases and access to NIIT Smartserve in Gurgaon for a demonstration of the Sesame team in action.

Chapter 3

1. Marx, K. and Engels, F. (2002 [1848]) *The Communist Manifesto.* Penguin Classics, London.

2. GECIS (GE Capital International Services) was floated from GE on 31 December 2004 with two private equity groups, General Atlantic Partners and Oak Hill Capital Partners, each taking a 30% stake, and GE keeping 40%. It was renamed GenPact on 30 September 2005.

3. Handy, C. (1989) *The Age of Unreason.* Business Books Ltd/ Century Hutchinson Ltd, London. Handy, C. (1995) *The Empty Raincoat.* Arrow, London.

4. Handy, *The Empty Raincoat*, op. cit.

5. Scase, R. (2000) *Britain in 2010: The New Business Landscape.* Capstone, Oxford.

6. Rifkin, J. (1995) *The End of Work: The Decline of the Global Labor Force and the Dawn of the Post-market Era.* Jeremy P Tarcher, New York.

7. Bridges, W. (1994) *Jobshift: How to Prosper in a Workplace Without Jobs.* Da Capo Press, New York.

8. Beck, U. (1999) *The Brave New World of Work.* Polity Press, Cambridge.

9. Gorz, A. (1999) *Reclaiming Work: Beyond the Wage-based Society.* Polity Press, Cambridge.

10. Bayliss, V. (1998) *Redefining Work.* Royal Society for the Encouragement of Arts, Manufactures and Commerce, London. A subsequent extension of the report, *Redefining Work 2*, was published by the RSA in 2003, available at www.rsa.org

11. Pink, D. (2001) *Free Agent Nation: How America's New Independent Workers are Transforming the Way we Live.* Warner Books, New York.

12. Department of Trade and Industry, Small Business Service statistics. Published on the internet at www.sbs.gov.uk

13. Shiv Nadar, interview with Mark Kobayashi-Hillary, 6 September 2005.

14. Devesh Nayel, email interview with Mark Kobayashi-Hillary, 9 July 2003. Infosys BPO was known as Progeon at this time.

15. Wikipedia, 'Joint venture', see http://en.wikipedia.org/wiki/Joint_venture

16. 'Xansa to commence JV with Department of Health (DH) on 1 April 2005'. Xansa press release, 30 March 2005, see www.xansa.com/shared/pressreleases/197303/

17. Willcocks has been consistently producing detailed analyses of outsourcing contracts throughout the 1990s and this decade, with 25 books on the subject to date. His most recent book is *Global Sourcing of Business and IT Services*, written with Mary C. Lacity, published in 2006 by Palgrave Macmillan, Basingstoke, UK and New York.

18. Galbraith, J.K. (1998) *The Affluent Society – 40th Anniversary Edition Updated and with a New Introduction by the Author.* Mariner Books/Houghton Mifflin Company, New York.

Chapter 4

1. Presentation by Guillermo Kopp, Vice President, Tower Group at the FT Business Events 2nd Annual Conference on 'Core Systems Strategies – Leveraging Technology to Compete in Financial Services', February 2005.

2. Bahadur, K., Desmet, D. and van Bommel, E. (2006) 'Smart IT spending: insights from European banks'. *The McKinsey Quarterly*, No. 6, Winter.

3. 'City of London goes WiFi', joint press release by The Cloud and The City of London, 20 February 2006, available at www.thecloud.net/content.asp?section=5&content=49&expand=282

4. The Aberdeen Group (2005) *Software as a Service Buyers Guide.* The Aberdeen Group, available at www.aberdeen.com/summary/report/benchmark/RA_SaaSBuyerGuide_BE_3305.asp

5. Kanakamedala, K., Krishnakanthan, V. and Roberts, R.P. (2006) 'Two new tools that IO's want'. *The McKinsey Quarterly*. Based on 'CIO Spending in 2006'. *The McKinsey Quarterly*, No. 7 Spring (2006).

6. TickIT is a certification process relayed to the application of ISO (International Organization for Standardization) 9001 (see www.tickit.org). The standard is about improving the quality of software and its application.

Chapter 5

1. Friedman, T. (2005) *The World is Flat: A Brief History of the Twenty-first Century.* Allen Lane, London.

2. See www.apache.org for a complete introduction to Apache and statistics on its use.

3. See www.deepnetexplorer.com for more information and download.

4. 'HCL Launches sub-10,000 rupee PC'. *The Hindu*, 15 October, available at www.hindu.com/2005/10/15/stories/20051015007 21600.htm

5. See http://laptop.media.mit.edu for more details on the One Laptop Per Child project.

6. Smith, D. (2003) *Free Lunch: Easily Digestible Economics*. Profile Books, London.

7. 'Google founder dreams of Google implant in your brain'. *The Register*, 3 March, available at www.theregister.co.uk/2004/03/03/google_founder_dreams_of_google/

8. Kellaway, L. (2006) 'Employers have little to fear from a spot of cyber-skiving'. *Financial Times*, 24 September.

9. Battelle, J. (2005) *The Search: How Google and its Rivals Rewrote the Rules of Business and Transformed our Culture*. Nicholas Brealey, London.

10. Ibid. The database of intentions is one of the key concepts in *The Search* – it runs throughout the book as one of the key changes in future advertising.

11. Barkham, P. (2006) 'Email agony as trainee puts on the Ritz'. *The Guardian*, 26 August, available at http://technology.guardian.co.uk/news/story/0,1858730,00.html

12. J.P. Rangaswami, CIO, BT Global Services, writing in *Computing Business*, June 2006, available at www.computingbusiness.co.uk

13. Battelle, *The Search*, op. cit.

14. There is a lot of analysis into the production process of this movie, but the best overall summary – with links to Josh Friedman's blog – can be found on *Wikipedia* at http://en.wikipedia.org/wiki/Snakes_on_a_plane

15. 'Arctic Monkeys make chart history'. *BBC News*, 29 January 2006, available at http://news.bbc.co.uk/1/hi/entertainment/4660394.stm

16. 'Best British album of all time revealed'. *New Musical Express*, 28 January 2006, available at www.nme.com/news/arctic-monkeys/22062

17. Anderson, C. (2006) *The Long Tail: How Endless Choice is Creating Unlimited Demand*. Random House, London.

18. Kaplan, J. (2005) 'Utility computing: a better model for outsourcing success', in Brudenhall, P. (ed.) *Technology and Offshore Outsourcing Strategies*. Palgrave Macmillan, Basingstoke, UK, pp. 259–74.

19. Michelle Lam, interview conducted via email and myspace on 1 January 2007.

Chapter 6

1. Sako, M. (2005) 'Outsourcing & offshoring: key trends & issues', Said Business School, Oxford University, November. Paper prepared for the Emerging Markets Forum.
2. Carr, N. (2003) 'IT doesn't matter'. *Harvard Business Review*, May.
3. Carr, N. (2004) *Does IT Matter? Information Technology and the Corrosion of Competitive Advantage*. Harvard Business School Press, Boston, MA.
4. Bahadur *et al.*, 'Smart IT spending', op. cit.
5. Hamish McRae (Associate Editor of *The Independent*), speaking at a CSC Leading Edge Forum membership conference in June 2006.

Chapter 7

1. MGI (2003) *Offshoring: Is it a Win-Win Game?* McKinsey Global Institute, available at www.mckinsey.com/mgi/publications/win_win_game.asp
2. OECD (2006) *The Share of Employment Potentially Affected by Offshoring – An Empirical Investigation*. Working Party on the Information Economy, OECD Directorate for Science, Technology and Industry, Paris, available at www.oecd.org/dataoecd/37/26/36187829.pdf
3. MGI (2005) *The Emerging Global Labor Market: Part I – The Demand for Offshore Talent Services*. McKinsey Global Institute, available at www.mckinsey.com/mgi/publications/emerginggloballabormarket/
4. Evalueserve (2004) *Impact of Global Sourcing on the UK Economy 2003–2010*, available at www.evalueserve.com
5. Evalueserve, *Impact of Global Sourcing*, op. cit., p. 5.
6. ONS (2005) *Labour Market Trends*. UK Office of National Statistics, London – see www.statistics.gov.uk/StatBase/
7. Codling, P. *et al.* (2006) *The Impact of Global Sourcing on the UK Software and IT Services Sector*. Ovum, London. The entire report can be downloaded from the DTI website at www.dti.gov.uk/files/file32496.pdf
8. Ibid., p. 4.
9. Ibid., p. 3.
10. In February 2006 Mark participated in a press conference at the NASSCOM annual conference in Mumbai. Friedman was making the case that everyone has to look out for their own career because the internet allows individuals to compete with individuals.

11. RentACoder offers a very simple reverse auction process connecting those who need some software to be written or modified with those who can do the job. Those with work announce the details of a project on the site and those looking for contracts can pitch for the business, directly connecting the buyer and seller of a software development service. See www.rentacoder.com

12. OECD, *The Share of Employment*, op. cit.

13. BCS (2004) *Offshoring – A Challenge or Opportunity for British IT Professionals?* BCS (2006) *Embracing the Challenge, Exploiting the Opportunities: Building a world class IT profession in the era of global sourcing*. British Computer Society Working Party on Offshoring. Both reports can be downloaded free from www.bcs.org/ positions/offshoring

14. BCS (2006) *Embracing the Challenge*, op. cit.

15. Ibid.

16. Full details of BCS's Career Builder can be found at www.bcs.org/ careerbuilder

17. BCS (2006) *Embracing the Challenge*, op. cit.

18. *Developing the Future: A Report on the Challenges and Opportunities Facing the UK Software Development Industry*. Report by the Initial Working Party for Developing the Future, 5 July 2006. Sponsored by British Computer Society, Lancaster University and Microsoft, available from the BCS website at www.bcs.org/ upload/pdf/developingfuture.pdf

19. The Skills Framework for the Information Age (SFIA) provides a common reference model for the identification of the skills needed to develop effective information systems making use of information and communications technology. SFIA enables employers of IT professionals to carry out a range of HR activities against a common framework of reference – including skill audit, planning future skill requirements, development programmes, standardization of job titles and functions, and resource allocation. See www.sfia.org.uk

20. BCS, *Embracing the Challenge*, op. cit.

Chapter 8

1. Friedman, *The World is Flat*, op. cit.

2. http://pmindia.nic.in/prelease/pcontent.asp?id=261

3. Harvey, O. (2005) 'Your life: for sale'. *The Sun*, 23 June.

4. Sparrow, E.A. (2004) *A Guide to Global Sourcing: Offshore Outsourcing and other Global Delivery Models*. British Computer Society, London. Vashistha, A. and Vashistha A. (2005) *The Offshore Nation: The Rise of Services Globalization*. Tata McGraw Hill, Columbus, OH.

5. Shaw, T.M., Cooper, A.F. and Ankiewicz, A. (2006) 'Emerging economics & global development in the new century: post-bipolar & NIC lessons from/for BRICSAM', unpublished draft paper, available at www.cpsa-acsp.ca/papers-2006/Shaw.pdf

6. Shaw, T.M. and Westhuizen (2004). *TMS* The Global Political Economy in Jeffrey Haynes (ed) Palgrave Advances in Development Studies (London: Palgrave Macmillan, 2005) pp. 249–267, especially pp. 264–265.

7. Keynes, J.M. (1920) *The Economic Consequences of the Peace.* Harcourt Brace Jovanovich, New York, available at www.worldebooklibrary. com/eBooks/WorldeBookLibrary.com/keynes1.htm

8. Friedman, T. (2000) *The Lexus and the Olive Tree: Understanding Globalization.* Anchor, New York.

9. For more information check the *Wikipedia* page on Samuelson, at http://en.wikipedia.org/wiki/Paul_Samuelson

10. Steve Ranger (2006) 'Indian outsourcer brings jobs to Northern Ireland', *silicon.com*, 14 June, available at http://services.silicon. com/offshoring/0,3800004877,39159541,00.htm

11. 'Biggest BPO deal in the UK Life Assurance market: Diligenta seals £486m deal with Pearl Group', press release from TCS, 25 April 2006.

12. TCS, 'The global network delivery model'. White paper, Tata Consultancy Systems, April 2006.

13. NOA press release, January 2006, available at http://www.noa. co.uk/predictionsrelease.htm

14. McCue, A. (2006) 'Dixons outsources IT to India in £150m deal'. *silicon.com*, 20 January, available at http://services.silicon.com/ offshoring/0,3800004877,39155797,00.htm

15. Azim Premji was talking at the inaugural Aditya Birla centre lecture at London Business School in November 2006. This was a response to a question on the convergence of the Indian and 'western' consulting firms posed to Premji by Mahesh Ramachandran.

16. Vashistha and Vashistha, *The Offshore Nation*, op. cit.

Chapter 9

1. Friedman, *The World is Flat*, op. cit.

2. Sako, M., Griffith, R. and Abrahamovsky, L. (2004) *Offshoring of Business Services and its Impact on the UK Economy.* AIM Research (Advanced Institute of Management Research).

3. Anderson, *The Long Tail*, op. cit.

4. Hallett, T. (2006) Editor's blog. *silicon.com*, 6 September, available at http://comment.silicon.com/editorsblog

Further Reading

Anderson, C. (2006) *The Long Tail: How Endless Choice is Creating Unlimited Demand.* Random House, London.

Battelle, J. (2005) *The Search: How Google and its Rivals Rewrote the Rules of Business and Transformed our Culture.* Nicholas Brealey, London.

Bayliss, V. (1998) *Redefining Work (I).* Royal Society for the Encouragement of Arts, Manufactures and Commerce, London.

Beck, U. (1999) *The Brave New World of Work.* Polity Press, Cambridge.

Bridges, W. (1994) *Jobshift: How to Prosper in a Workplace Without Jobs.* Da Capo Press, New York.

Brudenhall, P. (ed.) (2005) *Technology and Offshore Outsourcing Strategies.* Palgrave Macmillan, Basingstoke, UK.

Carr, N. (2004) *Does IT Matter? Information Technology and the Corrosion of Competitive Advantage.* Harvard Business School Press, Boston, MA.

Corbett, M.F. (2004) *The Outsourcing Revolution: Why it Makes Sense and How to do it Right.* Dearborn Trade, Chicago, IL.

Friedman, T. (2000) *The Lexus and the Olive Tree: Understanding Globalization.* Anchor, New York.

Friedman, T. (2005) *The World is Flat: A Brief History of the Twenty-first Century.* Allen Lane, London.

Gorz, A. (1999) *Reclaiming Work: Beyond the Wage-based Society.* Polity Press, Cambridge.

Handy, C. (1989) *The Age of Unreason.* Business Books Ltd/Century Hutchinson Ltd, London.

Handy, C. (1995) *The Empty Raincoat.* Arrow, London.

Keynes, J.M. (1920) *The Economic Consequences of the Peace.* Harcourt Brace Jovanovich, New York.

Kobayashi-Hillary, M. (2005) *Outsourcing to India: The Offshore Advantage*, 2nd edition. Springer, New York.

Kobayashi-Hillary, M. (2007) *Building a Future with BRICS: The Next Decade for Offshoring.* Springer, New York.

Marx, K. and Engels, F. (2002 [1848]) *The Communist Manifesto.* Penguin Classics, London.

Mitnick, K. (2003) *The Art of Deception.* Wiley, Inc., Indianapolis, IN.

Pink, D. (2001) *Free Agent Nation: How America's New Independent Workers are Transforming the Way we Live.* Warner Books, New York.

Rifkin, J. (1995) *The End of Work: The Decline of the Global Labor Force and the Dawn of the Post-market Era.* Jeremy P Tarcher, New York.

Scase, R. (2000) *Britain in 2010: The New Business Landscape.* Capstone, Oxford.

Sparrow, E.A. (2004) *A Guide to Global Sourcing: Offshore Outsourcing and other Global Delivery Models.* British Computer Society, London.

Vashistha, A. and Vashistha A. (2005) *The Offshore Nation: The Rise of Services Globalization.* Tata McGraw Hill, Columbus, OH.

Willcocks, L.P. and Lacity, M.C. (2006) *Global Sourcing of Business and IT Services.* Palgrave Macmillan, Basingstoke, UK and New York.

Index